WOLF

WOLF

U-BOAT COMMANDERS
IN WORLD WAR II

JORDAN VAUSE

NAVAL INSTITUTE PRESS
Annapolis, Maryland

Library of Congress Cataloging-in-Publication Data

Vause, Jordan.
  Wolf: U-boat commanders in World War II/Jordan Vause.
    p.   cm.
  Includes bibliographical references and index.
  ISBN 1-55750-874-7 (alk. paper)
  1. Sailors—Germany. 2. World War, 1939–1945—Naval operations, German.
3. World War, 1939–1945—Naval operations—Submarine. 4. Germany. Kriegsmarine—
World War, 1939–1945. I. Title.
D781.V38   1997
940.54′5943—dc20   96-43105

Printed in the United States of America on acid-free paper ∞

97 98 99 00 01 02 03 04 9 8 7 6 5 4 3 2

First printing

Passages from Herbert Werner, *Iron Coffins*, reprinted with permission
of Henry Holt and Company, Inc., New York.

Passages from Eric C. Rust, *Naval Officers under Hitler:*
The Story of Crew 34, reprinted with permission of
Greenwood Publishing Group, Inc., Westport, Conn.

To My Children
Joseph Gregory, Thomas Jordan, Mary Elizabeth,
Andrew Delaney, and Ellen Frances

Contents

Foreword

I T ALL happened about fifty years ago, in my first life. I think it is amazing that Mr. Vause has taken the trouble to stir up the past and to analyze the human beings involved and their actions. The public interest in literature concerning the war seems to be more intense in the United States than in Europe.

In my opinion, a U-boat commander should be well qualified, experienced, have a personal touch, and get a bit of luck as well. He must be able to apply what I call "psychical hygiene" in handling his crew because a good crew will support him in cases of near despair or in critical situations. Mutual confidence between crew and commander is essential—one is useless without the other. In addition, a good commander must be able to find, depending on the situation, a proper mixture of daring, caution, and forward vision. The submarine war is in a way like big game hunting; but within seconds the hunter becomes the hunted and has to run for his life. Being hunted requires what I call second-stage thinking, calculating what your opponent thinks you will do and then doing the opposite. This game is a matter of nerve and may last many hours, even days. Of course, if both sides have the experience and the patience, it may come to third-stage thinking, or more. The sub-chasing group may assume that you are trying to get away from a convoy after an attack, whereas you may think you are better off within or underneath it. Sometimes it is like a game of chess, especially if your opponent has experience and knows the rules of the game. The stakes are high, of course.

One gets caught by one's past. I am writing in the present tense, although about events that happened ages ago. But there is one more thing I would like to mention. In the beginning, a war is exciting; toward the end, it is a bloody gamble in which you try to achieve the maximum result with an acceptable risk so as to have at least some chance of staying alive. If the commander had had the ability to detach himself from the actual situation, if he had been able to look at himself as though on a movie screen and judge on that basis, his decisions might have been better.

You, the reader, have that ability. Please judge fairly.

— Jürgen Oesten
Commander of U-61, U-106, and U-861
Ritterkreuzträger (Knight's Cross recipient)

Acknowledgments

THIS book could not have been written without the assistance of many former U-Bootwaffe (U-boat service) officers. I must thank three of these men in particular: Jürgen Oesten, who responded to countless letters, reviewed several chapters of the book, and agreed to write the foreword to it; Victor Oehrn, who also answered one letter after another and graciously allowed me to use his unpublished memoirs; and Peter Hansen, who proofread every chapter for historical accuracy. My sincere thanks as well to Karl Daublebsky von Eichhain, Eberhard Godt, Gottfried König, Otto Kretschmer, Karl-Friedrich Merten, Theodor Petersen, Reinhard Reche, Hans-Diedrich von Tiesenhausen, Erich Topp, Herbert Werner, and Helmut Witte.

I am also grateful for the support and assistance of the following individuals and organizations: Captain Edward L. Beach, USN (Ret.), Horst Bredow, Gus Britton, Lothar-Günther Buchheim, Michael Hadley, Bodo Herzog, Peter Padfield, Jürgen Rohwer, Eberhard Schmidt, and the staffs of the Marineschule Mürwik, the Stiftung Traditionsarchiv Unterseeboote, the British Broadcasting Corporation, and the Deutsche Dienststelle. Some of those listed here will not like what I have written, but their opinions will never diminish my admiration for them and their work.

I would like to mention two gentlemen in closing. I regard them both as my friends—a definite asset in this line of work—and as professionals who would never trade the truth for friendship. Eric Rust, who received a letter from someone he had never met and responded as though he had known him forever; and Jack Sweetman, who treated a student as a colleague and a novice as a pro.

WOLF

Introduction

HORST Bredow, a short, stocky, owl-faced man with an impatient manner, is the founder and director of the U-boat archives in Cuxhaven-Altenbruch. These archives are generally considered to hold more data on U-boats and the U-Bootwaffe than any other place on earth, and Bredow has built them up from scratch, bit by bit, over the last forty years. It is his life's work. He will probably die there.

The archives are huge. They are crammed into a single, large, red-brick house in Cuxhaven. Outside, except for flagpoles and an anchor in the garden, the house looks much like every other house on the block; it is not an obvious repository for its contents. Inside is another world: dark, cramped, labyrinthine—much like the inside of a submarine. The rooms contain books, photographs, videotapes, war diaries, and personnel folders. There is a museum, an office, and a darkroom. There is a vault for the examination of classified Bundesmarine (Federal German Navy) material, for Horst Bredow, by virtue of his position, is privy to a lot of it. One room is devoted entirely to a re-creation of Otto Hersing's parlor, another contains nothing but correspondence. Each room bears the name of an ace—Otto Weddigen, Otto Kretschmer, Engelbert Endrass, Georg Lassen—excepting only the kitchen and the bedrooms (for the Bredow family lives in the same house). Bredow prowls constantly through this private world in his slippers and sweater, looking up the answers to inquiries from all over the world at $15 apiece. He is, he will admit, a driven man.

Bredow's single-minded devotion to his archives is understandable only if one is aware of his own background. He is haunted, he says, by the memory of his days as an officer in a U-boat and by a fate he should have shared but did not. In January 1944 he was assigned as a newly commissioned *Leutnant zur See* (ensign) to U-288. He knew the boat well. He had served in her as a midshipman, when her commander, asking him if he *really* wanted to learn about submarines, stripped him of his insignia and

1

Horst Bredow's U-boat archive, the largest repository of U-boat information in the world, is contained in this house in a residential neighborhood of Cuxhaven. The American flag is flying because of the author's visit, a courtesy Bredow extends to all his foreign guests. (Author's collection)

sent him below as a common seaman. He learned, and the commander had asked for him back. As U-288's second watch officer, or third in command, he became part of the crew; he fought with them, bled with them, sang with them, enjoyed the friendship and the camaraderie which so many who have never served cannot understand. Then one day he was wounded in an air attack and had to enter the hospital. U-288 left on her next patrol without him. On 3 April 1944 she was lost at sea. Her entire crew—all except Bredow—died.

Human nature tends to work with images. They are useful in remembering people or places. They allow us to describe things of which we have no firsthand knowledge. They serve to inspire us, to comfort us, to warn us, and to remind us of our history and our heritage. They make the dead alive again and the living vibrant.

Horst Bredow, deep in his archives, is protecting his image of the German U-boat sailor—the image of the men he served with, the commander who taught him, the crew who left him behind. It is a gentle image of good and noble men. It is the image of the U-boat commander as a "knight of the deep," a warrior who carried out his duty without complaint, fought honorably, and died bravely for his country. And Bredow is prepared to protect this image with his own labor, his money, his reputation, and his health from all who would harm it.

Of course, Bredow's is not the only image of the U-Bootwaffe that exists. It is certainly not accepted unanimously by the men whose lives are cataloged in his building or by their successors (many Bundesmarine officers today consider the archives a shrine dedicated to the past and avoid the place). It is not shared by the media in Germany or abroad, or by the community of historians who have written about the U-boats in two wars, or by the victims of German torpedoes. Michael Hadley, in *Count Not the Dead,* his 1995 analysis of the U-boat in literature and the media, shows that at least twelve distinct images have been projected by German writers over the years.[1] Most U-boat commanders, if asked, will offer their own images of themselves, and there were at least fourteen hundred commanders at one time or another in World War II. The images are numerous, and together they run the range from Bredow's noble knight to the worst of pirates, felons, and Nazi killers. Some of them are colorful indeed, and many of them are well known to the reader. But all of the images, including Bredow's, are wrong.

Though many have tried to describe the U-boat commander on the basis of one image or another, it is ultimately a frustrating exercise to portray him as anything but an individual. This becomes obvious very quickly when various commanders are singled out for closer examination. When I began to write this book, I had in mind a general study of the U-boat commander. Happily, I was warned off the idea, but one of my original theses was that, although no one image fit the U-boat commander of World War II, he might be characterized by comparing him to one or another of the images suggested above. I found that far from adhering to any particular image, the man was stubborn in eluding any image at all. With the series of portraits in this book I hope to prove that point, and as long as the reader finishes it by saying, "These men were less alike than I thought," the goal will have been met.

In studying such officers as Victor Oehrn, Karl Dönitz's planning genius, or Wolfgang Lüth, the second-ranking ace of the war, or Jürgen Oesten, a quiet skeptic who nevertheless was awarded the Knight's Cross, one sees common characteristics, shared experiences, and many similar ideas but never gets the impression that they are in any way alike. Otto

Kretschmer once compared Lüth to himself, but Lüth was nothing like Kretschmer. Oehrn admired Günther Prien, for whom he planned the Scapa Flow operation, but he did not emulate Prien. Oesten was closer in philosophy to Oskar Kusch, the only U-Bootwaffe officer executed during the war for sedition, than he was to his commander in chief, the tragic Karl Dönitz. Some commanders were so different that they progressed to the point of open warfare. Officers like Karl-Friedrich Merten and Erich Topp, for example, both highly decorated aces, were left quarreling in the media as they might once have done in a quayside tavern, hardly two minds conjoined in thought.

There were many reasons for this phenomenon. On the surface, U-Bootwaffe officers had very much in common, and this book will try to point these areas out as they come up. The Kriegsmarine (German Navy from 1935 to 1945) attempted to select candidates of a certain background and breeding. Educational requirements were strict. Training, at least in peacetime, did not vary much from one year to the next. But free spirits did slip through the net, and once the war began, lives and careers wound unplanned paths through places and situations that nobody would have associated with the world of the U-boat. The nightclubs of Paris and the streets of Rome, the harbors of Malaya and the deserts of Libya, the Chancellery and the prison camps, all tended to separate one officer from another, to split the monolithic groups of new officer candidates created by the service each year. Oehrn and Lüth had similar backgrounds and training, but Oehrn's wartime experiences were as different from Lüth's as Lüth's were from those of any Allied soldier. Lüth and Oesten were classmates who received identical preparation for war and who received their first commands at about the same time. Both men sailed boats from France to the Indian Ocean and back. But their differences in upbringing made one a confirmed National Socialist and the other an equally solid apostate.

Finally, in some cases any comparison is nonsensical because the similarities that may once have existed are gone. Herbert Werner, who became a commander in 1944, had by that time accumulated training and experience far different from that of his predecessors. He was so unlike Wolfgang Lüth, the man who handed him the orders to his first command, that any attempt to make them fit a common image—no matter how general or roughly drawn—fails utterly. The same is true for Theodor Petersen, who was one of Lüth's best friends, and Gottfried König, who was one of his protégés. Both men were closer to Werner than Lüth in their career patterns, and both now admit to opinions that would have placed them in opposition to Lüth, a man they would never wish to denigrate.

I have tried to follow these men through the months and years of the war, highlighting those aspects of their lives that truly set them apart, but to understand them better I felt it necessary to include several background chapters as well. The book begins with a brief summary of the U-Bootwaffe's history and traditions—the history and traditions they knew, not those we know today. There is a chapter on the crews and boats these men commanded: how they were formed, trained, and prepared for battle. There is a chapter on U-boat leadership and another on the U-Bootwaffe high command, specifically Karl Dönitz, the man they loved and feared more than any other. And there is a chapter on the image of the U-boats, their commanders, and their crews, for images matter even when they are false. Nobody who reads an account of the pitched battles between Karl-Friedrich Merten and controversial author Lothar-Günther Buchheim on the subject will doubt this. And though there is probably no single valid picture of the U-boat commander, the images that prevail are of some importance to those left behind.

Most images change over time—will these? Here too the subjects differ among themselves. "The history of U-boats will remain a saga in the last world war among related and civilized nations," wrote Reinhard Reche, commander of U-255. "As [with] the submariners of the western Allies, the U-boat men will be considered to have done their duty for their country." Eberhard Godt, the senior surviving member of the U-Bootwaffe in 1992, was more pessimistic: "What does Schiller say in the prologue to *Wallenstein?* 'Blurred by the favor and the hate of parties, / His image wavers in our history.' That goes as well for the reputation of the U-boat commander; now . . . and one hundred years from now." [2]

Horst Bredow hopes desperately for Reche's ending, but he expects that it is Godt's that will come to pass, and that is why he has spent his entire adult life working in the depths of his archives. He does not want the image of the men he loved to be forever negative. I do not expect either ending, nor do I believe that any of the images in current usage will last long into the next century. The men of the U-Bootwaffe, like most fighting men, will eventually be forgiven most of their sins and credited with most of the valor and self-sacrifice they demonstrated. Then, like most fighting men, they will fade honorably into the history of ancient wars.

This book will neither stop nor slow that fading, which is an inexorable part of life. At most, it may lend some understanding to a transient generation of readers, and toward this purpose I have tried to follow the words of Schiller so loved by Eberhard Godt:

> Blurred by the favor and the hate of parties,
> His image wavers in our history.
> But Art shall now bring him more humanly
> And closer to your eyes and to your hearts.

CHAPTER 1

The Monsters of the Sea

How wonderful Thy works, O Lord!
In wisdom Thou hast made all things, the earth is full of Thy handiwork.
There is the sea, great and wide; there creatures swarm without number,
animals small and great.
There roam the monsters of the sea.

—Psalm 104:24–26

THE complete name of Horst Bredow's archive is *Stiftung Traditionsarchiv Unterseeboote,* which translates roughly as the foundation for an archive of U-boat traditions, and indeed Bredow's image of the U-boat commander is steeped in the older tradition of the U-Bootwaffe and the German navies, the same tradition that most future U-boat commanders learned in their youths. It was well established by the late 1920s and early 1930s, when many of these men entered the service. The high command of the new U-Bootwaffe paid only lip service to its own tradition and eventually rejected its demands. Nevertheless, tradition would play a significant role in the life and career of any U-boat commander serving the Third Reich, and it is important that this role be understood from the start.[1]

Germans between the wars had a different view of the U-boat than we do today. Our images are almost always taken from the Battle of the Atlantic: black and white pictures of U-boat pens, brass bands, and flower girls; bearded men draped on periscope handles and newsreel footage of tankers burning; sharp young officers being decorated by Hitler; and bewildered sailors wrapped in blankets after a capture at sea. The books written about U-boats, the movies, and the television shows are all set in World War II. Our pictures are tinted with the ruthlessness and cruelty of

7

National Socialism. This is not surprising; World War II left a scar on modern memory unlike any event before or since.

But the man we now consider to be the definitive U-boat commander grew up with a different picture, that of the Imperial German Navy and its U-Bootwaffe. He followed their tradition. Even now, after another world war and another defeat, this tradition is still strong, and often predominant, in Germany. The huge flag behind Bredow's desk is the ensign of the Imperial Navy, not the banner of the Third Reich. This tradition was pervasive in the Reichsmarine (the German navy until 1935). It was part of the training received by all new officers and was reflected in the attitudes of the senior officers who led them. It was a tradition celebrated far beyond the service; most people knew about the performance of the kaiser's fleet in World War I, its battles, its victories, and its heroes. Although the story had been colored by postwar histories, memoirs, literature, and film, it was an impressive heritage, and much of it dealt with the exploits of the U-boats, of which almost four hundred were sent to sea and half were lost.

The history and achievements of the U-Bootwaffe were only part of its tradition. The tradition also included the spirit of the service, its burning loyalty, and the conduct of its members. And though most parts of U-boat tradition tended to unite the new officers of World War II, others would set each of them apart. Most often this difference was the degree to which each elected to follow the examples set by the U-boat commanders of World War I. The conduct of these officers was not always exemplary; in fact, in many cases, it was admittedly suspect. Some were careless, others cruel, and the incidents of atrocity seized upon by their enemies were often true. Most were competent men who acted like ordinary sinners. The best of them were models anyone on either side could emulate.

The tradition of the U-boats began almost as soon as the war did, and the man who made the first major contribution to it was also generally considered to be one of the best examples of military virtue in the Imperial Navy. Paradoxically, he had to inflict a naval defeat of terrible proportion to achieve these distinctions, a defeat he spelled out in his own words as it happened: "0600: Masts sighted to south. Dived. Subsequently made out a warship. Two additional warships identified, one to either side at about two miles. I decide to investigate. Warships identified as English cruisers, four stacks. Since there are no indications of a larger force in the area, I decide to attack; one ship after the other."[2]

With these words the era of submarine warfare opened. The story is well known, even now. On 22 September 1914, just seven weeks into the conflict, the small, obsolescent, gasoline-powered U-9 sighted the masts of three large Royal Navy armored cruisers. The commander of the boat, Otto Weddigen, decided to attack. In the course of the next ninety minutes he sank all three of them as he had planned and then escaped without a scratch. It was, in the words of the first lord of the admiralty, Winston Churchill, "an episode of a peculiar nature in human history." [3]

These three cruisers, HMS *Aboukir, Cressy,* and *Hogue,* were older ships, relegated to patrol duties in the North Sea and due in short order for the breaker's yard. Their crews were made up largely of overage reservists and young cadets. On that day they had been sent to sea without their usual destroyer escort, and most sources indicate that they were not overly concerned with submarine attack. When Weddigen sighted the masts of the *Aboukir* through U-9's periscope, the three ships were steaming insouciantly in triangle formation along an arrow-straight track. The *Aboukir* was hit first, amidships, with a single torpedo fired from a distance of five hundred meters. The *Cressy* and *Hogue* were each hit with two torpedoes as they lay dead in the water to pick up the *Aboukir*'s crew. Fifteen hundred men died on the three old ships that day, almost as many as had died on the *Titanic* two years earlier.

Otto Weddigen was not the first man to sink a ship from a submarine. That place in history goes to his fellow commander Otto Hersing, who three weeks earlier in U-21 had attacked and sunk the light cruiser HMS *Pathfinder.* But it was Weddigen, a new bridegroom "ready for any undertaking that promised to do for the Imperial Navy what our brothers of the army were so gloriously accomplishing," who in one swift stroke changed the face of modern war forever and planted a terrible fear in the minds of everyone who went to sea: the fear that a sudden invisible blow would rend the deck from beneath them and leave them to die in oil and flames. [4] And for that reason it is Weddigen, not Hersing, who has pride of place in U-boat tradition.

They were the first, and possibly the most famous, U-boat aces. Otto Hersing was the commander of U-21 throughout the war. He was noted for attacks on warships, and he later sank two battleships HMS *Triumph* and HMS *Majestic,* but he racked up an impressive total in merchant shipping as well. It is difficult to enumerate the decorations, citations, and testimonials given to him or to describe his popularity. Ironically, it was not

This photo of Otto Weddigen and the crew of SM U-9 was taken shortly after his historic attack on three British cruisers in 1914. Weddigen was one of the first heroes in U-Bootwaffe tradition. Every new commander was familiar with him, although not all tried to emulate his virtues. (Horst Bredow)

the sinking of the *Pathfinder* that made him famous, possibly because of confusion over whether she had in fact been hit by a torpedo or struck a mine. His fame, which was considerable, came later, and he survived the war to see it fade away. Otto Weddigen, by contrast, became famous at once, but he enjoyed his fame for only a short time before he was lost at sea. His was the streak across the heavens that poets and propagandists write about: a single heroic deed, a young and noble countenance frozen by the camera, and death at an early age uncorrupted by war. "In a brief career of a few months he had shown both the power and the vulnerability of this new weapon of warfare," wrote one historian after the war, "and he had also set a standard of decency in submarine operations, which unfortunately his brother officers felt no obligation to follow." [5]

The role of the U-boats in the war is well known and hardly needs more discussion here. For the first six months, German submarine operations were limited and carried out in compliance with the rules of commerce war. These rules, wholly unsuited to submarine warfare (and a nuisance for U-boats in both wars), provided for adequate warning, inspection of cargoes, the safety of crews, and strict observation of neutrality. In following these rules the commanders of the U-boats could be "decent," even gentlemanly, and observers on both sides could observe, as the London *Times* did when Weddigen died, "Our satisfaction at the occurrence is mingled with some regret at the death of a man who, so far as is known, behaved bravely and skillfully, and where it was possible displayed to his victims the humanity expected of seamen."[6]

This all changed when, in February 1915, the German government decided to initiate unrestricted submarine warfare within a prescribed zone around the British Isles. This was done for several reasons (not least of which was that a similar blockade had been initiated by Britain against Germany), but the decision backfired in May, when the British passenger liner *Lusitania* was sunk by Walther Schwieger in U-20, with the loss of eleven hundred lives.[7]

The *Lusitania* did not become a part of the U-boat tradition, even though Schwieger was celebrated in Germany for sinking her. A medal was struck for the occasion, and Schwieger was later awarded the Pour le Mérite, imperial Germany's highest award for valor. But the sinking was not a particularly heroic act. It involved neither long odds nor an armed enemy. Tradition does not accommodate actions that are, in the long term, embarrassing to those who hold to it, and the *Lusitania* was certainly very embarrassing for the U-Bootwaffe. Walther Schwieger was vilified by his enemies; any goodwill Weddigen had generated was lost at once. Germany was held accountable for the deaths of the *Lusitania* passengers, many of whom were neutral civilians, and was subsequently treated as an outlaw nation in the American press. As a result of the sinking, the policy of unrestricted submarine warfare was abandoned in September, and the next eighteen months of commerce war were relatively restrained.

During that time, however, German fortunes declined, both on land and at sea. The Battle of Jutland, though not decisive for either side, forced the German High Seas Fleet back into its harbors for the rest of the war.[8] German offensives on the Western Front, though costly, were not successful. The winter of 1916–17 was a terrible one for the German people. By the beginning of 1917 it had become clear to the German government that Germany's only hope for a positive resolution of the war lay in resuming the policy of unrestricted submarine warfare regardless of risk. They knew that the United States would likely go to war because of it, but they gambled that Britain could be brought to terms before American troops were in a position to make any difference in Europe. This gamble failed but not before a wild U-boat offensive that sent tonnage figures soaring.

Several important areas of U-Bootwaffe tradition began to develop during these halcyon months. The first was the idea of the U-boat as an underdog. After the effective neutralization of the German High Seas Fleet at Jutland, the U-boats found themselves alone with the Royal Navy in the waters around Great Britain. In spite of this overwhelming disadvantage, they managed in April 1917 to bring Britain to within six weeks of starvation. The second was the U-boat spirit. U-boat losses were rising, and crews now left their bases with a real fear that they might not return. "Morituri te Salutari" cheered the men of the Flanders flotillas during a visit by the kaiser: "We who are about to die salute you." But they continued to serve bravely, without question or complaint and with more success than might logically have been expected. They never lost this spirit; it survived the war intact, lasted through a bitter peace, survived a second war, and is evident in U-boat veterans today.

The spirit prospered in spite of increasingly bad press on the other side. Most of this, of course, was war propaganda and meant little. "The German submarine commanders have proved by their deeds that they commit excess from sheer love of cruelty, and not from any national necessity," raved an anonymous pamphleteer in 1918. "It is possible to carry out submarine warfare without barbarity, but the German submarine service appears deliberately to have chosen the methods of the barbarian." [9] But some criticism was richly deserved and would affect the public perception of the U-boat commander for at least eighty years to come. Incidents in which a U-boat was taken down with merchant crewmen standing on its weatherdeck, for example, were not the inventions of the press; they happened several times in the war. Several marked hospital ships were attacked and sunk by U-boats. Perhaps the worst offender was Helmut Patzig, commander of U-86, who was charged after the war with shooting the survivors of the hospital ship *Llandovery Castle* (which he had just sunk) and destroying their lifeboats. There seems little doubt that he was guilty, but he disappeared before his trial and was never seen again.

Men like Patzig represented only a fraction of the whole, but the Western image of the U-boat commander was based on them. It was an unfair appraisal because there were more than a few commanders who were worthy of respect on both sides. Otto Weddigen was one of them, possibly because he died so early in the war; Otto Hersing was another. Perhaps the most striking example was that of Lothar von Arnauld de la Perière, the former admiralty staff officer and would-be zeppelin pilot who took command of U-35 in November 1915. Over the next three years Arnauld sank almost two hundred ships—half a million tons of shipping—all the while following the highest standards of maritime law. After two wars he is still the "ace of aces," the highest-scoring submarine commander of any navy in history, and his reputation sparkled like the sun on the sea.

Much of U-boat tradition was built on men such as Arnauld, Weddigen, and Hersing, along with a second tier of officers including Walter Forstmann, Max Valentiner, Otto Steinbrinck, Hans Rose, Werner Fürbringer, and Bernhardt Wegener, who were all that Patzig was not. They were the modern knights that Bredow sees in every commander, and as knights they were invested with the chivalric virtues of bravery, integrity, honor, and mercy. Even today they seem to loom over their successors in World War II, most of whom, in spite of their own virtues, were officers of a lesser caliber.

It had become clear by mid-1918 that the strategy of unrestricted submarine warfare had failed. It failed because technology had begun to work against the U-boats. Merchant ships now sailed in convoy. Enormous minefields were sown across the U-boats' tracks in and out of Germany; the depth charge was developed; airplanes and blimps guarded convoys and spotted U-boats as they sailed on the surface. In April 1917 U-boats accounted for eight hundred thousand tons of shipping lost. One year later that figure had dropped by two-thirds. Nevertheless, the boats continued to sail, to attack, and to sink ships, even after the Americans had arrived in force, the last major German land offensive had collapsed, and clandestine peace negotiations had begun. When U-boat operations were finally halted on 22 October 1918, they had sunk fourteen hundred enemy and neutral ships of about twelve million tons—an extraordinary total by any reckoning.

The tradition of the U-Bootwaffe received a last bittersweet cachet just before the war ended. In October 1918 a mutiny broke out in the German surface fleet. It was a stain that the postwar naval establishment could not explain, expunge, or forget, and the obsession with it affected minds and drove policy for many years. The mutiny did not spread to the U-boats, however, and so it was left to a U-boat officer to break it up. Johann Spiess, commander of U-135 and Otto Weddigen's first watch officer in 1914, was directed to bring his boat into Wilhelmshaven harbor, the hub of the insurrection. Once inside, he pointed his bow at the huge battleship *Thüringen,* prepared to fire his torpedoes, sink the ship, and kill her mutineers and anyone else on board if they did not surrender at once. Spiess was determined that his boat would always be loyal even if loyalty meant turning on his own countrymen.

After the war ended, the success of the U-Bootwaffe brought the wrath of its enemies crashing down upon its members, their service, and their country. The Treaty of Versailles banned U-boats. Those already in existence were taken by the Allies, and Germany was forbidden to build any more. Some in the new Reichsmarine, however, doubted that they were gone forever. The officers and men of the U-Bootwaffe were gone as well: dispersed among a defeated and demoralized population to become bankers, barbers, farmers, and mechanics. All that was left were pictures—of Weddigen torpedoing his three cruisers, of Schwieger and the *Lusitania,* of the courtly Arnauld and the devilish Patzig, of burning ships, coffins on an Irish beach, and Spiess waiting eagerly to destroy the rebellious *Thüringen*—and silence.

Between the end of the war in 1918 and the return of the U-Bootwaffe in 1935, these pictures of the U-boats began to coalesce into a formal tradition. The process involved much debate and historical revision, and some of what resulted was doubtless enhanced by those who had a personal interest in it. Early histories of the war were not helpful. Historians who wrote from the enemy point of view naturally condemned the U-boats; German accounts were defensive and apologetic. By the late 1920s these negative attitudes receded as readers became more intrigued than appalled by the U-boats and U-boat veterans began to publish their memoirs. Michael Hadley identifies one turning point as the publication in 1928 of Lowell Thomas's popular book *Raiders of the Deep,* a collection of short portraits of the wartime U-boat aces.[10] *Raiders,* which was written without rancor in a tabloid-style prose and published in several languages, including German, treated the U-boat commander with interest and compassion. One poignant scene in the book involved Otto Hersing, the ace and hero who had done as much as anyone to inspire the U-boat tradition. Thomas had tracked him down to a small farm on the Baltic coast, where, bereft of fame and glory, Hersing poked at his potatoes and complained of arthritis.

By the time the first U-boat commanders of World War II began to trickle into the newly reconstituted U-Bootwaffe in 1935, the formal tradition of the U-boat was in place, well developed, widely known, and respected as much by Germany's former adversaries as by the Germans themselves. This tradition consisted of the history of the U-boats and

their success in the war, the integrity and honor of their best commanders, the high level of esprit de corps among their crewmen, and the loyalty
of the organization as a whole. The tradition failed to take into account
the unpleasant aspects of the U-boat war: the bad judgment, the cruelty,
the ruthlessness and atrocities that sometimes occurred, and the fact that
submarine warfare by its nature could be a gruesome exercise, wholly
unsuited to the concepts of chivalry and mercy. It was a handsome legacy
but not an entirely objective one.

This tradition was familiar to the new commanders, though they differed in their acceptance of it. For example, although everyone recognized that the model for a U-boat officer's behavior could be found in the
actions of someone like Lothar von Arnauld de la Perière, not everyone
set out to emulate Arnauld. Some, in fact, had no time for him and his
comrades. Their days were done, their glory gone. They were set aside in
favor of another image: the stirring portrait of a kind and stalwart face
over stiff collar and bow tie, with U-boat badge, Iron Cross, Blue Max,
and scribbled surname floating across brass buttons and gold braid—the
knight, the monster of the sea.

CHAPTER 2

"We Were a New Start!"

29 March 1933. . . . We spend our first afternoon looking around this beautiful island, still unknown civilians, still our own masters. . . . One meets old friends among new comrades and memories of the past are dragged out; one meets people from the same home town who share friends and acquaintances. Always there is the question "where from?" and each answer is different. They come from all over the Reich. It is a fine thing that the Navy can create such a community from all these different regions.

—Jürgen Oesten, on his first day in the Reichsmarine

WHEN Otto Weddigen sank three cruisers in 1914, Victor Oehrn was six years old. Most German boys his age knew of Otto Weddigen and his remarkable achievement, but Victor, because of his unusual circumstances, may not have. His father, an executive in the Siemens Corporation, was working at a factory in the Caucasus when Victor was born in 1907. Victor would not see Germany until he was fourteen, and he grew up among Russians, Armenians, Georgians, and Tatars. After the Bolshevik Revolution in 1917, his father was put on a list of the local "bourgeoisie," to be disposed of in one way or another. The Oehrn family was forced to move, first to another Siemens mine and then back to Berlin in 1921. "It was quite an adventure," Victor Oehrn remembers—especially for a youngster. At fourteen he had a thorough knowledge of both the Russian character and the Islamic faith. He spoke French and English and would later become one of only four Russian interpreters in the Kriegsmarine.

Victor Oehrn was an *Auslandsdeutscher,* a German citizen who was raised outside of Germany. People with such a background usually had several identifiable traits. Because of his trials in the Caucasus, for example, Oehrn hated communism with a passion not matched by most

16

Germans (he does not hate the Russian people, he will hasten to add, only the Bolsheviks, "strangers with Russian names"). For the same reason he was, and still is, very nationalistic; living outside of Germany and seeing it only from afar, he had formed a love for it that many of his contemporaries did not share. Finally, he loathed the Treaty of Versailles, calling it "stupid, short-sighted, unjust, and discriminatory." He believed it had left Germany weak and unprotected, "and this is the reason for my joining the military. I am an Auslandsdeutscher. I have experienced personally what it means to be defenseless. I wanted to do my part to change that." [1] In 1927, the year before *Raiders of the Deep* was published, Victor Oehrn joined the Reichsmarine.

His career over the next five years was typical for a junior officer in a small navy and rather humdrum. He finished his formal training in 1930, then served for eighteen months on the light cruiser *Königsberg,* winning his commission as a Leutnant zur See in September 1931 and developing an exceptional talent for the endless minutiae and relative ignominy of staff work. During this time he became well schooled in mining and torpedo operations, communications, naval artillery, navigation, and probably submarine warfare (though this last would have been limited to classroom theory). Apparently he had proven leadership skills as well because in September 1932 he was assigned to the Reichsmarine basic training base on the Dänholm. Six months later, as the *Kompaniechef,* or company officer, of a recruit training company, he was standing on an empty drill field to greet the new and confused recruits of Reichsmarine Crew 33.

MOST of the wartime U-boat commanders were trained in the decade before the war, and most of the famous ones were commissioned officers when the war began. The process they had to endure before their commissioning was difficult, thorough, and consistent across the year groups, or *Crews,* with which they entered. In the mid-1930s this process consisted of five stages and lasted approximately three years: two months of basic infantry training; three months of training under sail; an extended training cruise in a Reichsmarine cruiser; nine months of classroom education at the Marineschule Mürwik; and a probationary period in the fleet after formal training and before commissioning. The sequence was the same for earlier crews, like Victor Oehrn's, and later ones, though the duration of one stage or the next might vary and the overall course tended to shorten as war approached. All future U-boat officers followed it in lockstep with their surface navy counterparts.

Reichsmarine basic training—*Infanteristische Ausbildung*—on the Dänholm was the first step. The Dänholm is a small, windswept island off the Baltic coast of eastern Germany between the port city of Stralsund on the mainland and the larger island of Rugen to the north. Cold, barren, and remote, it was not a pleasant place, but it was well-suited for the purpose it served, which was to turn civilians into soldiers. In the last few days of March 1933 123 young men descended upon the Dänholm from every part of Germany, each with a suitcase, a bewildered look, and orders to report for induction. These young men together made up Crew 33, and they represented the entire intake of officer candidates for the year.

"And so we cross over to the Dänholm," wrote one of these new recruits, Jürgen Oesten, in the diary he opened on 29 March. "It is rather like a symbol: on one side is the old life, the first chapter; on the other side is the beginning of a new life." [2] Ever since he crossed over, Oesten continued to believe that a man's life can be divided into sections, like chapters in a book or acts in a play, or even that he might live several lives, each with a beginning and an end, before he died. It is not an uncommon idea, and it is shared by other U-Bootwaffe officers. And though they might divide their own lives up in different ways, for most of them a chapter closed as soon as they crossed over to the Dänholm.

Jürgen Oesten was six years younger than Victor Oehrn, and he barely remembers the war. His background was nothing like Oehrn's (or those of most of his new classmates). He was born in Berlin, where his father was a sculptor and a member of the city's large, diverse, and colorful artistic community; he still owns a bust his father made of him as a boy. Though his parents were tolerant people who instilled the same virtue in him, they disliked the newly powerful National Socialist Party and kept their distance from it. Oesten seems less agitated than Oehrn about such things as peace terms and treaty restrictions, and patriotism was not his primary motivation for entering the Reichsmarine. "Why did I enter the navy?" he wrote. "Well, I had been sailing on all sorts of boats and yachts—started at the age of twelve on lakes near Berlin and with bigger boats on the Baltic later on." *Aus Freude an der Seefahrt*, for love of the sea, were the words of another ace, but Jürgen Oesten cannot take it as seriously. "On the other hand," he continued, "for boys there are certain periods when they want to be pastry cooks or coachmen or sailors. Apparently I stopped at the sailor period." [3]

There were dozens of good reasons for a young man to join the military service, especially one as exciting and romantic as the Reichsmarine, and future U-Bootwaffe officers in various crews have given different reasons for doing so. Oehrn's patriotism and Oesten's love of the sea were only two of them. Others included the prospect of a steady job in the midst of a recession, the prestige and respect that went with a commission, and the urge to "get away from it all." For Karl Daublebsky von Eichhain, Crew 29, the Reichsmarine was the only way he could continue the seafaring tradition of his father and both grandfathers; that he was Austrian made no difference to him, even though one of his heroes, the Austrian U-boat commander Georg von Trapp, would eventually flee the country rather than have to make a similar decision. For Hans-Diedrich von Tiesenhausen and Helmut Witte, both members of Crew 34, the navy was an opportunity for travel and adventure. "I had joined the navy for the same reason as so many young boys do of all nations or countries," writes von Tiesenhausen. "All we wanted to do was see the world." And "to see the world at government expense," adds Witte, "since I couldn't afford to pay for it myself."[4]

The reason a man gave for entering the Reichsmarine was one of the few ways in which he differed from the rest of his classmates, for the process used by the Reichsmarine to investigate, examine, screen, and finally select its recruits was calculated to ensure that all of them were as alike as possible. This process had not changed at all since Oehrn had been accepted in 1927 and hardly at all since the days of the old Imperial Navy, and the unwritten rules it used to select new officer candidates for its ranks were extremely rigorous and more than a bit skewed. Theoretically, any German male with an *Abitur* (roughly speaking, a high school diploma, but harder to obtain) was eligible for the Dänholm, but the average recruit, according to Eric Rust, was more strictly defined: "[The new recruit was] born and raised in a sizable Prussian city not far from the sea; his parents Protestant and commoners, members of the middle class; his father an active or former officer with political ties to the DNVP [the most conservative of Weimar Germany's major political parties]; well educated, highly motivated, and physically fit; aware and supportive of the traditions of the naval officer corps; a supporter of Hitler's takeover on grounds of order, normalcy, and national revival, but with some misgivings over Nazi methods and the more radical aspects of the Party program."[5]

Members of Crew 33 came from all over the Reich and sometimes from beyond. But most grew up in the northern regions of Germany proper and lived within one hundred miles of the sea. Most were Evangelical Lütheran; only a fraction were Roman Catholic, and none were Jews.

Most came from the conservative middle-class families who sentimentally remembered the "old Germany," suffered through the war, disliked the postwar government, and loathed the communists. All of these characteristics were thought desirable in Reichsmarine officers. Not until later did it become clear that they would lead to an officer corps that willingly accepted the rise of National Socialism, applauded the early successes of Adolf Hitler, the rejection of Versailles, the renascence of the military, the territorial grabs, and, in the end, became a tragic group of men who could neither condemn nor reject their government until it was too late.

The future U-boat commanders in Crew 33 were no exception. The Bremen-born Reinhard Hardegen, for example, who would make his name along the East Coast of North America in 1942, met almost all of the implicit criteria listed above when he was selected as a member of the crew. Bremen was a *Hansestadt* and the second largest seaport in Germany. Hardegen's father taught in a *Gymnasium* and was one of a group, according to Rust, that contributed to the narrow education and conservative mind-set of Reichsmarine crews in the twenties and thirties. Hardegen was a Protestant, an *Abiturient* (and thus qualified to enter university), and a skilled yachtsman by the time he was in his teens. He also came highly recommended for the Reichsmarine by the former merchant marine officer, U-boat commander, and war hero Paul König, a family friend.[6]

The Reichsmarine selection process was indeed thorough, and there would have been dozens of young men like Reinhard Hardegen in Crew 33. Background, breeding, and education varied less among U-Bootwaffe officers than other factors simply because the service had such a high level of control over them. It was not perfect, however, and in spite of its rigor and perceived inflexibility, it did occasionally allow the odd rebel, square peg, or just plain weird person to slip through. It would be nice to think that this was done intentionally—diversity is the key to any good mix of good men—but more likely it just happened. At least two examples could be found in the new crew: Jürgen Oesten, who certainly did not fit the pattern, and Wolfgang Lüth, the son of a cloth merchant in Riga.

Victor Oehrn does not remember Jürgen Oesten; tellingly, he remembers Wolfgang Lüth very well, possibly because Lüth was so much like him. Lüth, like Oehrn, was an Auslandsdeutscher. His family lived in Latvia, members of a German community that had been present in the Baltic states since the days of the Teutonic knights. His Baltic accent was thick and set him apart at once, as did his odd appearance, and he had other less visible characteristics that were just as distinctive. Auslandsdeutscher by nature were conservative and nationalistic; in the case of the Baltic Germans these traits were charged and exacerbated by a genuine persecution of the community, first by the Russians and then by the Latvians themselves. Lüth was no exception to this rule and went further than most. Whether he was enthusiastic about National Socialism as a recruit is not clear, but later in his career he became one of its most vocal adherents. Like many of the true believers, he embarrassed himself more than once in the process. Not surprisingly, Lüth and Oesten were never close.

In April 1933, Jürgen Oesten, Wolfgang Lüth, Reinhard Hardegen, and 120 other young men were standing on the threshold of naval careers that would be interesting, exciting, often deadly, and uniformly tragic. Many of Germany's future U-boat commanders and several aces were in their midst, though none of them knew it. Many of them would die in their boats; none of them knew who. At that point they knew only that they had survived a difficult selection process and that they were having a miserable time on the Dänholm.

II Schiffsstammabteilung Ostsee (II SSO), the training unit to which the entire crew had been assigned, had been divided like an army battalion into companies, platoons, and squads. Each company was led by a commissioned Reichsmarine officer, and each squad, or *Korporalschaft,* by a noncommissioned officer (NCO). These two played different but complementary roles. The duty of the company commander was to provide moral and professional guidance for the recruits and to supervise, at a distance, their training. "It is the commander's duty to form and strengthen the spirit, the morale, of the young recruit," wrote Victor Oehrn. "One cannot do this with nice words, but only with an outstanding personal example. In the training of the officer candidate this duty is of the *highest meaning and importance* . . . a fine and important duty indeed!"[7] Aside from this, Oehrn kept an appropriate Prussian distance from his charges, all of whom, as recruits, were men of the lowest rank.

The hands-on training of the new recruits was left to the squad leaders. This training included close-order drill, weapons training, physical fitness, uniform and quarters inspections, and other day-to-day activities, as well as a liberal portion of unadulterated physical and mental punishment. Temporary power, along with the frustrating knowledge that they themselves were ultimately to be the subordinates, allowed the NCOs to do their job with relish, and new recruits were subjected to meaningless drill, sadistic exercise routine, and shouted abuse. Few look back upon the experience with any pleasure. In this regard, basic training on the Dänholm was no different from any other boot camp in any other service in any other country: it was designed and executed to weed out those who were unfit or unprepared for military service as quickly as possible.

The bonds formed on the Dänholm would last for years, through a terrible war, an equally difficult peace, and into the present day, in part because everyone recognized soon enough that the trials of the Dänholm were more easily overcome by sticking together and cooperating with one another. For those who survived—and most did—the misery of the island was one more thing that all of them, no matter where they went, no matter if they succeeded or failed in their careers or their lives, would have in common forever.

After basic training was complete the crew began to disperse. Not all of the original 123 men in Crew 33 were in training to become line officers, or *Seeoffiziere*. Some were to be engineering officers, medical officers, or administrative officers, and their training would take them elsewhere. U-boat commanders were without exception Seeoffiziere until late in the war. Many of the engineers would eventually find their way back into the U-Bootwaffe to serve with distinction, but they would never be watch officers or commanders. In a few cases large boats were assigned doctors, but this was not the usual practice, and they were never given command. (This segregation by career field was the source of some frustration, especially among the engineers. The Bundesmarine discontinued the practice after the war.)

For the future Seeoffiziere, a year of training at sea followed the Dänholm. Newly promoted to *Seekadetten* (naval cadets), they reported to Kiel in June 1933 for three months on the Reichsmarine sailing ship *Gorch Fock,* a brand-new three-masted barque. The intent of service on the *Gorch Fock* was to provide the officer candidate not only practical training in seamanship but some small insight into himself. The training was difficult, often frightening, and sometimes dangerous; swinging from a single line forty or fifty feet above the main deck in the teeth of a gale builds character if nothing else. On a practical level, the apprenticeship on the *Gorch Fock* appears only minimally applicable to the skills required for U-boat operations. The two platforms had little in common, and sailing ships, for reasons of safety and sentimentality, were rarely engaged by U-boats.

More useful were the subsequent training cruises on Reichsmarine warships, during which the Seekadetten played the roles of ordinary deck seamen. Both Oesten and Lüth were embarked on the light cruiser *Karlsruhe* in October 1933 in Kiel, which had been designated specifically as a train-

The Marineschule Mürwik. Built on the east bank of Flensburger Förde in 1910, it is the place where all German naval officers receive their formal classroom training. Most U-boat commanders spent at least some time in the "Red Castle by the Sea." (Marineschule Mürwik)

ing ship and given a reduced regular crew to accommodate the new arrivals. Over the next nine months, as the *Karlsruhe* steamed around the world and visited one foreign port after another, the Seekadetten observed and participated in most aspects of fleet operations, and by the time the cruise was over and they had disembarked, they had a good idea of how their own ships and those of their enemies would operate in wartime (the only area in which they had missed out, ironically, was antisubmarine warfare [ASW] because the heavy cruiser is not an ASW platform and there were no U-boats to play with). A major examination followed the cruise. Not everyone passed it, but those who did were promoted to the rank of *Fähnrich* (midshipman) and proceeded to the fourth stage of their formal training, the Marineschule Mürwik, for six months of classroom training beginning in June 1934.

If any single place can be considered the home of the German naval officer, it is the Marineschule Mürwik, the "Red Castle by the Sea." The Marineschule is the German equivalent of the United States Naval Academy, and although one usually spends only a short time there, it evokes in many the same air of mystical nostalgia. Its rust-red towers rise from the Jutland peninsula just north of Flensburg. Before it lie the peaceful waters of Flensburger Förde; behind it rests the small leafy suburb of Mürwik, from which it takes its name. It was founded in 1910 by Kaiser Wilhelm II in the midst of a tremendous and often bitter naval arms race between Germany and Great Britain; nevertheless, its methods were patterned after those of its British counterpart at Dartmouth as much as the entire Imperial Navy was patterned after the Royal Navy. The curriculum was designed to produce gentlemen as well as officers. The subjects taught at the Marineschule therefore included all of the usual ones associated with the naval profession—navigation, signals, marine engineering, naval history, tactics, leadership, and English—as well as several of the more esoteric pursuits often associated with the military officer as a member of the landed gentry or the idle nobility—dancing, fencing, riding, and yachting, to name a few.

The Marineschule, like everything the young men had experienced so far, was slightly apart from the real world. It was supposed to be an escape, a safe place in an ugly world. But it was here, amid the fencing and yachting, that the world first intruded upon the men of Crew 33. In the first week of August 1934 a hastily arranged ceremony was held at the Marineschule in which the entire crew was *neu vereidigt,* literally, "sworn in anew." Each member of the crew was required to take a new oath that day, the infamous *Fahneneid,* in which he pledged his loyalty and his obedience not to a country or a flag but to an individual; in the words of the oath, "to Adolf Hitler, the Führer of the German Reich and People [and the] Supreme Commander of the Armed Forces." This remarkable oath was taken by every man in the German armed forces within hours of Reich President Paul von Hindenburg's death and Hitler's elevation as head of state. Reinhard Hardegen, Jürgen Oesten, and Wolfgang Lüth took the oath at the Marineschule that day. Victor Oehrn took it on the Dänholm. Helmut Witte, Hans-Diedrich von Tiesenhausen, and the rest of Crew 34 took it on the deck of the sailing ship *Gorch Fock.* Indeed, every man in the service took the new oath that day, but few of them could foresee its ultimate tragic consequences.

It was one of the few times that the political earthquakes then occurring in Germany affected the Reichsmarine, but it did not seem to cause any moral or philosophical problems within the officer corps, and most of them took the oath without a murmur. It was a small price to pay for everything they could see happening around them; the accession of Adolf

Hitler to power, however terrible it would turn out for Germany in the future, was very good for them in 1934, for the Reichsmarine, after years of stagnation, was beginning to grow. After Hitler took power in January 1933, naval construction accelerated and recruiting went up. More ships were being laid down. Reichsmarine crews increased in size. And it seemed, for the first time in a decade and a half, that U-boats might once again be a part of the German fleet.

IN 1934, while serving as a training officer on the *Karlsruhe* with Crew 33, Victor Oehrn was asked if he had any interest in U-boat service. His reaction was an emphatic *nein*; he was sure that such duty would mean spending several years with one eye glued to a periscope, and he wanted no part of it. He would have preferred a small command of his own— perhaps a minesweeper—with little supervision and few rules to follow. In any case, it was an odd question to ask; rumors were heard, of course, but there were still no U-boats in 1934, and he probably gave the question no more thought.[8]

The Reichsmarine had tried from the outset to find ways around the ban on U-boats. As early as 1922, an office had been set up to deal officially with matters of ship construction but in reality with the continuation of research and development in submarine warfare. German shipyards in the late 1920s were building submarines for other navies, which was not strictly banned by the treaty. In October 1934 the first class of officers had begun training at the new U-Bootabwehrschule (U-boat defense school, or UAW). The UAW was a thinly disguised center for the training of prospective U-boat commanders. The attitude was simply that everything short of an official breach of the treaty regulations was to be attempted; it was cynical, but no more so than the German attitude toward a similar ban on an air force, which was circumvented by the establishment of flying clubs, a national airline, and so on. By 1935, therefore, all that allowed the Reichsmarine to claim adherence to the Treaty of Versailles was a lack of rivets.

This odd state of affairs did not last for much longer. On 18 June 1935 the Anglo-German Naval Treaty was signed by representatives of both countries. It was, in essence, a repudiation of Versailles on paper, for it gave Britain nothing and allowed Germany to increase the size of the Reichsmarine (or, as it was soon to be called, the Kriegsmarine), to build more ships of every type, to institute a new fleet air arm, and, most significant, to build U-boats on a basis of one for every two in the Royal

Navy. Almost immediately the parts of six new U-boats were clapped together, and in September the first U-boat flotilla of the postwar period was formed in Wilhelmshaven: Flotilla Weddigen. By the end of the year twelve U-boats, all of them brand-new type II coastal boats (the crews jokingly called them *Einbäume,* or canoes), were assigned to the new flotilla, and *Kapitän zur See* (captain) Karl Dönitz, a former U-boat commander and captain of the cruiser *Emden,* was chosen to be its first commanding officer.

The selection was portentous and would have effects that nobody at the time could have foreseen. *Time* magazine, on its cover of 10 May 1943, portrayed Karl Dönitz as a huge head of riveted steel plates mounted at the top of a periscope. All around him, in a black and stormy sea, were other periscopes, not with the heads of men but of serpents. It was the perfect metaphor because by then, more than any other military leader in the war, Karl Dönitz had become synonymous with the organization he commanded. He *was* the U-Bootwaffe. He is its personification in the public mind. The image and reputation of the U-Bootwaffe are tied directly to his own, and one will rise or fall with the other. One cannot understand the U-boat commander without an understanding, or at least a knowledge, of Dönitz, a man most of them knew simultaneously as "the Lion" and "Onkel Karl," the consummate warrior and the understanding second father.

His own experience with U-boats had been brief. He was commissioned in 1914 and spent the first two years of the war in the surface fleet. As a U-Bootwaffe officer, he was a politician rather than a prodigy. His former commanding officer in U-39, the ace Walter Forstmann, said of him in a private conversation: "He learned the business on U-39 apparently adequately, excessively ambitious and pushy at times with little consideration as to other people's feelings, somewhat stubborn and obtuse. A man of black and white, dislike[d] to compromise."[9] As a commander, he met with only faint success. In 1918 his boat, UB-35, was sunk near Malta; he was captured, spent time in Britain as a prisoner of war, and returned to Germany only after pretending to be insane. In 1920 he was invited to enter the Reichsmarine. His career over the next fifteen years was spent in various staff and surface positions, culminating with command of the *Emden.* In 1935 he was forty-three years old, a thin, gray, unremarkable man, more impressive in uniform than out, but of unimpeachable deportment and military bearing. He had many vices, but his principal virtue was his ability to lead men, and it is this trait that most of his former officers and men are apt to comment upon when they speak of him. "His men," wrote Victor Oehrn, "saw in him a comrade, who would always be there for them, as much as they saw a superior who had unquestioned authority over them." [10]

Despite the ban on U-boats, Karl Dönitz never lost his interest in submarine warfare or his conviction that U-boats would one day again be a part of Germany's fleet, and he never stopped thinking about their possibilities in a future conflict. When he took command of Flotilla Weddigen, he had already conceived of and documented U-boat operations and tactics that went far beyond its modest six boats to contemplate a fleet of hundreds. In the first war, for example, the U-boat had operated alone; in the next war he imagined huge packs of boats operating together, guided by radio. In the first war, airpower was not a factor in the undersea war; in the second he saw that the proper use of aircraft for scouting, support, and defense could be critical for the success of any U-boat offensive. In the first war the U-boat attacked enemy warships as well as merchant shipping. But it was clear to Dönitz that the U-boat could never win a fight against the Royal Navy. The primary target had to be the enemy's merchant fleet, and the sole purpose of the U-boat was to sink them faster than they could be replaced: "The *sinking of ships* was the only thing that counted," he believed, and "any diversion, however attractive, which resulted in a reduction of the number of ships being sunk was inadmissible." [11] It seems clear that Dönitz, from the beginning, knew exactly what he wanted and what he didn't want for his new U-Bootwaffe, and he certainly did not want the ways and methods of the old U-Bootwaffe.

Between the end of the war and the beginning of the National Socialist era in Germany, the dented image of the U-boat commander of World War I was being rehabilitated. By the middle of the 1930s, according to Michael Hadley, this image had regained its wartime luster, and the men behind the image, the old aces such as Weddigen, Arnauld, Hersing, and Forstmann, were heroes again, respected by the public and celebrated in the media. [12] The aura surrounding them was to be used with abandon by the propagandists of the New Order. Dönitz, however, felt that these men should be honored at arm's length.

That the new U-Bootwaffe accepted the tradition of the old was reflected in many of the customs that were adopted. In the late 1930s, for example, new U-boat flotillas were named for fallen aces, beginning with Flotilla Weddigen in 1935. New U-boats with the same numbers as the famous boats of World War I were designated *Traditionsboote* and often wore distinctive insignia (the second U-9 displayed Weddigen's Iron Cross on her conning tower). It became customary to invite veterans of the old boats to the commissioning of a new one. But people often just smiled at these "old men with the crowns on their badges," which illustrates a sad but interesting part of the U-boat tradition and those who inspired it. Many of the great aces had a formative effect on the young men who succeeded them. But this effect remained at a personal level; when the boats returned, the old men with the crowns on their badges were politely left aside. In the experience of Victor Oehrn, they no longer fit in.

"We respected these old captains highly," he wrote later, "but we knew that their time was over. Of course I met many of them, with due respect, but there is a great difference between submarine aces and able staff officers. Arnauld de la Perière, Fürbringer, Valentiner . . . they all impressed me but we were a new start!"[13] They were old, out of touch, and lacking in spirit. Neither embraced nor consulted by the new blood of the U-Bootwaffe, they finished their fading careers in Kriegsmarine backwaters or were pushed gently into retirement. Hersing never returned. Arnauld started the war as flag officer, Danzig. Forstmann was sent to a munitions command in Osnabrück, Rose to another one in Münster, and Valentiner found himself at a desk in U-Bootabnehmekommando (U-Boat Acceptance Command, or UAK).

Dönitz wanted younger men, unaffected by the past, anxious to learn, and loyal only to him. Victor Oehrn, to his surprise, was one of these men, chosen in 1935 to be the commander of U-14 and the junior man in a fairly junior group. Most of the twelve new flotilla commanders were midranking surface warfare officers with between eight and eleven years of seniority and an average age of thirty. Other than Dönitz himself, nobody either in the flotilla staff or among the commanders of Flotilla Weddigen had had any previous experience with submarines; none but him had served in the war. Within two years Dönitz was accepting officers from crews as late as 1933 and 1934, men for whom the deeds of the great U-boat aces were a dim memory at best and more likely the stuff of boys' books. As a predictable result, the U-Bootwaffe officer corps was loyal to Dönitz, accepting uncritically his way of doing things and willing to follow him, as Oehrn once overheard one man in Flotilla Weddigen say, "into hell."

The training, comprehensive, exhausting, and incessant, began as soon as Flotilla Weddigen was established. "We drilled in Mecklenburg Bight because of the depth," wrote Oehrn. "We drilled from Monday through

The first twelve commanders of Flotilla Weddigen in 1936. According to Victor Oehrn, it is the only photograph in existence that shows all of them. Sitting, from left: Rösing, Grosse, Looff, Loycke (flotilla commander), Eckermann, Freiwald. Standing, from left: Paukstadt, Fresdorf, Schmidt, von Stockhausen, Beduhn, Schütze, and Oehrn. (Victor Oehrn)

Friday, daylight drills, nighttime drills, drills to the limits of our physical and emotional beings. Dönitz supervised all of this, usually from the bridge of our tender, the *Saar*. He said to us more than once, 'If it should come to war you will be able to say that nothing was any worse than the Mecklenburg Bight.'"[14] But even though life for these happy few was hectic and tiring, their spirits were high and morale was stratospheric. "We were a new start." They had, in a lighter moment, found and read a copy of Lowell Thomas's *Raiders of the Deep* (a title, says Oehrn, that highly amused them). At the suggestion of the senior officer in the flotilla, Hans-Günther Looff, the twelve of them signed a telegram stating, in essence, "We're back," and sent it off to the British publishers of *Raiders* in London.[15]

On 1 July 1936 a second U-flotilla was formed, Flotilla Hundius. Karl Dönitz assumed command of both flotillas on 1 July and the title of *Führer der U-Boote* (Commander, U-Boats, or FdU). Flotilla Weddigen was given to Kapitän zur See Albert Loycke, and shortly after that the original commanders began to go their separate ways. The service was growing, and they were its new apostles; although they had been in command of their boats for only a short time, they possessed invaluable experience that had to be passed along to others who followed them. A photograph, believed to be the only one in existence, was taken of them with Loycke toward the end. They are standing on a pier at dawn, each wrapped in his own version of the navy dress blue uniform, each with the trademark white cap of the U-boat commander. They are a cheerful bunch but ready, as Oehrn said later, in the spirit of the gladiator, to die for Germany. Of these twelve men only two became great successes during the coming war. Viktor Schütze left U-19 in 1938 to take command of U-25, and over the next two years sank enough ships to end up in fourth place on the tonnage list. But he could never have been called a media star, and he died only five years after the war was over. Victor Oehrn would also achieve success during the war. Two or three others were competent officers, but several were abject failures. One of the most unfortunate was Looff himself. He sank one ship, a tanker, in June 1940, but his own boat was lost so soon afterward that he did not have time to report his first triumph before he died.

The U-Bootwaffe continued to grow slowly until the beginning of the war, and more and more men were accepted to serve in it. Despite the exertions of Dönitz to get more money and more resources, however, it remained relatively small. The problem was Adolf Hitler's limited vision and his equating of sea power with huge surface ships and big guns; in spite of everything that had been learned at tragic cost in the first war, he had decided to build battleships instead of U-boats. A series of naval construction programs had followed the signing of the Naval Treaty in 1935; each was more ambitious than the last, and each contained the promise of more U-boats. But U-boat construction always seemed to be the lowest of several priorities; cruisers, pocket battleships, battleships, and aircraft carriers, were all laid down in the years before the war, but the number of U-boats in commission rose very slowly. The last and most fantastic of these construction programs, created in January 1939, was the Z Plan, which promised Dönitz almost 250 boats of various sizes. The Z Plan was innovative in several ways, but it had flaws. The most serious of these was an assumption that war with Britain (a war that Hitler had already decided would be necessary to his plans) would not occur for at least five years and optimistically ten.

AFTER leaving the Marineschule in April 1935, the Fähnriche of Crew 33 had been sent to their first at-sea assignments, mostly in large surface ships. Wolfgang Lüth reported to the cruiser *Königsberg,* Jürgen Oesten to the *Karlsruhe.* Unlike the graduates of the United States Naval Academy, they were not yet commissioned officers; it was an old Imperial Navy practice that officer candidates had to serve at sea for a probationary period, after which they would be commissioned upon the recommendations of their commanding officers. In reality, it was unusual for a Fähnrich not to be commissioned a Leutnant zur See along with everyone else in his crew unless he was very stupid or incredibly unlucky, and most of Crew 33 was commissioned en bloc in October 1936 after about eighteen months in the fleet (it was not until the relatively lofty rank of *Kapitänleutnant* (lieutenant) that the promotion dates within a crew began to diverge significantly based on performance, seniority, and ranking). Toward the end of 1936 and the beginning of 1937, newly "striped" and with some measure of experience at sea under their belts, the members of Crew 33 began to trickle into the U-Bootwaffe. Within four months of his promotion Lüth was in Neustadt at the U-boat school. Oesten followed him four months later, but after both men had gone through the many months of training and several individual training commands, Oesten was the first to be assigned an operational boat. He became second watch officer on U-20 in October 1937; Lüth became second watch officer on U-27 almost nine months later.

What led a man to enter the U-Bootwaffe? None were compelled to do so; Karl Dönitz was a forceful recruiter, but by and large his officers were enthusiastic volunteers. (This was not the case during the war, however, a fact that is contrary to the image.) Each man had his reasons for joining, but unlike those they had for joining the Reichsmarine itself, they were similar and had a lot to do with their perception of the U-Bootwaffe as exciting, effective, the "cutting edge," the weapon of destiny for Germany in any future conflict. Travel, tradition, or *Freude an der Seefahrt,* were rarely motivations. "When England declared war," wrote Reinhard Reche, a member of Crew 34, "the Kriegsmarine was in no way prepared against the great sea powers. So we volunteered for the U-Bootwaffe, which seemed to be the most effective means for cutting [off] their supplies. . . . The U-boot commander had the means for defending against the overwhelming seapower of the British Navy, and I found that confirmed in action, a very positive image indeed." Hans-Diedrich von Tiesenhausen adds simply: "It was something very special and adventurous in those days."[16]

The training program for U-boat officers was among the most rigorous in the Wehrmacht but not as formal as the training already in place for Kriegsmarine officer candidates, and the time it took to get through it varied from officer to officer. The program did accomplish its objective, which was to prepare its subjects for war, as did the constant drills and exercises to which Dönitz subjected all his operational boats. The fact that he was now several layers removed from the boats themselves did not mean that the routine had slackened since those early days in Mecklenburg Bight. If anything, the regime became more rigorous as time went on and the indications of war increased. Regular exercises were held in the North Atlantic. The Spanish Civil War provided an excellent training ground; many of Dönitz's boats spent time in Spanish coastal waters. The U-Bootwaffe was placed on alert twice: in September 1938, during the Sudetenland crisis, and again in March 1939 after Germany occupied the western half of Czechoslovakia. Both alerts turned out to be false alarms, but they were opportunities for Dönitz to test the preparedness of his service.

Nervous rumblings from abroad came at the same time as a disconcerting social upheaval at home. The most troubling aspects were the actions being taken against the Jewish population of Germany. Most U-Bootwaffe officers plead ignorance of these things—they seemed too busy to notice. "We were at sea," recalled Erich Topp, a member of Crew 34, "and only received news filtered by the Propaganda Ministry. If we had doubts about these activities, we were quite prepared to rationalize them." [17] Sometimes, however, they were so blatant and so awful that they could be neither ignored nor rationalized. Jürgen Oesten was on leave in Berlin during the night of 8 November 1938. The next morning, after thousands of Jewish homes, shops, and synagogues had been burned and tens of thousands of Jews beaten and robbed in the streets, he put on his best uniform, walked through the wreckage to the home of a Jewish family friend, and apologized as best he could for what would someday be known as the "Night of Glass," the Kristallnacht. [18]

By the late summer of 1939, war was assured. Plans were being completed in Berlin for the staged provocation that would allow German troops to enter Poland, and the final touches were being put on a nonaggression pact with the Soviet Union that would leave Germany's eastern advance undisturbed and her new borders secure. The German army and the Luftwaffe were ready for war, at least as much as any military force will admit to being ready. The Kriegsmarine, marooned in the first year of a ten-year rebuilding program, was not ready, and Karl Dönitz, having been promised 250 U-boats to fight the greatest fleet in the world, had 57, of which only a third were operational at any given time and another third could have been broken up for scrap metal. The material state of the U-Bootwaffe was grim. Thankfully, it was more fortunate in its men.

By 1939 there existed a solid base of several thousand well-trained and highly motivated U-boat crewmen. They were the U-Bootwaffe's most valuable asset, and in forming the nuclei for hundreds of later crews, their influence would extend like fruitful vines throughout the war. They were led by a cadre of professional officers, well educated, equally motivated, trained under the supervision of Dönitz himself and a small band of commanding officers who would come to be known as the first generation of the World War II U-boat command. This group, a few score at most, consisted traditionally of officers who had a boat when the war started or who (like Victor Oehrn) had one before the war and then moved on to other things. Dönitz once called them "the old guard of my U-Bootwaffe, upon whom my heart has always dwelt and still dwells." [19]

Granted, there is a certain cachet attached to the term "first generation" and little doubt that those men had an influence beyond their number in shaping the wartime perception of the U-boat commander, but all the same it is an unhelpful designation. It was arbitrary. The dividing line between those who were in the first generation and those who were not wanders capriciously through the officer corps with no regard for talent or seniority. It cut Crew 33 in two: Jürgen Oesten was in command of U-61 by September 1939, but Wolfgang Lüth, who ranked higher than Oesten, was first watch officer in U-38 and would be for some time. It was unfair because it implied that those in the first generation were somehow better qualified than those who were not. Although many of them were very successful, others were completely unprepared for war and performed miserably. The fate of Hans-Günther Looff is a good example. Finally, it detracts from the qualifications of the next level: the embryonic second-generation commanders who often had the same training and in many cases became just as good officers as their predecessors.

Rather than simply the commanders, it would be better to evaluate the entire U-Bootwaffe officer corps of September 1939, for they were still more alike than not. Their backgrounds were very similar. Their training, which lasted from three to five years between entry and commissioning, followed a common path from the Dänholm through Flensburg. All were volunteers, highly motivated and supremely confident in their service, their leaders, and their own capabilities. They were well trained in submarine operations, tactics, and weaponry; all of them were familiar with, and prepared to follow, international law regarding commerce warfare and prize regulations. None had ever served in wartime, but all shared a wartime tradition. They were taught to emulate in their conduct and performance the heroes of the first war: to be courageous, faithful, and good, to reject cowardice and cruelty. For this reason they considered themselves gentlemen as well as officers. They accepted the National Socialist government and tolerated its excesses because of its accomplishments. They were prepared to die for Germany and her leaders and particularly for their own leader, Karl Dönitz.

Finally, they shared the same spirit that had been shouted to the kaiser by the men of the Flanders flotillas in 1916. It was not a happy spirit, or blithe, or buoyant, or even necessarily courageous. It was grim, resolute, and fatalistic. It resembled less the inspiration of a saint in a leper colony or the bird that sings in the rain and more that of a dog who has taken a man's leg in his jaws and will not let go even after repeated heavy blows. It made the U-Bootwaffe appear ruthless and fanatical to the outside observer, but it allowed it to accomplish things far beyond what could reasonably have been expected from a military unit in war or peace. Indeed, it was the spirit of these men—nothing else—that enabled the U-boats to drag themselves through the last two years of war.

When the war broke out, Dönitz had grave doubts about the prospects of victory. His commanders, however, possessed of this remarkable spirit, knew they were as ready as they would ever be. In September 1939, Wolfgang Lüth was first watch officer of U-38. In a book he published in 1944 he described how his boat left Germany in August, ostensibly on a huge exercise; how the crew listened to the radio when Poland was invaded; how they waited to see what Britain would do. The boat was ready for combat. The crew was trained almost to the point of becoming a single entity. "We reached our assigned sector and waited for the moment of decision," he wrote, solemnly and without a trace of cynicism for the exercise of writing propaganda. "The war would not find us unprepared."[20]

CHAPTER 3

The Epiphany of an Ace

Nothing works without an idea. The idea is the important part.
—Victor Oehrn

ONE of the first things all new Fähnrichen were shown after they reported to the Marineschule Mürwik was the impressive entrance hall just inside the main doors, a combination museum and shrine in which, draped from the bulkheads, resting on columns, and enclosed in glass cases, was kept what could easily have been called the history of the German navy in its several incarnations. Most of the display is gone now, stolen or destroyed or taken away in pieces by the British for their own museums, but in 1933 it was intact and at least as inspirational as the similarly laid out Memorial Hall of the United States Naval Academy.

> In the light of brightly colored windows the visitor to the memorial hall is greeted by battle ensigns from every period of the navy, model ships of every kind under glass; a collection of invaluable mementoes from past wars and conflicts speak silently of great days and great deeds in German naval history. There are fragments of armor plate torn from German warships by English guns in the Battle of the Skagerrak, shrapnel from English heavy shells, fittings from the [cruiser] *Emden,* . . . on the walls hang life rings from German and English ships sunk in the war, an ensign from the Russian warship *Slava,* many pictures of famous men and famous ships.[1]

One display amid this panoply of banners and busts may have seemed—at first glance—incongruous to the observer. In the center of the room, under glass and cushioned like a copy of the Magna Carta, lay several old and discolored pages taken from a *Kriegstagebuch,* the war diary or deck log of an Imperial Navy warship. Such pages would not have been an uncommon sight for the Fähnrich; the format of the German naval war diary, plain and unadorned, was the same in both wars and he had seen it before. He probably would not have known what made these pages special, however, unless he recognized the date on the first page—Sunday, 22 September 1914—and the simple words underneath it: "Masts sighted to south. Dived."

It was, of course, the log in which Otto Weddigen described his first torpedo run on the British cruiser HMS *Aboukir*. If any single act of war by any submarine could have been characterized as pivotal, seminal, without parallel, an event rich in image and portent, it would have been the sinking of those three old warships one September morning in the Broad Fourteens, and Weddigen, even though he was neither the most successful nor the most fortunate of aces, was and remains the most famous for sinking them. His attack initiated many changes in 1914, and it set the tone of submarine warfare for the next four years. In 1939 he was long dead, but in his steely countenance there was a warning: history does repeat itself sometimes, if only imperfectly. Not everyone learned from Weddigen's attack or even remembered it, and to Britain's great sorrow, in the first two months of World War II an incident occurred that was tragically similar in its audacity, its shock, and its bloodshed.

VICTOR Oehrn sat alone in the office under a cone of yellowish light. Before him, on the wide expanse of wooden desktop, was spread a chart of the North Sea, marked in several places with coffee cup rings and punctuated with little holes. On each side of him were piled books, charts, folders, and papers. On the wall to his right was pinned a huge chart of the North Atlantic Ocean, and in front of him was a single large window, through which, in daytime, the sun poured into the room and the lowing of cows could be heard. But it was after midnight now. The window was dark and the cows were asleep. He looked at his watch and rubbed his eyes. He went back to the chart, concentrating on one spot now, a well-worn smudge just to the north of Scotland and due west of Bergen. With his left index finger still on the chart, Oehrn picked up one of the folders and expertly flicked it open to scatter several photographs onto the desk. They were aerial pictures of the same spot, taken from a long-range German bomber and only a few days old: they showed a group of small islands, bright, jagged spots in a sea of black. They were marked *Geheime Kommandosache*, and then, *Scapa Flow*.

By August 1939 Victor Oehrn, the erstwhile Kompaniechef on the

Dänholm and one of Dönitz's first commanders in Flotilla Weddigen, had risen through several positions to become *Erster Admiralstabsoffizier,* deputy chief of staff for operations, at FdU headquarters in Wilhelmshaven. His desk was located in the FdU operations room (called by its inmates the *Schnorchelbude*) in a plain wooden building set among green fields in a suburb of Wilhelmshaven called Sengwarden. The small staff consisted of Oehrn and four other officers reporting to a chief of staff. Each of the five officers, designated by number, was assigned a specific duty. Oehrn, for example, unofficially known as "A1," was concerned chiefly with the planning of FdU operations and the movements of the boats. It was a sound arrangement, and it would not change appreciably during the war.

Next to Dönitz and his chief of staff, a conservative and rather acerbic officer named Eberhard Godt, Victor Oehrn was the most important man in Sengwarden. But he was not altogether happy. From time to time, as he planned operations for other boats, he found himself wishing he were back at sea, back in command of a boat of his own, as in the old days in Mecklenburg Bight.

Given Karl Dönitz's prescience, it was surprising that his staff was not in Sengwarden when Germany entered Poland on 1 September 1939. "Come at once," he telegraphed to Oehrn at his home in Swinemünde after the invasion, and Oehrn, at the breakfast table, put down his fork, got into his car, and headed west. The journey took fourteen hours, and as he drove, he thought about what might happen in the next few days. Earlier in the year, Great Britain had promised to defend Poland against a German attack. Would she honor that commitment? He did not know, but he was aware that something had happened from which Germany could not easily extricate herself, not by bluff, as in the Rhineland, or by paper, as in the Sudetenland. "We have opened a door," a friend told him the day before. "I don't know who will close it and when." [2]

Oehrn arrived in Wilhelmshaven at nine o'clock in the evening and set to work at once. "Are you here already?" asked Dönitz with surprise. "You said at once, Herr Kommodore," he replied without hesitation. [3] Two days later, after Germany had ignored a final demand to leave Poland, Great Britain declared war, and for the second time in a quarter-century the two countries came to blows.

England against Germany—for the U-Bootwaffe it was as simple as that. The U-boats sailed against England in both wars, even after the Soviet Union was attacked in June 1941, even after Hitler declared war on

The North Atlantic Ocean, crested with the ships of an Allied convoy. Although the U-boats hunted from Murmansk to Sydney, the center of the battle, the elusive "front," was always in the well-traveled shipping lanes that linked Britain and North America. (National Archives)

the United States in December 1941, even after the war and well into the present day. The song of the U-boats was not a hymn to the Reich but the cheerfully anglophobic *Englandlied.* The resolve of the commanders at the time was tinged with regret that they would be fighting the navy upon which their own was patterned, and even Dönitz, when he finally addressed his staff on 3 September, spoke only of England: "So now we know; the war with England has started. It will be a very long and hard war. It will demand all of our strength. But the enemy is not new to us. We know him from the first war. We know better now how to handle him. We have developed a weapon and a tactic with our U-boats; with these we can strike at England, and if we all do our duty together, then we will defeat her. Go now to your work and look to the future."[4] He had been promised that no such war would begin for at least five more years. He

knew that war in 1939 would be dangerous for Germany, probably unwinnable, and certainly tragic, and he knew that his own service was not prepared: "Seldom indeed had any branch of the armed forces of a country gone to war so poorly equipped. It could, in fact, do no more than subject the enemy to a few odd pin-pricks. And pin-pricks are no means with which to try and force a great empire and one of the foremost maritime powers in the world to sue for peace." [5]

Because there were so few boats at that time and because, as in the first months of World War I, they were trying to operate in accordance with the strict rules of commerce war, sinkings were few and mistakes were made. No sustained campaign against enemy shipping was possible, and the swarms of wolfpacks that would appear in later years did not exist. Most shipping made it through to Britain and the Continent without any trouble. Britain had instituted a convoy system at once, and it was believed, perhaps prematurely, that the combination of convoy and the primitive sonar systems then in use would keep the U-boats away from the shipping lanes. It was assumed that existing ASW tactics were sufficient to protect the fleet against U-boat attack. Thus it would not have been surprising if public opinion of the U-boat commander had remained somewhat neutral, less favorable than the affable veterans described by Lowell Thomas—after all, they were the enemy—but certainly more so than the sociopath of 1918 wartime propaganda. But this was not to be the case. The U-boat might have been less than effective in the earlier months of the war, but it did accomplish very quickly the second destruction of its own image in the West.

Within six hours of Dönitz's signal, Kapitänleutnant Fritz-Julius Lemp in U-30 had attacked and sunk the British passenger liner *Athenia,* killing several hundred people. It was a stupid mistake; it broke every rule in the book, and it put both the U-Bootwaffe and the Reich Propaganda Office on the defensive immediately. At this early stage Germany still cared very much about its image, and when the old pictures of the *Lusitania,* of innocent passengers drowning, of U-boats sinking and killing with no regard for the rules of war, flashed back into the public consciousness, she reacted almost instinctively by trying to salvage the U-boat's reputation. Joseph Goebbels, the Reich propaganda minister, instead of saying nothing, or yes, the *Athenia* had been sunk by a German U-boat and war is hell, tried to blame everything on Winston Churchill, the new first lord of the Admiralty. At the same time, Karl Dönitz was performing a classic cover-up, having every reference to the sinking erased from Lemp's war diary and swearing his entire crew to silence. Lemp remained at sea and later became an ace.

On 17 September Kapitänleutnant Otto Schuhart in U-29 penetrated a screen of British destroyers to sink the aircraft carrier HMS *Courageous.* The ship went down in seventeen minutes, killing almost half her crew, and the notion that the U-boat had somehow become less dangerous between the wars or that current ASW tactics were adequate defense against it was dispelled quickly. Schuhart, like Lemp, went on to become an ace, but having achieved fame at the beginning, he settled into a career better characterized as satisfactory than superlative.

Neither incident seemed to change anything, least of all the perception of the U-boat commander in Britain. In the case of the *Athenia,* outrage had to compete with confusion. The sinking happened so fast (on the same day the prime minister went on the radio to announce that Britain was at war) that it did not register as it might have done later; unlike the sinking of the *Lusitania,* arguably its parallel, it was strenuously denied by Germany, and the man who sank her, Lemp, was unknown to the public. The loss of the *Courageous* was accepted more or less as any military defeat: a tragedy, but the ship was at sea, Schuhart had behaved honorably, and no rules had been broken. That a British submarine would have done the same thing went without saying.

It was in these first scattershot weeks, however, that a remarkable military operation was conceived and planned—an operation that would change everything. On 14 October 1939 a single U-boat under the command of Günther Prien entered the Royal Navy fleet anchorage in Scapa Flow and sank the battleship HMS *Royal Oak.* Not every naval operation can be considered history-making on its own; Weddigen's was one, and the sinking of the *Bismarck* in 1941 was another. The sinking of the *Royal Oak* is perhaps the best example. It was the most significant, most documented, most famous single U-Bootwaffe operation of the war, and it made most of those who participated in it just as famous. It revealed the nature of the battle to follow as clearly and as suddenly as had Otto Weddigen's act a quarter-century before. It created an immediate legend for the German people, and it helped to define the public image of the U-boat commander for the rest of the war and well afterward.

Scapa Flow, a natural deepwater harbor in the Orkney Islands, was the most important and most secure fleet anchorage in the British Isles. It was a huge body of water, irregularly shaped, ten miles across at its widest, and surrounded by three islands: Pomona, the largest of the islands, to the north, Hoy to the west, and South Ronaldsay to the southeast. All seven entrances were well guarded or completely blocked. The British believed it was impenetrable. To the Germans it must have seemed so; twice in World War I, in 1914 and again in 1918, U-boats had attempted to enter Scapa Flow, and both times they had been detected and destroyed. Dönitz, in search of a military victory and a propaganda coup for his service, resurrected the idea in 1939 and directed his staff to find a solution.

It was Victor Oehrn who first saw the way into Scapa Flow, probably during a close examination of aerial photographs taken over the small islands between Pomona and South Ronaldsay in September 1939. There were two narrow passages between these islands: Kirk Sound to the north and Stronsay Firth to the south. Both were closed by blockships, steel hulks filled with concrete, tied together with heavy chains, and sunk. The idea was that a submarine could not enter underwater without running into a blockship or on the surface without being stranded or having her bottom torn out. On the photographs Oehrn could pick out both entrances, and he could pick out the blockships. He saw that Stronsay Firth was definitely closed. But he also saw that a gap of at least fifty feet separated the two blockships that almost, but not quite, closed Kirk Sound. An experienced U-boat commander, through skillful shiphandling and with a favorable current, could slip into Scapa Flow between the blockships and the shore and escape the same way (what he did inside depended entirely upon him). The devil, as they say, lay in the details, a myriad of details that had to take into account everything from the murky bottom of Kirk Sound to the oddly reflective surface of the moon, and it was in these details that Victor Oehrn found himself immersed late that evening in the Schnorchelbude.

"A staff officer has no name." This statement, which Oehrn attributes to Helmuth von Moltke, is one of his favorites. It was not meant to be pejorative, nor did it mean that the staff officer was to be given no recognition for his work. It meant simply that everything he did as a staff officer, good or bad, was done in the name of the commander he served, and as far as the world outside was concerned, the commander took responsibility for it. For that reason, Oehrn has not received the recognition he deserves for planning the Scapa Flow operation; most people believe it was Dönitz himself, and the fact that Dönitz takes full credit for it in his memoirs does not help. Oehrn, who is both loyal and modest, graciously yields that credit to Dönitz and Godt, but he does lay quiet claim to the inspiration and much of the initial planning.[6]

Doubtless such an arrangement would not have been acceptable to every officer in the U-Bootwaffe (they were not, as a rule, noted for their humility), but Oehrn, seemingly born for staff work and certainly well trained for it, gracefully accepted his station. The officer chosen to carry out Oehrn's plan was of a different mind entirely. For Kapitänleutnant Günther Prien, commander of U-47 and the only man seriously considered by Karl Dönitz for the Scapa Flow operation, was as different in nature from Victor Oehrn as Oehrn was from a white rabbit.

Günther Prien, the "Bull of Scapa Flow," is without a doubt the best-known and most celebrated U-Bootwaffe officer in World War II. Nevertheless, he is a man about whom little is known and less written, and the events of his wartime career were for many years uncertain and shrouded in rumor. His autobiography, *Mein Weg Nach Scapa Flow* (My Road to

Scapa Flow), published during the war, is described by historian Dan Van der Vat as an "appalling" book. Michael Hadley is more circumspect in his treatment of *Mein Weg*, but he has little time for the other popular biography of Prien, Wolfgang Frank's *Prien Greift An* (Prien Attacks), which he considers propagandistic and without critical substance. Secondary sources about Prien are sketchy and contain little personal information. The best summation of his life, written by Van der Vat in 1992, is ten pages long.[7]

Günther Prien was born in Thüringen in 1908. His father died when he was young, and his mother's financial situation after the war was precarious, so when he was fifteen he left home and entered the Handelsmarine, the German merchant marine. During his first voyage on the sailing ship *Hamburg*, a passage around Cape Horn to Chile and Peru for nitrate, Prien served as the ship's "Moses," the youngest member of the crew. He was given "every dirty, filthy, nasty, and undesirable job aboard the ship," he received no pay, and he had to fight continually to survive among an older crew. All of this only made him more resolute, for Prien, if nothing else, had a grim determination to rise above his circumstances. The *Hamburg* was followed by other ships. Prien rose from cabin boy to seaman to officer, and he was given his *Kapitän auf Grosser Fahrt*, master's papers, in December 1931, but he never lost the determination that got him out of the galley.

That characteristic was to serve him well, for when depression hit the Handelsmarine in 1932, he could no longer find work. He had to start again from the bottom, literally from his mother's house. He was aided this time, however, by an incident beyond his control: in the summer of 1932 the Reichsmarine training ship *Niobe* capsized and sank in the Baltic, taking one-third of Crew 32 with her. Suddenly there was a critical need for new officer candidates, and the ranks of the Handelsmarine seemed a logical place to find them. Merchant officers with papers were accepted into the Reichsmarine as *Handelsschiffsoffiziere,* or HSOs, allowed to skip both the sail training and the world cruise (after all, many of them had been around the world more than once already) and placed into an existing crew, in Prien's case Crew 31. HSOs were used to augment several crews in this way. The loss of the *Niobe* was the first reason, but the Reichsmarine was expanding so fast in the early 1930s that HSOs were the quickest and most sensible source of the additional officers required. The strategy paid off handsomely. "Virtually all the HSOs turned out during the war to be outstanding officers and high class seamen," wrote Peter Hansen, a U-Bootwaffe officer who spent much of his time working for Admiral Wilhelm Canaris in the Abwehr and consequently knew more about most people than they would have liked. "I don't know of a single failure amongst them, contrary to the academically prepared [junior] officers, where some terrible flops developed."[8]

In 1935 Günther Prien was commissioned and accepted into the U-Bootwaffe. He served as a watch officer in U-3, one of the first boats in Flotilla Weddigen, then U-26. Finally, on 17 December 1938, after having finished both torpedo school and U-boat command school at the top of his class and only six years after joining the Reichsmarine, Günther Prien took command of U-47 at the Germania yards in Kiel. It was the most important day of his life. In spite of a system that was designed to exclude men like him, he had achieved a commission, a command, and a measure of the respect he had always wanted. "Despite his lack of a proper educational background and training," wrote Hansen, "and largely through sheer willpower and self-determination, he finally felt that he had arrived and was totally accepted."[9] When Günther Prien became famous, he often told people that 17 December was his birthday.

Short, scrappy, and moon-faced, Günther Prien was not the ideal physical representation of a U-boat commander. Temperamentally he was perfect: stubborn, cocky, impatient with those who could not measure up to his standards, and able to utter without noticeable cynicism such bon mots as "I get more fun out of a really good convoy exercise than out of any leave." His nickname at FdU was *Bumskopf*, "crashhead." "It was by no means a term of derision," says Victor Oehrn; "he was a simple man, clear-thinking, not given to arguing."[10] His temperament did not always endear him to others, of course. His crew, whom he drilled to the point of exhaustion, disliked him. He was rather distant toward his fellow commanders. "I met him at various occasions," wrote Jürgen Oesten, then the commander of U-61. "My impression was that he was cool and to the point, [but] not exactly likable."[11] But Prien's temperament appealed greatly to Dönitz, whose favorite commander Prien was, and it enraptured the press, for whom he would become a superstar.

On Sunday, 1 October 1939, Prien stood at attention in front of Karl Dönitz's desk on the submarine tender *Weichsel*. Dönitz tossed Oehrn's folder down in front of him, the operational order, the photos, the charts, the tables, everything. "Come back in two days and tell me what you think." Prien returned to U-47's tender, the *Hamburg*, and locked himself in his stateroom with a new stack of charts. He then went through every word of Oehrn's plan. He compared Oehrn's charts to those in front of him; he recomputed Oehrn's figures. He examined the intelligence reports, some compiled by other U-boats in the area as recently as Thursday. He looked at the photographs over and over again. First thing Monday morning he was back on board the *Weichsel,* just as Dönitz knew he would be, a faint smile on his round face and the Scapa Flow file in his hand.

With Prien's expected consent, preparations for the Scapa Flow operation, now called Special Operation P, began in earnest. Prien was ready. He had been ready, it seemed, since the day he joined the Reichsmarine. His crew (who would not be told about Special Operation P until the last minute) were also ready, drilled by Prien to the point of distraction, and willing, though they hated him, to follow their commander wherever he wanted to go, whether it was Scapa Flow or the gates of hell. Only the boat needed work. U-47, a type VIIB, was not the vessel best suited for such a mission; if anything, she was too large to fit into Scapa Flow and would therefore have to be specially prepared. This was done without much secrecy by the shipyard personnel in Kiel. The boat was made lighter by pumping fuel oil and fresh water out of her tanks. A large part of the crew's provisions followed. Her old air-driven torpedoes were taken off, to be replaced with brand-new electric ones, "the latest thing in weapons technology," Prien was assured. New onetime cipher wheels were distributed. Finally, several strange unmarked boxes were taken aboard. They were explosive charges: if U-47 were to become trapped inside Scapa Flow, Prien was to take her to where she could do the most damage and blow her up.

Special Operation P, with a few minor problems and one glaring exception, went entirely according to Oehrn's plan. It began on Monday, 8 October 1939, when the *Letzte Ölung,* the last rites, were administered to Günther Prien on the pier in Kiel. The Letzte Ölung was not a religious ceremony but rather a ritual briefing by an officer from FdU staff in which he would offer a few words of encouragement, then hand over the commander's orders, written on water-soluble paper and sealed in a brown paper envelope; only later in the war would the dark irony of the term become apparent. Shortly afterward, and without fanfare, Prien left Kiel, headed west through the Kaiser Wilhelm Canal to Brunsbüttel, and began to make his way quietly across the North Sea, avoiding all traffic and diving whenever he saw so much as a plume of smoke on the horizon.

Nothing of note happened during that time, although as the boat approached Scotland the crew was puzzled to see Amelung von Varendorff, the second watch officer, toss overboard all the code and cipher documents, and slightly disconcerted as the chief engineer, Hans Wessels, began to place his anonymous wooden boxes in various places throughout the boat. Rose Ness light on South Ronaldsay was sighted in the late evening of Thursday, 12 October. At approximately 0430 the next morning, Friday, the engines were stopped, the communications equipment was turned off, and U-47 drifted quietly to the bottom of the sea to wait for fifteen hours until nightfall and the scheduled attempt to break into Kirk Sound. At that time, dawn on Friday, the entire responsibility for the success of Special Operation P shifted from FdU—from Victor Oehrn and Karl Dönitz—to Günther Prien.

Prien told his crew about Special Operation P shortly after they went to the bottom. As a result, they could not sleep and occupied their time preparing for capture. Someone had the idea that the British would not give them any cigarettes so they all wrapped up their own cigarettes and matches in oilcloth and tucked them into the nooks and crannies along the inside of the conning tower. Someone suddenly thought he might need a handkerchief in the prisoner of war (POW) camp, and before too long everyone in the crew had a handkerchief tied around his neck. Even Prien thought about the prospect of being captured. "What do you think," he asked von Varendorff at one point. "Do we fly the *Kriegsflagge* or not?" If they were captured without it, they could be shot as spies, but von Varendorff thought it might affect U-47's speed in diving. "The hell with it then," smiled Prien, "and be it on our heads." [12]

At 2330 on Friday evening Prien brought U-47 to the surface again and began to make his tortuous way into Scapa Flow. No one had expected the operation to be easy, and it wasn't. The type VIIB boat was seventy meters long, with a draft of five meters and a fuel tank bulging from either side, and she was very wet on the surface at slow speed. On his first attempt Prien entered the wrong sound and then, while U-47 was pirouetting slowly among the blockships in Kirk Sound, visible to anyone on the shore, the current caught her and pushed her aground. Finally, at approximately 0030 on Saturday, 14 October, Günther Prien entered the vast basin of Scapa Flow. "We're through," shouted First Watch Officer Engelbert Endrass down the hatch to U-47's crewmen, each of whom had been standing or sitting at his post completely ignorant of what was going on topside; a muffled cheer arose as Prien turned west and chugged slowly out toward the very center of the anchorage to choose his targets, cursing a display of the aurora borealis that lit up the water around him like New Year's Eve on the Ku-Damm.

The northern lights would not be the only problem for Günther Prien that night, and compared to what came next, they were trivial. It was necessary, but unfortunate, that he had remained out of touch for so long the day before because if FdU had been able to contact him, they would surely have done so to cancel the operation for a completely different reason. The worst thing that could have happened—outside of Prien himself being lost or captured—had happened, the one glaring exception in Oehrn's carefully laid plan. A new report had come into FdU: the latest reconnaissance photos showed that a large part of the Home Fleet had weighed anchor and left Scapa Flow, leaving the vast basin empty and bereft of targets (in fact, the fleet had departed on Wednesday for Loch Ewe). As a result, the mood in Sengwarden on Friday evening was grim. Everyone was up and milling about, smoking, checking watches, playing endlessly with dividers and parallel rulers as they stared glumly at huge charts of Scapa Flow.

Oehrn waited patiently. There was absolutely nothing he could do. Certainly he could not help Günther Prien, who, four hundred miles away, slouched over the bridge coaming, smoking a cigarette, and fuming with anger, had rapidly determined the same unpleasant facts as FdU. He had steamed back and forth across the empty anchorage for half an hour. U-47 was now back where she had started: just inside of Scapa Flow at Kirk Sound. Nobody had seen anything at all. The option of leaving Scapa Flow without any sinkings had doubtless occurred to Prien by that time; under the circumstances it would have been a justifiable move. There is equally no doubt that to him the idea would have caused great irritation. He turned U-47 around again and continued to search, not to the west this time but northwest, along the Pomona coast toward Kirkwall, where some smaller ships might have been moored, destroyers perhaps, or minesweepers. It was a lucky move, for within ten minutes of setting the new course von Varendorff saw a shadow in the distance. U-Bootwaffe officers were trained to recognize enemy warships by their silhouettes, and both Prien and Endrass knew at once that they had come across a Royal Navy battleship.

HMS *Royal Oak*, a 31,000-ton battleship of the *Royal Sovereign* class, was commissioned in 1915. She was a true dreadnought, one of the great leviathans designed and built during the long naval arms race between

Britain and Germany that preceded the war. She was a veteran of Jutland and had been one of the long line of ships that watched the German Imperial Fleet steam into captivity in 1918. She remained in service between the wars and was likely to last through another one, even though she often needed repairs and was just slow enough to be a drag on her newer sisters. Ironically, it was for minor repairs that she had been left behind in Scapa Flow that day. The *Royal Oak* was past her prime when von Varendorff spotted her, but neither age nor speed altered the fact that she was still a valuable ship of immense power with eight fifteen-inch guns and a crew of eleven hundred.

So complete was the surprise Günther Prien achieved, so complacent his opposition, that he was able to make two separate torpedo attacks on the *Royal Oak* that night. He had to do this because the first run, during which he fired three torpedoes at the *Royal Oak* and one at the ship behind her, failed. Prien was no amateur. The run had been perfect, distance and bearing were correct, the torpedoes left the boat without incident and headed in silver streaks toward the battleship. But two of them went wide, and the third hit the *Royal Oak* low and forward, sending a column of white water up her side but doing no apparent damage. Many of her crew were not even awakened by the noise. The general impression was that an accident had occurred within the hull; the ship did not go to action stations, and, more significantly, no alarm was raised.[13] Prien, annoyed, brought U-47 completely about and emptied his stern tube at the *Royal Oak*. That one missed too.

Now Prien was furious. He had done everything correctly. He had fired four of his brand-new G7e electric torpedoes from the very close range of six hundred meters, three of them missed, and the fourth had done no damage. The *Royal Oak* quietly occupied the same space she had before. To make such a mistake was both embarrassing and puzzling to him, especially because the *Royal Oak* was the only target he had and the only difference between the complete success of his operation and its ignominious failure. For that reason another attack was assured, certainly before the last torpedo of the first attack ran out of fuel and went to the bottom, probably much earlier than that—Prien's nature made it impossible for him to do anything else. Twelve minutes later, the boat was back in position and the order to fire was given again.

Four more torpedoes leaped from U-47's tubes. This time they did not miss. Within twenty seconds a huge flash of fire burst forth upon the water, followed a second later by the ear-splitting double crash of high explosive underwater. "We saw one waterspout after another," Prien was to relate afterward, "followed by a series of huge explosions—white, red and green lights in a fireworks display such as I had never seen before. Pieces of deckwork, masts and smokestacks flew up into the air, giving the impression that the entire ship was blown completely to smithereens. The whole thing was over in thirty seconds."[14] The *Royal Oak* had been hit amidships by three torpedoes simultaneously. Within twenty minutes she rolled over and sank. As the smoke spread and sparks rained down upon her copper hull, the harbor came alive; sirens sounded, searchlights began to play upon the water, and patrol craft started out of the darkness. Prien could not afford to savor his triumph. He turned, headed back toward Kirk Sound at high speed, battled the current past the blockships, and within thirty minutes of the *Royal Oak* turning turtle, U-47 was outside of Scapa Flow and ready to begin operations against enemy shipping.

When the *Royal Oak* sank, she took with her almost nine hundred men.

The first indication of Günther Prien's attack on the *Royal Oak* came into the Schnorchelbude not from Prien himself, nor from German intelligence sources, but from the British media, in a broadcast by the BBC at 1300 (British Summer Time) and monitored in Germany: "Here is a news bulletin," said the calm and detached voice. "The Secretary of the Admiralty regrets to announce that HMS *Royal Oak* has been sunk by what is believed to be U-boat action. It was learned at the Admiralty that a list of the survivors of HMS *Royal Oak* will be published as quickly as possible."[15] The bulletin did not say anything about the capture or destruction of a U-boat inside Scapa Flow; in fact, Scapa Flow was not mentioned by name. Prien had obviously escaped. Special Operation P had succeeded, and when Victor Oehrn finally stepped out of the Schnorchelbude on Saturday morning for some fresh air, the essence of the U-Bootwaffe had changed. Probably he did not notice it at the time, nor did anyone except perhaps Dönitz himself, but something had very definitely changed.

OEHRN'S plan, to get a U-boat into Scapa Flow for the purpose of sinking enemy ships, had succeeded brilliantly. Dönitz's plan, to get a boat into Scapa Flow for the purpose of celebrating the U-Bootwaffe, now began. He had sensed the importance of such a move at once, indeed as soon as he had issued the order, as a means to gain more respect for the U-Bootwaffe, to capture the attention of his superiors, especially Hitler, and thereby to elicit funding for new boats and tactical support from the rest of the Wehrmacht for current operations. Now that the operation had succeeded, he threw his considerable talents for manipulation of the media into making all of those things reality and in the process turning Günther Prien into a superstar, the first in a war that would create hundreds.

Upon his return, Prien was directed to hold his boat at Brunsbüttel Locks so that Kriegsmarine Commander in Chief Erich Raeder could travel from Berlin to award him the Iron Cross (First Class). But the Iron Cross did not seem enough now that all this attention was being dumped on him—it was rather ordinary, after all. Happily, a new and more prestigious decoration had only recently been instituted: the Ritterkreuz, the Knight's Cross of the Iron Cross.[16] The Knight's Cross was meant to be exclusive—difficult to get and distinctive to look at—and it stayed that way throughout the war. There was no more logical choice than Prien, argued Dönitz, to be given one of the first Knight's Crosses and nobody better than the Führer to give it to him.

Günther Prien and his crew were flown in Adolf Hitler's personal airplane, the *Grenzmark,* to Tempelhof airport on the morning of 17 October, where they were greeted by a cheering crowd and whisked off in a convoy of ten Mercedes Benz limousines to the plush Kaiserhof Hotel. After checking in for a quick refurbishment, they were taken to the Chancellery for a noontime meeting with Hitler. There Günther Prien was awarded the Knight's Cross and the crew was praised lavishly. "The men before me today," said Hitler, "achieved a unique triumph in the same spot where the entire German fleet once was handed over by a weak government. . . . This great daring deed has only strengthened the whole German people in their unshakeable faith in victory."[17] Outside the Chancellery a crowd roared their approval of Prien, the sinking, and everything in general. The award ceremony was followed by an invitation to a private lunch, which proved, because of Hitler's taste in food, to be one of the few low points of the day. "Just a plate of soup," complained one man, "and a piece of bread. I guess we made some pretty long faces."[18]

After lunch Prien and his crew were taken to the Ministry of Propaganda for a press conference, and this was perhaps the most unusual part of the entire celebration. The press conference, by its nature a product of the twentieth century that had never before been used to showcase a military officer as junior as Prien, was seized upon by the ministry as a valuable propaganda tool, the most efficient way to display heroes to as many representatives of the media as possible, especially if the heroes were well

Günther Prien, the man who sank the *Royal Oak* in October 1939 and created a new image for the U-boat commanders. "A simple man, clear-thinking, not given to arguing," wrote Oehrn. "Cool and to the point," agreed Oesten, "[but] not exactly likable." (National Archives)

rehearsed and the exchange of information was properly controlled. The crew of U-47, all of them "looking somewhat tired and bewildered after a day of publicity unprecedented in the annals of the German submarine force," trooped into the press room and sat at tables that had been arranged in a large horseshoe.[19] Prien was introduced by Otto Dietrich, the ministry press chief, then he stood and delivered a short but factual account of Special Operation P. Unlike his hosts, he did not brag, nor did he criticize the enemy. Questions from the assembled reporters were kept to a minimum, and after the conference was over the crew filed out of the room as silently as they had entered. That evening they went to the Wintergarten for a vaudeville show, where the audience, apparently overcome by affection for Prien, rose spontaneously and sang the *Englandlied*.[20]

In spite of its brevity and obvious artifice, the importance of this press conference cannot be discounted, for it revealed the face of the U-boat commander to the world. Before Scapa Flow the identities of commanders and their boats were routinely withheld from publication. Not even Otto Schuhart, the man who sank the *Courageous,* was known in the West by name. Thus it was Prien who formed the initial image of the U-boat commander in the public mind, and it was an image not entirely negative. "Slight, blond, and youthful with a shrill sharp voice," said the *New York Times* of Prien. His crew were "young men all, some with blond clipped beards, others new shaven and rosy cheeked." To *Time* magazine Prien was "a one-time Hamburg-America Line cabin boy"; his crewmen were "boyish" and filled with "suppressed amusement" at their commander's statement. One of the few dissonant voices belonged to the American journalist William Shirer, who called Günther Prien "clean-cut, cocky, a fanatical Nazi, and obviously capable."[21]

Even in Britain, where Günther Prien could have expected utter execration, the reaction was mixed, "a melange of fear and respect, and with the Hitler shadow a little bit of loathing."[22] The U-boat was seen once again as a sinister, sneaky, and extremely dangerous weapon, capable of more than anyone could have suspected, but Prien himself was accorded grudging praise by none other than Winston Churchill himself. In a short statement to the Commons he called the attack "a remarkable exploit of fear and daring," possibly to deflect some of the mounting criticism he was receiving. As much anger was being directed toward him and his government as toward Prien and the U-Bootwaffe. It was "a disgrace," said one newspaper, that the *Royal Oak* was lost in what was supposed to be Britain's safest and most secure anchorage. It meant that no place was safe or secure from the U-boat, and the idea that the Admiralty had any inkling whatsoever of the threat was at the bottom of Scapa Flow with 883 officers and men of the Royal Navy.

The German media was enthralled with their new hero. When U-47 entered Scapa Flow, said Engelbert Endrass, his commander's frowning face and hunched shoulders reminded him of a bull in a ring. Günther Prien therefore became known in the press as the "Bull of Scapa Flow," and the figure of a bull, kicking its hind legs and blowing steam from its nostrils, became U-47's insignia, painted prominently in white under her bridge coaming. The nickname did not start a trend; the insignia did. Few other commanders had nicknames, and none was known by a name other than some form of his own, but after Scapa Flow almost every boat in commission sported something on its tower, from swastikas to flowers to Winston Churchill being stepped on by an elephant.

The public's love affair with Günther Prien and his crew did not end when they left Berlin. Presents began to flow in: money enough for Prien to open a trust account for the crew (it was worthless after the war ended), furniture, wine and cigarettes, clothing (especially knitted socks), and invitations to visit cities and towns. There is a story that all this publicity annoyed Günther Prien. "I am a submarine commander," he is supposed to have grumbled, "not a movie star." This is false. Prien loved the spotlight and basked in its glow; the real story is that Dönitz had to tell Prien almost exactly the same thing: "Remember, Prüntje, you are a submarine commander, not a movie star."[23] Later in his career, which turned out to be brief, the media attention and the adulation seemed to have become less enjoyable and more oppressive to Günther Prien. In October 1939 the Bull of Scapa Flow stood astride his world like a latter-day colossus and laughed.

In the end, almost everyone in Germany gained from Günther Prien's attack in Scapa Flow. On the strategic level, it meant only a small shift in the balance of power between the Royal Navy and the Kriegsmarine, but it had a profound effect on morale. The English had been hurt; the Tommies were not invincible after all. This boost in spirit extended to the German public, for whom Prien became an idol and a media sensation, the first of the war (admittedly his image was enhanced by Goebbels and the Propaganda Ministry, but the process of making heroes was not unique to Germany). As Dönitz had hoped, however, the organization that gained most was the U-Bootwaffe. The publicity was invaluable. The demonstrated ability of the U-boat to affect events, to achieve benefit far beyond its cost, to instill fear and respect in the enemy, was just what he needed to deal with a leader who had so far failed to see the potential of the weapon. Funding for U-boats increased after Scapa Flow, as did support from other branches of the Wehrmacht, particularly the Luftwaffe. Günther Prien was clothed in glory and became a legend; so to a lesser degree did every member of his crew. Karl Dönitz was promoted from Kapitän zur See to *Konteradmiral* (rear admiral) soon afterward and received a new title, *Befehlshaber der U-Boote* (commander in chief, U-boats, or simply BdU). And in a routine ceremony two months after Scapa Flow, Victor Oehrn, the man who conceived an operation that shook the world, was given the Iron Cross (Second Class).

Ironically, Oehrn was the only one left with something he had never wished for, while the thing he really wanted—a command at the front—seemed as far away as ever. He had always considered the Iron Cross a decoration for valor in combat; he accepted it out of respect for Dönitz, but as soon as the ceremony was over he put it into his coat pocket and would not wear it again for several weeks.[24] It did not matter. He had the satisfaction of knowing that he had contributed to a successful military operation, that without him it would most likely not have happened, and to a good staff officer that was reward enough. He later wrote: "The idea [of Scapa Flow] itself, how the operation could be done, how to get in, how to take advantage of the opportunity, that was mine. In hindsight it all seems so easy. The hard part was the execution, and any credit rightly belongs [to Günther Prien]. But nothing works without an idea. The idea is the important part."[25]

CHAPTER 4

On Patrol with the
Westward Ho!

So give me thy hand, thy fair white hand, ere we sail away to conquer Eng-el-land.
—*Englandlied (Wir Fahren Gegen England)*

THE six-month period after Scapa Flow in October 1939 was, in comparison to later events, a quiet one at sea. The only surface engagement of any significance was an unfortunate one for Germany, involving the scuttling of the pocket battleship *Graf Spee* in the River Plate. The U-boats, still bottled up in German ports from where they could enter the Atlantic only with difficulty, managed to sink between 100,000 and 200,000 gross registered tons (GRT) per month, a substantial amount but not enough to close the shipping lanes. Most traffic managed to get through. The U-boat threat was recognized by Britain as real but not critical, by no means as dangerous to her sovereignty as the German army, overpowering in Poland, or the Luftwaffe, against which few at the time thought she could put up effective opposition. It was very definitely a war of pinpricks, a war in which the potential of both navies remained largely hidden.

Throughout these months Victor Oehrn labored faithfully behind his desk in Sengwarden, torn between his joy at working for a man he admired and his exasperation at not being able to do what he really wanted. He had followed Dönitz since 1935. His respect—his love—for the man was boundless, and he would have served on BdU staff without complaint for the duration, drawing up Dönitz's rigorous operational plans, tracking the boats at sea, administering the Letzte Ölung to the commanders he envied so much. He even took to wearing his unearned Iron Cross after Dönitz had expressed personal disappointment at its absence from his coat, for he was loyal as well as diligent, and he could not bear to think he had offended his commander. It was a situation that might have dragged on for years except that war has a tendency to change plans and alter careers in ways nobody can expect. Günther Prien could easily have testified to that.

This first and relatively inconclusive stage of the war at sea ended in April 1940 with Operation Weserübung, the German invasion of Norway and Denmark. Weserübung was a stunning victory for Germany and a remarkable success for her land forces, but it was achieved at the cost of a large number of Kriegsmarine warships that were sacrificed, and it was a debacle for the U-boats, a force for which such an operation should have been tailor-made. It also got Victor Oehrn out of Sengwarden and into his dream.

The Kriegsmarine was heavily involved in the Norwegian part of the operation, and most of the U-boats available at that time were strung out along the jagged coastline of Norway to protect the invasion forces and interrupt the enemy supply lines. Oehrn, as usual, had planned their movements. He estimates that approximately one-third of the Royal Navy units involved in the operation could have been damaged or destroyed by the U-boat attack, and his estimate was grounded in several facts that were highly favorable to the German side.[1] ASW practices on the part of the Royal Navy were primitive. British warships, including aircraft carriers, battleships, heavy cruisers, and fleet auxiliaries, steamed blithely across the North Sea and up and down the Norwegian coast as though the submarine as a weapon did not exist. Commanders on the German side, led by Günther Prien, were all first-generation veterans, well trained and deadly.

Unfortunately, Operation Weserübung did not go according to Victor Oehrn's plan. His original estimate of the situation had been correct; the coast of Norway might well have been the naval review at Spithead, as one warship after another passed through the crosshairs of the U-boats, each well within range. His estimate of success, however, had been drastically wrong. U-boats made more than forty attacks on Allied warships and transports. All of them failed. Four boats were lost. And the high level of self-confidence with which the U-Bootwaffe entered Weserübung evaporated like the morning fog.

What went wrong? The U-Bootwaffe was an organization that relied on technology, perhaps more as the war went on than any branch of the Wehrmacht. In Norway, ironically, it was betrayed by technology. The problem lay neither in the commanders' abilities nor in the direction they received but in the torpedoes they had been given. In World War I the torpedo was a relatively simple weapon that exploded when it hit a solid object; the detonator, called the contact pistol, had its flaws, but it was battle-tested and it worked. In 1939 a new torpedo was released with a magnetic pistol that detonated when it passed through the magnetic field around a ship's hull. It was not tested properly, it often failed, and the lost opportunities of Operation Weserübung were the result.[2]

A sense of despair overwhelmed the service, leaving the crews morose and their commanders despondent. They sat idly on their boats, hovering at various levels of depression and anger and grumbling to themselves of defeat. So moved was Dönitz at their appalling loss of confidence that he made it a point to visit, personally, every boat he had, both to explain what exactly had happened and to promise that the situation would change immediately. He had those responsible for the new torpedoes brought before a court-martial. And one day he called Victor Oehrn into his office and asked a simple question: How long would it take for a peacetime U-boat commander to retrain with a new boat for combat? This was not unusual; normal planning required that such hypothetical questions be asked all the time. Oehrn made the calculation and gave Dönitz his answer without thinking much about it. It would take five days. Within thirty minutes he was told that he, Victor Oehrn, was the hypothetical commander in the question and that he would leave as soon as possible to take command of U-37. "But," said Dönitz, "you can have more than five days if you want. Take as long as you need."[3]

The plan was straightforward. Oehrn was to inaugurate a new U-boat campaign—the first one since Weserübung. He was to demonstrate the continued effectiveness of German torpedoes by sinking as many ships as he could with them. He was to restore the confidence of the officer corps by proving that even a staff officer (albeit BdU's best staff officer and a onetime commander) could succeed in submarine warfare and therefore that the battle-hardened first generation now sulking in their boats could, if they trusted themselves and their weapons, accomplish more than anyone had thought possible. Quite simply, Victor Oehrn had been ordered to jump-start the Battle of the Atlantic, and anyone can be forgiven for wondering why Dönitz would have selected a man who had never commanded a U-boat in combat to undertake such an important and delicate assignment. The most obvious answer was that Oehrn, by virtue of *not* being a commander, was not affected by the overall sense of gloom that pervaded the service. As a member of BdU staff, he had what is now called the "big picture." He knew exactly what Dönitz was trying to do, whereas a commander at the front would not. Finally, there was something noble, almost biblical, about Dönitz sending out one of his most valuable staff officers to do such a job.

What Oehrn thought of the idea is unknown, but he was a proud man. He had personally told Dönitz that a new U-boat commander would require only five days to prepare for patrol, so he took only five days. Fortunately, the boat he had been given, U-37, had a seasoned crew and an enviable record. Under her previous commander, Werner Hartmann, she had sunk nineteen ships of almost 80,000 GRT, a truly remarkable total for anyone at this point in the war. All Oehrn had to do was take U-37 out of Wilhelmshaven and around Heligoland a few times, and that more for his own benefit than anyone else's, and on 15 May, resplendent in dress blue uniform and white scarf, his crew lined up stiffly on the weather deck and the words *Westward Ho!* painted proudly in English on U-37's tower, he left for the North Atlantic.[4]

So began Victor Oehrn's career as a wartime U-boat commander.

Dönitz wanted his staff officers to have combat experience. This was not possible with the staff he had assembled in Sengwarden at the start of the war, but as time went on these men were slowly "swapped out" for veterans. There were good reasons for this change. The differences between the perceptions of a staff officer and the experiences of a commander at the front were often critical and in some cases could lead to incorrect directions from the Schnorchelbude. There were some things that a staff officer, however gifted, could never appreciate until he had lived through them: a chase by enemy destroyers, a depth charge siege, the sinking of a ship. Victor Oehrn had the mind of a staff officer: efficient, orderly, and slightly detached from the reality of the fleet. He did not at first have the mind of a battle commander. He learned quickly and sometimes jarringly that the front was not as he imagined and that BdU staff, as well informed and professional as they might have been, were not always in touch with reality.

On his second day out, for example, he had to decide whether to proceed into the Atlantic via the prescribed route—the "Fair Island Gap" between the Orkney and Shetland Islands—or to take a longer but safer route north of the Shetlands. As deputy for operations, he had always instructed his boats to run the gap, and for that reason he decided to do so himself, even though now, as a commander, he saw that it might be safer to go around. On the third day, just west of Fair Island, U-37 was sighted and attacked by a British bomber so accurately that its crew reported her sunk. Because Oehrn applied the rules he used at his desk to a situation at the front, he almost lost his boat, and he made a mental note that henceforth all boats would be directed to avoid the Fair Island Gap.

He sank his first ship four days after he left Wilhelmshaven: it was the Swedish motor ship *Erik Frisell,* which he sighted just west of the Outer Hebrides on 19 May. Within a week he had damaged a second ship and sunk a third. In two of these attacks Oehrn used the electric torpedoes that had failed in Norway. As Dönitz had suspected, they did not perform well (for that reason gunfire was used to sink the *Erik Frisell,* and the second ship, the British *Dunster Grange,* escaped him). In his third attack, during the night of 23–24 May on the Greek steamer *Kyma,* Oehrn finally used his older torpedoes—the type G7a torpedoes armed with contact fuses— and they worked perfectly. His findings, along with his tonnage totals, were duly sent back to Wilhelmshaven. The patrol went well for almost two weeks, much better than he had hoped when he set out, but then Oehrn's lack of combat experience became apparent once more. He made a minor slip. It involved people, not tactics. There was no danger to his boat or his crew, nobody was hurt, and nothing was changed. But he cannot forget it.

On that day he sighted the British merchant *Sheaf Mead* sailing alone about two hundred miles northeast of the Spanish coast. He attacked and succeeded in hitting her. The ship began to go down, her bow high in the air like a whale coming to the surface—and then exploded. Most of the crew had already left the ship when it happened; of those still scrambling about on board, he remembers, "two men—I can see them now—flew high into the air and then, in great arcs, down to the water." He decided to come alongside one of the lifeboats to ask for information and perhaps to offer assistance. What exactly he expected from the miserable crewmen of the *Sheaf Mead* when he began to ask questions nobody knows, but when he entered the sea of wreckage within which her survivors huddled in lifeboats and clung to fragments of flotsam, he found them uncooperative. "They did not answer my question 'what ship?' and just looked at us angrily. . . . We could not help. The weather and the hazardous area prevented any kind of rescue attempt. I just turned and left." [5]

Victor Oehrn had no idea how a merchant crewman would act after his ship was sunk from beneath him. The stories he would have read of World War I, especially those of the great aces, described jolly encounters in which regrets were shared, food, water, and medical supplies were handed over, and directions were given. He may have approached the boats of the *Sheaf Mead* in anticipation of a civilized conversation, and instead he was given the quiet rage of desperate and frustrated men for whom he was a ruthless killer. The discontinuous image of combat entertained by those who had not seen it was a different, and much more significant, problem than that of taking the wrong passage into the Atlantic. In that case the error was noted, adjusted for, and forgotten, but his encounter with the survivors of the *Sheaf Mead* made a lasting impression on Oehrn and did nothing for his self-confidence. "The entire affair had moved me deeply," he wrote, "and I described it in my war diary in somewhat more detail than usual. Place yourself in the position of a young commander . . . who has not yet become used to war. What hardness he has to have in order to follow his orders and carry out his mission!"[6]

Oehrn's actions were those of a novice in combat. He would not repeat them. Obviously a more experienced—or less sensitive—officer would have acted differently, having learned that there is little time in war for charity toward one's enemy. An example offers itself. Despite Oehrn's mission, there was another boat at sea when the *Westward Ho!* left Wilhelmshaven. It was the small type II U-9, commanded by one of his former recruits, the Balt Wolfgang Lüth. By the time Oehrn reached his area of operations, Lüth had dispatched three ships in a manner best described as clinical. By the end of the month he would have completed two patrols in the English Channel, sunk a fourth ship, and escaped an almost certain death under four British destroyers off the Norfolk coast, all before Victor Oehrn and the *Westward Ho!* had returned from what was to have been the initial blow in Karl Dönitz's new U-boat campaign (not surprisingly, in view of Oehrn's anointed role as the U-Bootwaffe's savior, Lüth was given little credit for it). No twinges of conscience, no hint of regret, no need to talk to survivors can be found in Lüth's deck logs, in his own written recollections of the sinkings, or in the accounts of his subordinates for any of these ships. As he said to his first watch officer after vaporizing the French submarine *Doris*, it was a simple case of "them or us."

The rest of Oehrn's patrol, which lasted almost four weeks, went well, and he returned to Wilhelmshaven on 6 June 1940. He had sunk ten ships for a total of 41,000 GRT, admittedly a better patrol than either of Lüth's and a very successful one in anyone's reckoning, and Dönitz set out to make as much out of it as he could. Oehrn was given the Iron Cross (First Class); his crew received lesser decorations. Media coverage was extensive, again at Dönitz's instigation, for he had long since learned how to

Victor Oehrn celebrating with his crew on the bridge of U-37. He is returning from the first of three war patrols he made in 1940, the patrol that is said to have restored the shattered morale of the U-Bootwaffe. (Victor Oehrn)

use the press for his own purposes. "'Westward Ho!' Returns," blared the *Nordische Rundschau* on 12 June: "The report that a German U-boat is once again returning from a successful patrol has reached us from far out at sea. . . . The boat is in sight! 'Ten this time!' and everyone's gaze goes up to the white battle pennants over the tower. This time? Yes, this boat, on whose tower the words 'Westward Ho' are written proudly, is returning home from its fifth successful patrol! The boat has sunk

Oehrn's former subordinate Wolfgang Lüth on U-9. For several weeks in the spring of 1940, Lüth was Oehrn's only rival at sea, but political and propaganda considerations ensured that Oehrn would get most of the attention. (Horst Bredow)

43,000 tons on this last patrol and sets a new record [for one boat] of 150,000 tons!"

Because of this patrol, Victor Oehrn is given credit in many histories as the man who saved the morale of the U-Bootwaffe (and therefore the U-Bootwaffe itself). This is only partially true. Nobody could deny that the black despair of April had disappeared by the time U-37 returned to Wilhelmshaven, but this could easily be credited to the progress of the war in general, which by that time had swung decisively in Germany's favor. France was on the verge of collapse when Oehrn returned to Wilhelmshaven. The French army had been routed, and most of the British Expeditionary Force had been evacuated from the beaches of Dunkirk (surprisingly, without any U-boats in the area to stop them). By 14 June troops of the German Fourth Army were marching down the Champs Elysées. A German soldier could not help feeling good about all these events, and so, presumably, could the men in the U-boats.

But something had restored the morale and the confidence of the U-boat commander and his crew in themselves, in their boats, and in their weapons. Something had broken the link they had made for themselves between *Schicksal,* inevitable fate, and the purely technical problem of a badly designed torpedo. "The spell of bad luck had been broken," wrote Dönitz, who was not usually given to such praise. "The fighting powers of the U-boat had once again been proved. My convictions had not played me false. It will be readily appreciated that I was particularly grateful to the commander of U-37 for what he had achieved, for he, too, understood how much depended upon the success or otherwise of his patrol. Now, however, the other U-boats put to sea convinced that what U-37 had done, they, too, could do."[7]

WHETHER Oehrn was responsible for a change or only benefited from one, there is no disputing that every aspect of the undersea war—the morale of the U-Bootwaffe, its success, and its strategic situation—began to improve just as he brought the *Westward Ho!* back to Wilhelmshaven in June. It was the beginning of what historians like to call the "Happy Times" of the U-Bootwaffe, and for most of those who were at the front during the second half of 1940 it was indeed a happy period, a golden age during which everything went their way, and success, instead of having to be searched out and caught, fell into their laps like the autumn leaves.

After France surrendered on 22 June 1940, Great Britain found herself in a difficult position. She was alone. Germany occupied the Continent.

The Soviet Union was still, ostensibly, on the German side, and the United States was still neutral. Britain had no supply lines on land. Anything she could not provide her people at home or her forces in battle had to be imported by sea from North America, over a rainbow of shipping lanes originating in Sydney, Halifax, Boston, New York, and Baltimore and converging into a huge triangular section of the North Atlantic northwest of Ireland called the Western Approaches. Earlier in the war German U-boats had to operate from Germany, usually from Wilhelmshaven. To get into the Atlantic a boat had to risk a long and perilous passage around Scotland; for that reason most U-boats stayed in the North Sea, and the shipping lanes were relatively safe. But as soon as France surrendered, Dönitz was able to move his boats into forward bases along the west coast of France from which they could enter the North Atlantic more easily. The Western Approaches, and particularly the bottleneck at the northern channel into the Irish Sea and the harbors of Glasgow, Liverpool, and Belfast, could now be reached in twelve hours after a fairly safe passage up the coast of the Irish Republic.

Sinkings increased almost immediately. Allied shipping lost to U-boat attack during the first eight months of the war averaged about 120,000 GRT per month. Total losses in May 1940 were about 63,000 GRT. Over the three months of summer 1940, however, average losses doubled to an average of 250,000 GRT per month, and in October, the first month of a bloody autumn, ninety Allied and neutral ships totaling 350,000 GRT— almost triple the first figure—would be sunk by U-boats.

Not everyone was happy during the Happy Times. The rise in U-boot-waffe fortunes corresponded almost exactly to Wolfgang Lüth's having to leave U-9 for a new boat under construction in Kiel, and the prospect of being on the sidelines for three months irritated him to the extreme. He was one of many who feared that the war might end without him. Dönitz had warned on the first day of hostilities that the war would be long and the outcome uncertain; nevertheless, with the surrender of France, the ongoing Battle of Britain, an incipient invasion, and the raging U-boat war, many U-boat officers who should have known better were afraid that Germany might win the war before they could get to the front. Lüth was one of them. Others were more circumspect, and some, like Jürgen Oesten, were almost derisory.

By the end of June 1940 Oesten had been in command of the Einbaum U-61 for almost a year. Like Wolfgang Lüth, he had completed several war patrols by that time, including one during Operation Weserübung, and like Lüth he had four ships to his credit. Unlike Lüth, he had spent the month of May in port, along with most of his fellow commanders. Two months after Lüth left U-9, Jürgen Oesten was relieved from his command and sent to Kiel, also to commission a new boat, in his case U-106. Unlike Lüth, who feared that the U-boat war might end while he was away, Oesten knew very well that it would not. "I don't think that there were many of the older and more experienced German submarine people who thought that this would be a short and easy operation," he wrote. "It was quite clear right from the beginning that the odds were against us." [8]

"*Leinen Los!* We begin to move." Victor Oehrn had no such trivial worries as Lüth or Oesten. He had a successful boat, a good crew, the confidence of his commander in chief, and more fame than a man with one war patrol under his belt had any right to expect. Oehrn's first patrol had kicked off the Happy Times. Now, on 1 August 1940, he was leaving Wilhelmshaven for his second. The sequence Oehrn describes below would soon become a ritual in the U-Bootwaffe. It reflects his own exuberance and the stratospheric level to which morale in the service had quickly risen: "The escort vessel takes station in front of us. We get three cheers from those we leave on the pier. The band plays one stanza of the *Deutschlandlied*, then one of the *Englandlied* . . . and then, since France had just surrendered, that English song about the *Westwall*: 'We will hang out our washing on the Siegfried Line.' Finally there comes the point where the escort turns back, and from now on we are alone with God." [9] The last line, a sobering reminder that gaiety cannot replace good, was significant, for three weeks after he left Wilhelmshaven, Oehrn found himself "alone with God" in a most profound way.

OEHRN was certain he had just committed a crime. Was it a dream? "*Schiff! Rot sieben null! Siehe da drüben!*" In the early evening, six hundred miles west of the Irish coast, a lookout on his boat had seen the masts of a large freighter. Oehrn clambered up onto the bridge, his binoculars knocking against the ladder. Following the lookout's outstretched arm he saw the ship, a medium-sized freighter of no distinction. "About 5,000 tons, I think," he said to his first watch officer, Nico Clausen, who had come up just behind him, "*Aüserste Kraft voraus.* All ahead full. I'm going to attack."

He took the boat to periscope depth. An approach was made, torpedoes were fired, the ship was struck and began to sink; it was a textbook attack. "What do you think," he suggested to Clausen as they took turns at the periscope. "Shall we come up now to watch?" The watch officer frowned. It was *leichtsinnig,* he realized later, very silly, but they had done it anyway, and they climbed up onto the bridge just in time to see the ship's bow rearing up slowly in the water like a huge black spear. Men were still on board.

"The gun, Herr Kaleu!" someone shouted. "They're going for their gun!" Oehrn spun. He had been seen by the men on the freighter. Even though the ship was going down fast, several figures were running toward her deck gun. "Open fire!" he screamed down to his gun crews, and almost at once a roar and a puff of smoke issued from the 105mm cannon mounted forward of the bridge.

What happened next was a living nightmare. Oehrn could see everything through his binoculars. He saw the gun on the sinking ship disintegrate. He saw a lifeboat, filled with men, as it dropped down the side of the ship and hit the water with a splash. He saw the side of the ship vanish in flame as a shell from his cannon hit her directly above the lifeboat. The freighter went down quickly, and the lifeboat drifted away, but many of the survivors inside, having taken the full force of the blast from the errant 105mm cannon shell, were clearly injured.

As he watched all of this, Victor Oehrn was seized with a terrible thought. He could not let these men survive. He could not let the picture of a German shell hitting a helpless lifeboat get back to the media, where it no doubt would have spread like a cancer. To shield his country and his service he would have to destroy the lifeboats.

Oehrn made his preparations calmly. He ordered everyone below except for two of his oldest and most experienced men. They were directed to man the gun, which immediately began a slow turn away from the bow of the ship and toward the lifeboat and its wretched inhabitants. The watch officer at his elbow looked at him; the question was never uttered, but he knew what it would be. The men in the lifeboat were looking at him also, unarmed, half-dressed, burned and broken. Anger and apprehension were in their faces, but they said nothing. They knew what he was thinking, just as his watch officer did, so they just looked at him and waited for the first shot.

Everyone waited. The silence was complete, overcoming even the sound of the wind and the sea. "Herr Kaleu," ventured Clausen gently. "You have to do something. The gun is ready. Give a command." Everyone, the men on the bridge of the *Westward Ho!,* the men on her guns, and the men in the lifeboats whose ship he had just sunk, waited for Victor Oehrn to give the command to fire.

Oehrn's mind raced as he thought of his limited options. How far was he obliged to go for his country? His mission was to sink ships. He had fulfilled it by sinking this ship quickly and economically. Hitting a lifeboat with gunfire would look very bad. But his mission was *not* to protect Germany's reputation; after all, he thought with more than a little regret, the reputation of his own country in the West was probably beyond redemption. He was justified in firing his guns. A single lucky shot from the ship could easily have punctured his pressure hull, preventing U-37 from ever diving again, or her fuel tank, leaving her marooned and helpless at sea. His men had aimed at the ship, not at the lifeboat hanging from the falls in front of her. He was not justified in killing the men in the boat afterward, no matter who saw him or who did not.

Slowly, as all this went through his mind, Oehrn began to reconsider, and when he finally spoke, after what seemed like hours, it was to offer life, not death. "Gun crews stand down. Half ahead." The gunners stepped back. The *Westward Ho!* began to move slowly toward the wreckage. Nico Clausen, a possible witness to a war crime, whistled slowly and pulled out a cigarette.

The boats Oehrn had almost fired on belonged to the British steamer *Severn Leigh,* which he sank on 23 August 1940. It was a frightening encounter on both sides. Some readers may consider it evidence of the U-boat commander's innate cruelty that he considered such a thing at all, that it took a positive act of will not to proceed. Others may conclude that he was simply not up to his mission, that he should have stayed at his desk in the Schnorchelbude. Neither is true. Oehrn was not a cruel man, nor was he out of his depth. He was a sensitive man confronted with a dilemma, and the initial reaction to a dilemma is often a quick rehearsal of possible solutions, however extreme. In wartime the consideration of any solution involves material preparation. A foot soldier hears a noise in the underbrush; whatever he decides to do, he is unslinging and aiming his gun while he is thinking about it.

Oehrn obviously brought this dilemma upon himself. His decision to approach the *Severn Leigh* was ill-advised, as he admits. But the confrontation that followed may have been aggravated by an event that had occurred five days earlier. On 19 August 1940, Adolf Hitler had declared a zone around the British Isles in which all shipping, including that of neutrals, was subject to attack without warning. In effect, he had reintroduced the policy of unrestricted submarine warfare so hated by the enemies of imperial Germany in 1915. It was not, admittedly, a sudden decision; Germany's adherence to the strict rules of commerce war had been eroding ever since the war began. But it could only reinforce the public image of the U-boat as a sneaky and underhanded weapon and the U-boat commander as ruthless and wanton. Oehrn was not stupid. He was aware of Germany's past mistakes and of current public opinion. He knew that the reputations of his country and his service would suffer because of Hitler's announcement of unrestricted submarine warfare. He knew also that specific events like the destruction of a lifeboat had a tendency to work against Germany, especially when the perception was one of willful intent. One of the solutions that flashed before him, therefore, was to remove the evidence and forget all about it.

He made a different, and much more charitable, decision in the end.[10]

VICTOR Oehrn ended his second war patrol on 30 August 1940 in the Breton coastal port of Lorient. Eight pennants fluttered overhead as he conned the *Westward Ho!* up the Scorff estuary and into the harbor. The officers on the bridge tried to look as businesslike as they could after thirty days at sea; the crew, paraded on the weather deck, quietly discussed their options as regarded the night life in Lorient, the women of Lorient, the next train out of Lorient. Everyone was pleased. It had not been a bad patrol: eight ships were sunk, two damaged, and Oehrn now had 75,000 GRT to his credit, very close to the theoretical minimum of 100,000 required for the coveted Knight's Cross.[11] He was well on his way to becoming an ace, a fact he could now contemplate with some pleasure.

U-boats were eventually based out of several French Atlantic ports, from Brest in the north to Bordeaux in the south, but of these the city most often identified with the U-Bootwaffe in World War II was Lorient, the "Port of Aces" and BdU headquarters from 1940 to 1942.[12] It seemed in 1940 that every officer with a reputation had taken his boat into the Scorff estuary and tied up alongside one of the old wooden hulks then being used for temporary docks in Lorient harbor, starting with the redoubtable Fritz-Julius Lemp and ending with the man who was still undisputed primus inter pares in the U-Bootwaffe, Günther Prien.

One officer who had not yet reached the Port of Aces was the man who kept the whole operation moving: Karl Dönitz. He had visited Lorient soon after it had been taken by German forces with a view toward moving his headquarters (he had chosen a little chateau in Kerneval, just outside of Lorient, for this purpose), but throughout the summer of 1940 the U-boats continued to be controlled, with no obvious ill effects, out of Sengwarden. Dönitz was still in Sengwarden when he decided to implement the tactic that was to have perhaps the single most significant impact on the war at sea. This tactic, which had been conceived in theory some years before the war and practiced by the U-Bootwaffe at length in peacetime, was called *Rudeltaktik*—the wolfpack.

Since the beginning of World War I the U-boat had been a solitary hunter, finding her prey and killing alone. But enemy merchant ships were now sailing in convoy under escort; some of the fast eastbound convoys, fully loaded with arms, ammunition, and oil, had thirty, forty, or fifty ships in their columns. What would happen, asked Dönitz, if a U-boat, having found a convoy, did not attack at once but called for assistance from other boats? If a single U-boat could sink two or three ships from a convoy, ten boats could cut a convoy in half. The convoy escorts would be forced to divide their attention, becoming less effective and more confused, and the psychological effect of enemy torpedoes coming from every direction would be overwhelming. A convoy could be destroyed—wiped from the sea.

BdU's first attempts at Rudeltaktik in 1939 and early 1940 were ignominious failures, but time and practice brought efficiency. By late September, after Dönitz had vacated Sengwarden for Paris, the real effects of Rudeltaktik were immediate, compelling, and total. During that month ninety ships were sunk by U-boats: fifteen of them in one day, four, five, or six routinely in an hour. Oehrn's total of ten ships in May was considered fantastic at the time; in September Hans Jenisch sank seven ships in a week. Only days before Oehrn's departure, a single convoy, the fast eastbound HX 72 from Halifax, had lost eleven ships in twenty-four hours. Three of them were sunk in as many minutes. Ships no longer disappeared in singles but in clusters: on 9 October Viktor Schütze sank two ships and damaged a third in two minutes, and Heinrich Bleichrodt accomplished the identical feat on 17 October in no time at all.[13]

New heroes were produced: Schütze and Bleichrodt and Jenisch; Engelbert Endrass, Prien's first watch officer in Scapa Flow; Joachim Schepke, the handsome commander of U-100, and Heinrich Liebe, the equally plain commander of U-38; Fritz Frauenheim, Hans Rudolf Rösing, Joachim Matz, Herbert Wohlfahrt, and Herbert Schultze. The best and most dangerous officer in wolfpack operations was no longer Günther Prien but the forbidding Otto Kretschmer, the son of a Silesian schoolmaster and the commander of U-99. In the last six months of 1940 he sank more than thirty ships to become the most successful World War II submarine commander of any navy in the world; it was a position he would not relinquish in the five years remaining before Germany's surrender. Unlike Prien, the media star, Kretschmer did not brag or posture. He had no personality to speak of. He just sank ships, and he sank them like a robot: one after the other, seemingly without fear or feeling, four, five, six at a time.

Kretschmer was the pivotal commander in the most significant victory for the U-Bootwaffe in 1940, a two-day Atlantic convoy battle in mid-October that would forever after be known in naval history as the "Night of Long Knives." During this battle, which began at about noon on 18 October, two eastbound convoys were attacked by U-boats as they approached the North Channel and were torn to pieces. The first convoy, SC 7, left Sydney, Nova Scotia, with thirty-five ships, of which twenty-nine remained when she steamed past Rockall Bank on 18 October. *Eight* managed to limp into British ports over the next two days. The rest, twenty-one freighters, tankers, refrigerator ships, and ammunition carriers, were lost from convoy SC 7 overnight. Otto Kretschmer sank eight of them. The second convoy, HX 79, with forty-nine ships and an escort of ten Royal Navy destroyers, corvettes, and minesweepers, followed SC 7 by one day and lost thirteen ships overnight.

These two nights were by far the worst in the battle so far; in percentages, they would be the worst ever. Karl Dönitz was quietly exultant. The defining moment of the U-Bootwaffe had arrived; his trust in the service and his faith in the tactics he had espoused for years, particularly Rudeltaktik, now seemed fully vindicated. For Britain, and especially for the British Admiralty, the season was a disaster, and October was the worst in a series of very bad months, "the very nadir," according to Royal Navy officer and historian Donald Macintyre, "of British fortunes in the Battle of the Atlantic."[14] Rudeltaktik had caught them unprepared, and they admitted as much: "[This] development was, from the British point of view, full of the most serious implications since the enemy had adopted a form of attack which we had not foreseen and against which neither tactical nor technical countermeasures had been prepared."[15]

Victor Oehrn did not take part in the fierce convoy battles of mid-October. He was at sea during the Night of Long Knives, midway through his third war patrol, but he was nowhere near the area of the fight. He was fast approaching the 100,000-GRT mark in enemy shipping, but he had lost the spotlight that was his in June and the *Westward Ho!* was once again simply U-37, an older boat that leaked. One of the effects of Rudeltaktik had been to change the U-Bootwaffe from an irritant into a deadly killing machine, but another had been to change the image of the U-boat commander from a man with a name and a face to a nameless synthesis of many different men. Wolfpacks were anonymous. Unlike Günther Prien in 1939, most of the newer aces were not well known outside of the service; the men who fought against them did not know their names, and people in the streets of London and Liverpool—or Berlin and Kiel—did not know what they looked like. As a result, any fame Oehrn might have achieved with his first patrol was gone by his third. It did not bother him as long as he could keep his boat and his crew—after all, he wanted only to be at the front, to be with his men and to fight another day for Germany.

Otto Kretschmer, "Silent Otto," the man who would become the single highest-ranking submarine ace of World War II. During the last three months of 1940, Kretschmer sank fifteen ships—more than most aces would sink in a career. (U.S. Naval Institute)

Staff work was certainly important and I enjoyed it, but the staff officer is always in second place. First place belongs to the man at the front; it has to be that way and it always was with us. . . . The responsibilities of a U-boat commander gave me great joy, to be out alone under the eyes of God (and those of Dönitz, who, thousands of kilometers away in port, always had us in his heart). . . . I liked being responsible for a boat and a crew, both of which I held above everything else; these magnificent men, who trusted me, and whose wives and children, standing on the pier in Wilhelmshaven, used to look up at me as if to ask: "will you bring everyone back to us safe and well." [16]

Victor Oehrn entered the Scorff for the second time on 22 October 1940. Karl Dönitz was waiting for him, and after the boat was tied up the crew was formed quickly into ranks for his inspection. Oehrn and Clausen stood at the front, looking like nothing so much as two tramps leading a platoon of sewer workers: dirty, odiferous, a month's worth of beard, and Oehrn with an incongruous bunch of fresh flowers. Dönitz smiled at his deputy. "A successful patrol, Oehrn?"

"Moderately so, Herr Admiral." Dönitz motioned and another officer came forward with a box. "Kapitänleutnant Victor Oehrn," he said, so that everyone could hear him. "In the name of the Führer and Commander-in-Chief of the Wehrmacht I award you the Knight's Cross of the Iron Cross." Everyone applauded as he placed the red, black, and silver ribbon around Oehrn's neck and laid the large black cross, a confection of silver and steel coveted by every commander in the U-Bootwaffe and for which some were prepared to risk their lives, their crews, and their boats, under his throat. "My congratulations, Oehrn."

"And I have another announcement," he continued. "Effective immediately Kapitänleutnant Oehrn is relieved from command of U-37 and reassigned to BdU staff. The new commander of U-37 will be Oberleutnant zur See Nicolai Clausen." Clausen blinked. Oehrn did not move. He had just lost his boat.

He should have seen the move coming. It was inevitable. He knew how Dönitz thought and how BdU operated. He had been sent to sea in May to correct a serious problem. Now the problem was gone, and therefore so was his reason for being in command. Britain, having weathered the best of the German army and the Luftwaffe, was reeling before the U-boats. Her navy was confused, undermanned, overtaxed, and frustrated. The U-boat commanders who had once been sulking in their boats were now fighting to be sent back to the front. Oehrn was one of those commanders, and he had done well, but he was also an excellent staff officer, and because increased U-boat activity at sea dictated a similar increase in the workload at BdU, he was needed at his desk again—the sooner the better. Probably Oehrn was allowed to stay in command of U-37 as long as he did only because the experience made him a better staff officer and the Knight's Cross made him more content—a cynical view, but there was a war on, and Dönitz had no time to humor anyone's sensitivities.

Victor Oehrn had always wanted to be a U-boat commander at the front, to do the things he often planned for others, to have his great adventure in the great war, to fight for Germany. It was something he had trained to do. It was something both nature and upbringing had demanded that he do. But now he was back to being a man with no name, alone in his office with memories.

The adventure, it seemed, was over.

CHAPTER 5

The Capturing of Souls

There she was, quite near us and stopped dead in the water. It was exciting to see this long, narrow tube of steel and iron pitching and rolling in the long swell. On her conning tower I could see a couple of suntanned boys with unshaven, laughing faces waving to us. What a magnificent picture! . . . I stared at the U-106 in awe.

—Otto Giese

THE commander of a U-boat was an individual, but his achievements were the collective achievements of several dozen men. They could do nothing without him and he could do nothing without them, a fact he was ill-advised to forget, and neither he nor his crew could do anything without a well-built and well-operated boat, a machine so complex and so demanding that one had to follow a ten-step process to flush the toilet.[1]

A commander, his crew, and his boat were so tightly bound together that the three often became a single entity under the commander's name. It was the commander who was tracked in the huge plotting tables at Kerneval: "Kretschmer is now moving into Quadrant AL 6581." It was the commander who was decorated for the performance of the crew as a group or excoriated for their failure. It was the commander, not the boat, to whom the crew attached themselves (unless he was a complete embarrassment to them): "I served in U-Hartmann in 1943." In a way, the commander *became* the crew and the boat, just as Karl Dönitz became the U-Bootwaffe in many minds.

Because every crew and every boat in the U-Bootwaffe was different, just as every commander was different, the relationships they formed were unique and lasted only as long as everyone stayed together. A U-boat crew might change completely with a new member; a commander might change

74

with a new crew, a new boat, even a shiny new piece of equipment (the torpedo fiasco of 1940 would tend to prove this). But fragile as they were, these relationships were the strength of the U-Bootwaffe, and many of them were strong enough to survive the war. They still exist today, fed by affection rather than by necessity. Informal associations and newsletters are common among U-boat crewmen, regular reunions are held, and long-dead commanders are discussed as if they were still alive.

This alloy of men and machinery was a magical thing. Some understood it better than others. Everyone knew it was there.

OBERLEUTNANT *zur See* (lieutenant [junior grade]) Jürgen Oesten was a large man, six feet tall, according to his prisoner of war index card. His height, his brown hair, his blue eyes, and his sharp features made him look like a latter-day Viking, a far cry from the cherubic bust his father had carved in Berlin so many years before. He was twenty-six years old in August 1940, and when he was relieved as commander of U-61 that month he had sunk seven ships of 20,000 GRT, won the Iron Cross (First and Second Class), and lost none of his skepticism. He still distrusted the government, and he still had his doubts about the war. In fact, he had just made a bet with his father-in-law that the Americans would be in on it before too long.[2] He was not troubled about leaving the front, and when he received his orders to report to the shipyards of Deschimag AG Weser in Bremen to commission a new boat, U-106, he went with regret but not disappointment.

It was U-Bootwaffe practice for a new commander and his crew to arrive at the shipyard several weeks, or even months, before their boat was due for commissioning so they could learn about the boat and its inner workings during the construction process. When Oesten arrived in Bremen on 27 August 1940, he knew that U-106 had only recently been launched and looked nothing like the fighting weapons one saw at sea. Only her massive hull was complete. As he looked at her for the first time, drifting lazily in the filthy waters of the Deschimag yard, he could not help but be impressed by the small battalions of yardworkers crawling in, out, over, and around her like tiny ants on a floating corpse, wiring, welding, hammering, sawing, painting, and riveting. As he crawled through her narrow passageways, his senses were captured by golden showers of sparks, by the smell of diesel fumes and smoke, by the terrifying noise and the crunch of metal shavings underfoot.

The period of intensive training that ran in rough parallel with a boat's construction was called her *Baubelehrung,* literally, "build instruction." During a boat's Baubelehrung her crew would work side by side with her builders to learn everything they could about their new command and about the equipment they would be using on board: how it was built and installed, how it worked, how it might malfunction, and how to repair it. They were able to look at things from different perspectives, see parts of the boat they would never see after she was finished, and enter spaces they would never enter at sea. It was training from the keel up, available only once, impossible to teach in a classroom. Every new boat, even those built toward the end of the war, had a period of time set aside for Baubelehrung. It always proved worthwhile.[3]

Oesten was not the first to report for Baubelehrung. That distinction belonged to his new chief engineer, Oberleutnant (Ing) Herbert Panknin, who, along with the chief petty officers in charge of the boat's diesel plant and electrical systems and most of its engineering personnel, had been in Bremen since the boat was launched. The chief engineer of a U-boat, the *Leitende Ingenieur,* or LI, was the senior engineer on board, responsible directly to the commander for all technical matters. He had no prospects of command himself, having been trained as an *Ingenieuroffizier* rather than a Seeoffizier, but a commander was ill-advised to ignore his advice. Panknin, a regular officer of Crew 34, was probably the busiest man in the yard, having not only to learn every nut and bolt of the boat himself but to make sure that all his men did as well. For that reason, he spent most of his time crawling around inside U-106's hull with a flashlight and a clipboard, and he rarely had time for pleasantries.

A U-boat, or any submarine, is not really a submarine but a submersible: a boat that spends most of her time on the surface but can dive below the water for short periods if necessary. She can do this because she is simply a large watertight metal capsule, allowed to float by the air inside her tanks or allowed to sink by expulsion of the same air, driven on the surface by diesel engines and underwater by electric motors. The stability of the boat, her tendency to remain on an even keel, was controlled by her rudder, by diving planes (which were simply rudders turned sideways), or by trim tanks, small water tanks scattered around inside the hull which could be filled or emptied as required. She looked like a boat because the first watertight hull was enclosed by a second boat-shaped hull that stopped her from wallowing too much and allowed her to move more economically through the water, and she could stay at a certain depth only as long as she kept moving. If a submarine stopped moving—lost way—for too long, her options were limited: pop back up to the surface like a jack-in-the-box or sink to the bottom. Sinking, Panknin might say, hands suddenly clasped as though he were squeezing an orange, often meant the collapse of the hull. This always had a certain effect on the uninitiated.

A U-boat was simple enough in principle, but it was very difficult to build, and a well-built boat was a sublimely complicated creation. U-106, a type IXB boat of 1,173 submerged tons, was actually a big step for Oesten. She was much larger than the type IIC Einbaum U-61, more powerful, and more advanced in design. Of the approximately eleven hundred U-boats built between 1935 and 1945, the type IX was one of the largest. She ranged in size from the type IXA of 1,153 tons to the huge type IXD2 of 1,804 tons and in length anywhere from 76 meters to 86 meters (about the length of a standard American football field). U-106, one of the smaller of the type, nevertheless had three mounted deck guns, six torpedo

Jürgen Oesten. A good commander and an honest man, he always looked warily on those who were running his country and his service. (Jürgen Oesten)

tubes, a range of eight thousand nautical miles, and a crew of forty-eight. U-61, a boat of one-fourth the displacement, would have fit comfortably within her hull. Going from one boat to the other would require some adjustment for Oesten. The type IX boat was more sluggish than the type II, harder to turn, slower to respond, even slower to dive, but the inside, wrote Wolfgang Lüth, who made an identical move from the type II U-138 to the type IXA U-43 in November 1940, reminded him of a hospital after the tiny spaces and cramped tower of his old Einbaum (he was especially pleased to have a washbasin to himself).[4]

U-106 was laid down in December 1939 and launched in June 1940. Most likely the engineers had arrived before launching, while the boat was still on the ways; it was the last chance for them to see the entire hull. The diesel mechanics spent most of their time in the engine room, where the boat's two 2200-horsepower main diesel engines were bolted down. The electrician's mates could examine the batteries under the deck-plates or the two 500-horsepower electric motors they were wired to. The torpedomen, the gunner's mates, and the radiomen came later, after the hull was finished. The torpedomen were able to see how the torpedo loading mechanisms were bolted into the forward and after torpedo rooms for the boat's six torpedo tubes. The seamen saw how her guns, a 105mm cannon forward, a 37mm gun aft, and a 20mm antiaircraft gun in the raised superstructure abaft the tower (usually called the *Wintergarten*), were secured to the hull, how they were loaded, and how they were cleaned and protected from the elements. The radiomen were shown how the hydrophone worked and how the communications gear was wired; in later years they had to learn how to set up and operate the myriad radar and radar detection devices being churned out by German laboratories, but U-106 had no such equipment on board when she was built. The last to arrive, logically, were those who had the least interest in the construction of the boat: the boatswain's mates, the cook, and the doctor, if they were lucky enough to have one (Oesten was not). After all, a stove was a stove, a line was a line, and *Treponema pallidum* was *Treponema pallidum* in any boat.

The rest of the boat's officers arrived in Bremen at various times during the summer. After Oesten came Hermann Rasch, the first watch officer, Grünberg, the second watch officer, and Böttcher, the *Obersteuermann* (one of two men Oesten had been able to bring with him from U-61). The atmosphere at Deschimag was no doubt enlivened considerably by the appearance of Hermann Rasch, a large, loud man with an inspired disregard for authority and a liking for malodorous black cigars. Rasch, whose father had been captain of the ill-starred battle cruiser *Goeben* in 1914, was Oesten's second in command, and because U-106 was a type IX boat he was the man most likely to succeed him when he left. His carpet-chewing manner was probably an asset in the position; disconcerting to the unsuspecting seaman, most of it was bluster. "His bark was worse than his bite," wrote Peter Hansen, who interviewed downed pilots with him. "He was a practical joker, a great tease in every respect, especially when it came to Karl Dönitz or Eberhard Godt, both of whom were somewhat sober types who did not catch on quickly when someone tried to pull their legs or made sardonic comments to them with a straight face." [5]

U-106's Baubelehrung came to a close on 24 September 1940, the day she was commissioned. The commissioning, or *Indienststellung*, of a new U-boat was the ceremony in which she was turned over to the Kriegsmarine by the yard and placed into active service. An Indienststellung had several meanings. It was a true change of ownership: Deschimag AG Weser was no longer responsible for U-106 and was not required to pay for further work on her, although as a practical matter some yards did so and some did not. It was a symbolic milestone in the life of the boat: her commissioning made her a fighting unit in the Kriegsmarine and a weapon against the enemy. It could be a memorable moment for the new commander or any member of his crew. Günther Prien often gave 17 December as his birthday simply because that was the day in 1938 that his boat, U-47, had been commissioned. Jürgen Oesten, not as enthusiastic as Prien but still mindful of the occasion, took command of U-106 in front of a small audience that included the workers who built his boat and the manager of the yard, the commanding officer, Kriegsmarine-Dienststelle Bremen (the wives and families of the crew were not present). He had only a few words to say. He thanked the yard, mentioned the first U-106, a boat of the Imperial Navy that had hit a mine in October 1917 and gone down with her entire crew, reminded his own crew that they had a hard task ahead, and was sure, he concluded, that everyone would do his best.[6]

U-106's crew stood in ranks facing Oesten as he spoke: the officers, Rasch, Panknin, Grünberg, and Böttcher, with gloves and ceremonial daggers, the enlisted men to Bottcher's left, ramrod straight and arrayed in order of rank from the senior petty officers to the boat's Moses, the youngest seaman on board. They could not respond, of course, but in any case they knew, as he did, that the words were only for the ceremony. Speeches were all well and good, but a crew could be won over only by actions, by example, and mostly by success, as Oesten and his officers were well aware.

Happily, they were products of a training system remarkably enlightened in the way it treated the relationship between an officer and the men he would eventually command. The strict divisions of rank in the Imperial Navy and the lack of communication between them were thought to be a major cause of the 1918 mutinies, and the Kriegsmarine went to great lengths to ensure that they would not happen again. Officers were encouraged, even required, to learn as much about their men as possible. Karl-Friedrich Merten, commander of U-68, when he was assigned to the pre-dreadnought battleship *Schleswig-Holstein* as a training officer in 1938, compiled a huge book of the names, descriptions, and photographs of the two hundred Seekadetten in his charge and memorized it.[7] Officers were reminded that their men had needs and worries of their own. If he responded to these, they would respond to him. Erich Topp, the commander of U-552, stopped a patrol and returned to port so that his navigator might retrieve a good luck charm he had forgotten.[8] Wolfgang Lüth would help to find living quarters for the families of former crewmen long after he let his last boat.[9] "Officer life *alongside* the men," wrote Merten, "had become streamlined to a life closely *with* the men."[10]

The commander was to be dignified yet approachable, strict but caring, a parent in loco parentis. It was the perfect leadership model for life in the confined spaces of a U-boat. "There is no ship at sea in which the place of the commander as *Maitre apres Dieu* [Lord after God] is so obvious as in a U-boat," wrote Oesten after the war. "[He] is the pivotal figure, and the nature of his position far exceeds that which is normally associated with a unit commander in any military hierarchy." The relationship between a U-boat commander and his crew is based squarely on the concept of a benign autocrat who is all-powerful but who nevertheless requires trust and confidence from below so he can rule effectively. The process by which one is obtained and the other inspired is what Oesten likes to call "the capturing of souls," or *Seelenfang*.[11]

This process varied from one commander to another. It was often difficult and almost never short. It started for Oesten as soon as the boat was commissioned (not, as one might have suspected, during Baubelehrung) and lasted for several months, slowed, he believes, because there were only two men in U-106 with whom he had previously served. It took a long time, he writes, to understand the substance of a man, his potential, his failings. For that reason it was better to start with men one already knew.

In later years, after he had gained in prestige and pull, he made sure to keep as many as he could.[12] Oesten was aided by the fact that U-106 was a new boat with a grace period behind the lines. Some commanders, like Lüth, did not have time for capturing souls. "I don't know you" was all he could say to his crew upon taking command of U-43, an operational boat, "and you don't know me. We will become better acquainted at the front."[13] According to Merten: "You cannot do anything to create sympathy [on purpose]. The only thing any commander can do is to be open-minded and to behave naturally according to his character and not to try to be an actor and to play a role as a heroic commander. Usually your crew will have a sensitive feeling for the true genuineness of your nature. They will find it out in the first dangerous position."[14]

Danger, said Merten, was the only test of a commander. His behavior under stress forms the crew's impression of him. This impression is critical, and once made it is very hard to change. U-106, of course, was not yet in combat, but the interminable hours of shakedown and training provided many opportunities for Oesten to operate, and the crew to observe him, in situations resembling those of combat: extreme stress, hard work, intense boredom, and serious danger. From the date of her commissioning to the beginning of her first war patrol three months later, U-106 went back and forth between Bremen, Kiel, Danzig, Gotenhafen, Stettin, Memel, and Wilhelmshaven no less than eleven times, during which she went through dozens of tests, trials, and exercises, was attached at one time or another to four major commands, and was involved in a collision at sea. Any man who could lead a boat successfully through all that, as Oesten did, could not help but create a positive first impression.[15]

After her commissioning and three days of various trials in Bremen, for example, U-106 sailed through the Kaiser Wilhelm Canal to Kiel for two weeks testing at TEK (Torpedoerprobungskommando, or Torpedo Trials Command) and then to Danzig for two weeks testing at UAK. Nothing could test a new crew like combat, but the experience of having to go through time trials at UAK with the formidable Kapitän zur See Günther Sachs on board was almost as bad. Sachs, a veteran of the Imperial U-Bootwaffe who would not be fooled in technical matters, but a "terror and a pest" so stout he could not fit through the tower hatch, would perch on the bridge with one petty officer and scream a command down to the control room. After the maneuver was complete, a single shouted "failed, do it again" would invariably follow, and everything would have to start over from the top. After several iterations of this procedure, everyone was ready to bite each other's head off, and Oesten himself, who had to react calmly and professionally to each scream, was closely watched by crew and examiner alike.[16]

The collision occurred during UAK testing on 19 October, the Night of Long Knives, when U-106 rammed another boat on trials, U-134. "And not our fault," Oesten hastens to add, "since U-134 was submerged and had to give way."[17] For crewmen who could not see anything outside the hull and who trusted their officers completely to find the way, the sound and feel of one boat hitting another must have been frightening indeed. The prospect of having one's boat sink to the bottom with everyone inside was pressure of a kind not found on the Dänholm, or in a classroom, or in the shipyards of Deschimag AG Weser, and again, the performance of Oesten in this situation was critical to his success as a leader. During the war more than twenty boats were involved in fatal collisions. Fortunately, nobody was seriously hurt in this one, and everyone got a four-day break while U-106 went back into the yards for repairs.

While Oesten was trying to win the trust he needed to command, his men were trying to get along with each other—not, in all cases, an easy process. The same stressful months that would establish his relationship to them would eventually forge them into something approaching a single unit, a machine within a machine, but under the circumstances (as Oesten himself had once remarked about Crew 33) it was a wonder that it ever happened. The composition of a U-boat crew was at least as remarkable as that of a Reichsmarine crew—perhaps more so because of its relative heterogeneity.

Most U-boat crewmen were young, in their early twenties, but they might range in age from the late teens to least the mid-thirties (Victor Oehrn allowed a man of fifty to sail with him in U-37). They came from every walk of life. Most of the sample in one limited study had worked in industry rather than agriculture, commerce, or the services. A majority had been skilled craftsmen—mechanics, machinists, metalworkers, electricians, and plumbers—but there were also cooks, barbers, accountants, and train drivers. They came from every part of the Reich. Most of the study sample were from central Germany and the great industrial regions of the Ruhr, Westphalia, and Saxony, but others came from East Prussia, Berlin, Baden, Wurttemberg, Bavaria, the Saar, and Austria. According to Hansen, there was a deliberate policy to recruit from the inland regions rather than the coast for the simple reason that those who lived by the sea knew its dangers and would defer. Often the most enthusiastic were those from small towns and farms, which made for an interesting problem. "These fellows from the villages and countryside spoke only heavily accented German with various local dialects. I know of cases where the men could hardly communicate properly with each other." [18]

Their backgrounds probably did not differ from those of the general public: middle or lower class, of average education, Protestant. The same applied to politics: U-boat crewmen were probably as tolerant, and as unenthusiastic, about National Socialism as any man in the street. But because the average crewman during the war was only in his early teens when Adolf Hitler became chancellor, he was more heavily indoctrinated in the ideology than his elders (including his officers) had been. Most men in the U-Bootwaffe, for example, did not finish their education until the late 1930s, long after National Socialist thought had permeated the school system, and many had been in the Hitler Youth or the Reich Labor Service or both. Few could remember the "bad old days" of the Weimar Republic and so had no basis for comparing the government to any previous one. Oesten could at least say to himself that things before National Socialism had been no better. His men, even if they had similar reservations, could not (no doubt it was for this reason that Wolfgang Lüth spent so much time giving lectures to his younger crewmen about the horrors of Weimar and the accomplishments of the Third Reich).

Despite many opinions to the contrary and the prevailing image of the U-boat sailor as some kind of troglodyte, there does not seem to have been any particular U-boat "type." This is not to say that the general idea of U-boat life as being wet, miserable, and short is wrong. It was all of that. But Jürgen Oesten does not see that misery as requiring any special character, and he states the opposite quite plainly: "To my opinion there is nothing special about serving or leading aboard submarines. It is a profession as many others, where the same qualities are required. Human beings are adaptable, and once you have found your bearing aboard submarines, it is just a bloody trade. The fact that it happens submerged sometimes may have a certain attraction for young boys or so, but it should not affect sensible people." [19]

Under normal circumstances such a disparate group might have separated like shrapnel, but suddenly they found themselves thrown together in a metal shell the size of a small apartment, in which they worked, ate common meals, slept literally in each other's bunks, grew rank and dirty together, and remained so for weeks at a time. There were no secrets. Each man knew everyone else intimately and soon found himself depending on

Members of Oesten's crew paraded on the weather deck of U-106. Oesten is in the white cap, looking more scruffy than the others. "In my opinion," he once wrote, "there is nothing special about serving or leading aboard submarines. It is a profession as many others, where the same qualities are required." (Jürgen Oesten)

everyone else for his life. If he made a mistake, others suffered for it, meaning that Kapitän Sachs might start one of his endless drills over again, that an enemy ship might escape, or that the entire crew might die. Since nobody with any personal pride or sense of self-interest wanted to make that mistake, everyone did his best and learned to work in concert. In an emergency dive they moved no longer as fifty men but as one, and during a torpedo run their voices and actions complemented each other's like the tiny pieces of a watch. As they sat in their bunks during mealtimes they found they could read each other's thoughts and anticipate each other's words. They began to develop reputations and sprout nicknames. Although they had worked together for only a matter of weeks, it was as though they had lived together all their lives.

Of course, they began to take a perverse pride in having to endure this situation and soon developed the cocky attitude that characterized the U-boat sailor. They even had an identifying mark, for during those hectic months the boat's insignia was conceived and painted across the tower: two smiling sawfish crossed at the tips of their noses. Like most such insignia (beginning with Prien's bull), it was drawn as a caricature, but the adult sawfish is a large, unpleasant fish that loiters in shallow water and uses its serrated six-foot snout as a slashing weapon. Its use as a symbol for the boat made her crewmen, each of whom wore a smaller sawfish on his blue garrison cap, feel formidable and slightly evil as well.

By late December 1940, a process that had started in June and lasted more than six months was almost over. The tests and the trials were done, the collision damage had been repaired, and the boat was judged ready for the front. The crew was well trained and confident. Oesten was satisfied, at least as much as any commander would admit. Christmas Day was spent in Wilhelmshaven, taking on provisions, and on 4 January 1941, after degaussing at Brunsbüttel and one final passage through the Kaiser Wilhelm Canal to Kiel to pick up her orders, U-106 departed for her first war patrol. She was not yet ready for combat—no boat was ready—but she had done all that might be expected to prepare for it, and most of the credit must go to Oesten. "Three months between commissioning and departure on the first war patrol was a very brief time," wrote Peter Hansen, "it usually required four to seven months. Only an experienced commander with a core of front-experienced men could have managed it." [20]

U-106 had finally become a *Frontboot,* a unit assigned to an operational U-flotilla and available for battle service. The lengthy process of the Baubelehrung shakedown and training that she had gone through was not unusual. All new boats went through the same tests and trials, their crews had to endure what is now called, with some tedium, "the bonding process," and their commanders had to hunt, like Oesten, for the souls of their men. For U-106 it was worthwhile. She did well under Jürgen Oesten. For most boats it was useful. But it was not a magic formula for success, and in some cases it failed utterly to prepare a boat.

IN AUGUST 1941 Hans-Joachim Rahmlow, commander of U-570, gave up his boat without a struggle to aircraft of 269 Squadron, RAF Coastal Command. It was the first time a U-boat had been captured and taken back safely to an Allied port.

Rahmlow had commissioned U-570 after one short and messy war patrol as commander of U-58. He took her and his crew through the same trials and tests as Oesten did, and he was sent to sea. But Rahmlow, a pedantic man who tended to get seasick, was not a good leader and neither were his officers. He did not capture the souls of his crew. He was uncomfortable with them, and they loathed him. There is evidence to suggest that he was unfamiliar with the characteristics of his boat and that quick and decisive action on his part might have saved her. The fatal panic that caused him to throw up his hands as soon as he was engaged by an astonished Lockheed Hudson was just icing on the cake.

The Admiralty, of course, was delighted with the capture, and so was British Intelligence. U-570 was taken over by the Royal Navy, rechristened HMS *Graph,* studied, analyzed, and used in her original capacity as a submarine until spare parts ran out. She made several war patrols under the White Ensign, which caused some confusion on both sides. In the process, the British learned more about the U-boats they had been hunting than from any amount of secondary intelligence. The discovery that the thickness of the steel in the German hulls allowed them to dive below the normal settings of British depth charges was doubtless responsible for the loss of many German lives in the following months.[21]

In an objective sense it would have been better had Rahmlow and his crew gone down with the boat. But he lived, and he paid for his mistake. He narrowly escaped a secret court-martial for cowardice when news of his capture leaked into the British POW system. After the war, he was ostracized by his fellow officers, and he spent the rest of his life in ignominy. Horst Bredow was once asked his opinion of Rahmlow. He cocked his head, looked at the questioner, and slowly gave a politically correct answer: "I suppose these days he would have been exonerated due to a temporary incapacity. Unsuitability. Insanity. Something like that." The shrug that followed was eloquent. "But what do *you* think about him?" he was pressed. "I would have strung him up," he replied. And that, correct or not, is the opinion of most men in the U-Bootwaffe.[22]

Perhaps nothing could have saved Hans-Joachim Rahmlow from his fate. Some men are destined for tragedy. But Baubelehrung and the subsequent months of testing at sea were designed to bring a crew up to a minimum standard of readiness or, failing that, to reveal the unsuitability of a commander before it was too late. With Rahmlow the system had failed, and there was no room for failure. The Happy Times were over, and the U-boats were fighting for their lives.

CHAPTER 6

The Tide, the Games

Don't envy men because they seem to have a run of luck,
Since luck's a nine day's wonder. Wait their end.

—Euripides, *Herakleidai*

ON 23 October 1941 a convoy of forty-three ships left the Newfoundland port of Argentia for Great Britain. According to the numbering system used for convoys, it was designated HX 156, meaning that it was a fast eastbound convoy originating in Halifax, Nova Scotia. It was not the 156th convoy to sail; there were several large gaps in the series. Nor was it very fast—between nine and fifteen knots, which was all that such a jungle of steamers, tankers, reefers, ammunition ships, troopships, and oilers could make without breaking formation or running into each other. But the cargoes carried in the holds of HX 156 were life itself for Britain.

Accompanying HX 156 was Escort Group 4.1.3, made up of five destroyers selected at random from the various squadrons of the United States Atlantic Fleet. These were as disparate as the ships they guarded. They ranged in size and power from the brand new *Benson*-class destroyer USS *Hilary P. Jones* to the old four-stacker USS *Reuben James,* commissioned in 1920 and slowly falling apart. Their escort tactics varied. One ship might patrol vigorously while another steamed stolidly in station for the entire passage. Their command and control was lacking, their ASW equipment was primitive, their very presence in the convoy lanes was a matter of controversy. For HX 156, however, they were the only protection to be had against the monsters of the sea.[1] The last ship to leave sight of land was probably the *Reuben James.*

ON 24 February 1941 *Vizeadmiral* (vice admiral) Lothar von Arnauld de la Perière, the most successful submarine commander in history, died in an airplane crash at Le Bourget in Paris on his way to take command as *Admiral Südost* (flag officer southeast). He was fifty-four years old. His sudden death was, by all accounts, not made much of, either at BdU or in the U-Bootwaffe at large. His funeral at the Invalidenfriedhof in Berlin was attended by Erich Raeder but not by Karl Dönitz.

Arnauld had taken no direct part in the U-boat war. Senior to Dönitz by seven years, he was unable to serve under him at BdU, but even so there is no reason to believe that he would have fitted into Dönitz's staff or his philosophy. In his position as Kriegsmarine commander in Brittany, he had been instrumental in securing the Breton U-boat bases; his diplomacy, his congenial manner, and his French background had secured for the U-Bootwaffe the full cooperation of the local workforce and the French navy in supporting these bases for at least two years. Dönitz gave him scant credit, and his contributions are not widely known today. Lothar von Arnauld de la Perière was "an inspiring personality, a diplomatic achiever, a smooth and pleasant operator," known to the men he commanded as "Arno von der Pier" and throughout the service as a gentleman. His reputation is assured. His death proved a harbinger of things to come and a warning, whispered as slaves whispered in Roman parades, of the transience of glory.[2]

By the end of 1940, Karl Dönitz's best commanders had been at the front for over a year and he had to start making decisions about their futures. Many of them had enjoyed great success, and most of them, fortunately, were still alive, but the odds against their continued success mounted every day. Sooner or later, he knew, one of them would make a mistake, die at sea, or end up a prisoner of war, and neither fame, success, nor skill would save him. In March 1915, just six months after his moment of triumph in the Broad Fourteens, Otto Weddigen's boat was ignominiously rammed and sunk by HMS *Dreadnought* off the coast of Scotland. Weddigen and his entire crew were lost. It was a lesson in fate not lost on Dönitz, and in 1941, resolved not to wait any longer, he began to pull his "old guard," the men of the first generation, back from the front.

In February 1941, sixteen months after he entered Scapa Flow and paraded through Berlin, Günther Prien was still at sea, having exceeded Weddigen's life span as a German hero by almost 200 percent. He lived, but the price of survival was high. He was, according to more than one source, tired and depressed, and his notoriety was weighing on him. Only five of the famous crew he had taken into Scapa Flow were left. The letters still came in, many of them from German schoolchildren, but they went into the trash unopened. He had been aghast at his autobiography, *Mein Weg Nach Scapa Flow,* which was written for him by the Ministry of Propaganda. Dönitz, sensing a problem, had already talked to Prien once, at Kerneval in December 1940, about a training assignment ashore. He nagged, he cajoled, he argued, but he did not, in the end, order him to take it, and Prien, uninterested, would commit to leaving U-47 only if he could have another boat. Neither man was satisfied with the outcome of the conversation, but the combination of Baubelehrung and shakedown, Dönitz knew, would at least keep Prien away from the front for several months, and in the meantime he would be allowed to make one final war patrol in his beloved U-47.[3]

Two weeks later, on 8 March 1941, Günther Prien was dead, lost with his boat and his entire crew in a convoy battle south of Iceland. Nobody seems to know the exact cause of the loss: U-47 was reported variously to have been sunk by depth charges, because of an accident during an emergency dive, or by a rogue torpedo fired from another boat during the height of the battle. Her end was as enigmatic as Prien himself.

Shortly after he talked to Günther Prien at Kerneval, Dönitz had a similar conversation with Otto Kretschmer, his most successful ace. It was as urgent an exchange but more bizarre, in that it took place entirely in Dönitz's staff car during a drive from Lorient to Cologne for Christmas. Dönitz sat in the front, Kretschmer in the back next to Wolfgang Lüth, and for several hours, as the car rushed through the wartime darkness of France and Belgium and the two officers tried to stay awake, he nagged and pleaded with Kretschmer to accept a position similar to the one he had just offered Prien. When the car arrived in Cologne, Dönitz was frustrated and Kretschmer was still on sea duty.[4]

Three months later, just ten days after Prien was lost, Otto Kretschmer's boat U-99 was bombed to the surface by HMS *Walker.* So sudden was the attack that Kretschmer did not even have time to radio his last six sinkings back to BdU. He and most of his crew were taken prisoner and sent to Britain. During the same battle, Joachim Schepke, the matinee idol who commanded U-100, was killed when HMS *Vanoc* rammed his boat and cut him in half. A defiant poem, written by an anonymous U-boat crewman shortly afterward to commemorate the loss of Otto Kretschmer, closes with the following lines:

Two hundred thousand tons at least,
now from the enemy we've torn.
We take them with us as we die,
as to our Führer we have sworn.

A final "Heil" to the Reich,
a final kiss to home we gave.
Give us, who die on honor's field,
in honor, also one last wave.[5]

Within two weeks Dönitz had lost three men who were arguably the mind, heart, and soul of his service. The closest parallel would have been the simultaneous loss in World War I of Weddigen, Hersing, and Arnauld, for only they had enjoyed the same success, the same public adulation, the same aura of epic fame, but not even these three had been invested with the propaganda value of Dönitz's new trinity, and perhaps wisely so. The death of Schepke and the capture of Kretschmer were not reported to the German public until April. The death of Günther Prien, the idol of his country and the favorite of his commander in chief, was not announced until 23 May, and so hard was the news to accept, so deathless had Prien become in the public mind, that people did not believe it. Fifteen years after his death, the German press was still dealing seriously with rumors that he and his crew had been seen alive after the war. Dan Van der Vat wrote: "It was all without foundation. It amounted to the secular canonization of a popular war hero without equal in the bleak and bloody history of the Third Reich."[6]

And still the fates were unsatisfied. Another officer who had been at the front since the war began was Fritz-Julius Lemp, who had sunk the British liner *Athenia* within six hours of Britain's declaring war. Lemp was now the commander of U-110. He had, since the *Athenia,* led a quiet but fulfilling career in the North Atlantic, sinking enough ships to win the Knight's Cross but never again breaking the surface of wartime anonymity. There is no record that Dönitz ever asked Lemp to take a shore assignment, perhaps because of the *Athenia* blemish. But if he could have withdrawn a single commander from the front in 1941, it should have been Lemp, a man who was to lose the Battle of the Atlantic as surely as if he had run over Karl Dönitz with a two-ton truck.

On 8 May 1941, six hundred miles southwest of Iceland, U-110 was brought to the surface by a combination of depth charges and gunfire by HMS *Aubretia* and *Bulldog*. Fritz-Julius Lemp and his crew escaped the boat, but Lemp drowned or was shot, never realizing that U-110 was not sinking. After the remainder of the crew were hustled belowdecks, a boarding party from the *Bulldog* searched U-110 thoroughly and emerged with an Enigma cipher machine and settings for three months. The Enigma machine was used in one form or another throughout the Wehrmacht. The capture of a Kriegsmarine version allowed the Admiralty to read BdU signals almost as soon as they were sent, and although occasional changes in the machine or the cipher may have temporarily obstructed the resulting flow of intelligence (called Ultra by the British), BdU communications were never secure again.

One cannot, as Medina Sidonia once observed to his cook, win them all. But not everyone went the way of Günther Prien. As the long, gloomy spring of 1941 dragged to a close, an increasing number of first-generation U-boat commanders found themselves on shore and still alive. Victor Oehrn was back in his position as BdU A1, Otto Schuhart had been head of officer training at the U-boat school in Neustadt since February, and in August Viktor Schütze would become commander of the Second U-Flotilla. Even Jürgen Oesten was moved. U-106 left Lorient in October on her fourth war patrol, but neither the fish on her tower nor the commander inside was the same as when she had steamed so resolutely out of Kiel in December, for Dönitz's distrust of the odds and his need for qualified men ashore had prompted him to relieve Oesten and replace him with the boat's first watch officer, Hermann Rasch. In two years Oesten had sunk a reported 110,000 GRT of enemy shipping. In March, having reached the necessary plateau, he had been decorated with the Knight's Cross by the Führer (the two sawfish on his tower were promptly given the same medal). Now, like so many of his comrades, he was behind a desk, the new commander of the Ninth U-Flotilla.

By the end of 1941, a definite shift had occurred in the U-Bootwaffe away from a predominance of first-generation commanders and toward the second. From that point on, the surviving members of the old guard would occupy supporting positions on shore, their places at the front filled by men who had been their subordinates, their students, and in many cases their protégés. There is no doubt that Karl Dönitz had a special attachment to this relatively small group of officers. They were the men who had made his service the fearsome weapon it had become; they were his media stars, the executors of his Rudeltaktik, the architects of the Happy Times, his "lords of the sea," and his heart, he once said, would always be with them. Their departure from the front marked the end of the Happy Times as clearly as any event in 1941. Things were not the same, said the Old Man in *The Boat,* now that the old gang was gone.

Joachim Schepke in control of an audience. Handsome and debonair, Schepke was a willing idol and a good National Socialist in the bargain. His loss in March 1941, along with that of Prien and Kretschmer, marked the end of an era in the Battle of the Atlantic. (National Archives)

There is no evidence, however, that their collective relief had any objective impact on the course of the battle. The convoy lanes were just as hazardous without Prien or Kretschmer hunting in them, and the ships continued to sink as before.

The second generation was as deadly as the first, and for good reason. Their training, still conducted in peacetime, was as structured and as thorough as that of their predecessors. In a sense, the war shielded them from initial failure. Rather than having to make their own mistakes under fire, they had the opportunity to observe another man and learn from his. They enjoyed a more favorable climate for success, having missed the first dreary months of the war and the dispiriting torpedo failures of 1939 and 1940 and getting their commands after the French ports were taken and the Happy Times had begun. Finally, it is entirely reasonable to believe that a good commander was born, not made, and that it did not matter when he first took command. There is an interesting statistic in this regard, probably unscientific but worthy of passing note: five out of the ten most successful U-boat commanders of World War II, Kretschmer, Schütze, Schultze, Liebe, and Prien, had commanded U-boats before September 1939. Together during the war they would sink 162 ships of approximately 930,000 GRT. The other five officers on the list, Lüth, Topp, Merten, Lassen, and Heinz Lehmann-Willenbrock, had all been watch officers in September 1939. After they received their commands, they would sink 156 ships of about 940,000 GRT, almost exactly the same amount.[7]

ON 27 October 1941, approximately halfway across the North Atlantic, convoy HX 156 turned south to avoid a reported convoy battle raging around westbound convoy ON 28. The seas through which the miserable ships sailed were high and a force ten gale had sprung up. The *Niblack* was tossed so badly that her propellers kept rising out of the water. An officer was washed over the side of the *Hilary P. Jones*. The mood was one of wary caution, and nerves were frayed for more reasons than the weather. The *Kearny* had been attacked only ten days earlier. Everyone in the escort group knew that they, as well as their unruly charges, were in constant danger of attack by U-boats. Everyone prayed that the filthy weather conditions would keep the boats away. With luck, they would not be found.

At that moment the man who would find them was four days away.

THE most successful of the second-generation commanders was Wolfgang Lüth, who was second behind Otto Kretschmer, both in tonnage and in ships sunk, and who spent more time at sea, was more highly decorated, and was promoted faster and further than any man in the U-Bootwaffe.

Erich Topp. Neither his glowering formal portrait nor the cheerful shot of him returning from a war patrol in 1941 fully reflected his complicated nature. (National Archives, U.S. Naval Institute)

For more than one reason, however, Lüth was not the most representative commander of his generation. That distinction belongs instead to Erich Topp, the third-ranking commander of the war, who has achieved fame greater than all but a very few men in the U-Bootwaffe.

Erich Topp was born in Hannover, the son of an engineer. He entered the Reichsmarine in 1934, the U-Bootwaffe in 1937, and he became first watch officer of U-46 in 1938. In June 1940 Topp was given his first command, the Einbaum U-57, but after only three months she was accidentally rammed by a Norwegian freighter outside the Brunsbüttel locks and sank in ten fathoms of water. Absolved of blame, he was given another boat, the new type VIIC U-552, which would be known in history as the "red devil boat" because of the two scarlet demons painted on her tower. His old crew, most of whom had managed to escape U-57 ahead of Topp through the bridge hatch, came with him. In mid-1941, after six war patrols in two boats, Erich Topp was both a seasoned commander and a new Ritterkreuzträger, with fourteen ships of some 90,000 GRT to his credit.

Some of his detractors have emphasized his faults, and no doubt Topp had several. He was a formidable figure nonetheless. With his sharp features and piercing stare, he looked every inch the classic U-boat commander, so much so, in fact, that a photograph of him as he stood draped over the handles of his periscope was reprinted on a German postage stamp in 1944. In public he was reserved and aloof, but to his men he was an inspired leader, prepared to go to great lengths to keep them happy and motivated. The sight of them shivering on the beach as they asked his permission to accompany him to his next boat is proof of their loyalty. He was ruthless, not cruel necessarily, although there was that element in several of the great aces, but at the same time he was never given to worrying about the things he did for the U-Bootwaffe, for his government, or for his country. He knew it was all for a good cause. He was an idealist, as he himself admits, although he has never been able to call himself what his friend Lothar-Günther Buchheim has called him. When the war began, says Buchheim, Erich Topp was a Nazi.[8]

The association of the U-boat commander with the politics of National Socialism has been almost impossible to break. It existed during the war, remained after the war, and is there today, in some minds, after fifty years of goodwill. Those who care about the image of the U-boat commander can hardly be blamed for despairing that this association will ever disappear, especially after they read statements from a generation who cannot remember the war. "As we reminisce," wrote a *Daily Express* columnist in 1993, fifty years after the Battle of the Atlantic was lost, "there is a tendency to forgive a bit and forget a lot. But most of these men, in their time, were steely Nazi fanatics who glorified in their merciless destruction."[9] Actually, very few officers in the U-Bootwaffe were "steely Nazi fanatics," and most were not Nazis in any but the broadest sense of the word. Here, as in so many things, every man was different.

Günther Prien, for example, has been called a Nazi, apparently because he was determined, ruthless, and willing to cooperate with the Propaganda Ministry, but it is hard to determine his politics. He did join the Nazi Party in 1932 after he left the Handelsmarine, but he had to resign when he entered the Reichsmarine. He did allow himself to be used in German propaganda, but he did not like it. "He was not untypical of his service," wrote Dan Van der Vat, "ruthlessly patriotic, but not [a] slavering Nazi." In the same book, however, Peter Padfield calls him a "fanatically Nazi commander," which echoes William Shirer's flash judgment of him in 1939 and contradicts Peter Hansen's assessment of him as less a

National Socialist than a "very proud *Deutscher Nationaler* who had achieved his dream of rising to the top." Prien, who died young and probably with regrets, remains a mystery.[10]

Otto Kretschmer was a nationalist for whom Germany, even a National Socialist Germany, was everything. According to Bodo Herzog, he did not approve of National Socialism, he did not participate in the propaganda exercises, and he spoke up from time to time about the intrusions of party orthodoxy upon the day-to-day affairs of the U-Bootwaffe. He fought, not for the New Order but for his country. When he was captured, wrote Peter Padfield, he was not at all the ideologue the Royal Navy had expected to see (and it kept very good records on U-Bootwaffe officers) but a polite and reserved man who made no attempt to defend National Socialism and who had actually become rather bored with the endless slaughter of the convoy battles. "[He] gave us the impression of being far from the fanatical Hitlerite we had half-expected," wrote Donald Macintyre, the captain of HMS *Walker.* "Indeed, as a professional naval officer and a most skilful one, he had much the same attitude to politics as we had ourselves and preferred to restrict himself to his duties and lament the mess the politicians had made of things."[11]

Joachim Schepke is harder to explain. "Unlike Prien," states Michael Hadley flatly in *Count Not the Dead*, "Schepke was a National Socialist." He offers only Schepke's wartime book *U-Bootfahrer von Heute* (Submariners of Today) to support his statement, but it is an unfortunate product and Schepke's militant tone is disturbing, "stridently polemical . . . noteworthy for its exploitative style and for the often mindless commitment to political ideology."[12] The uncharitable references to Jews would be troubling to any modern reader. But no U-Bootwaffe officer, not even Schepke, could release a book in Germany without the "assistance" of ghostwriters and editors from the Ministry of Propaganda, and to condemn a man for having done so would be premature. There are better examples than Schepke of officers whose public utterances, edited or not, have betrayed them.

One of these was Wolfgang Lüth. If his own published statements are to be believed, he came to admire National Socialism early on. Like his peers, he liked the good things about it and tended to ignore the bad, but as an Auslandsdeutscher whose family had been persecuted by other governments (first the Russian, then the Latvian) he felt a much stronger attraction to the nationalist tenets of National Socialism than they did. During the war years he became outspoken in his support for the party, much more so than any officer, even a successful one, was expected to be. "If our men are led into action united with revolutionary ardor in the National Socialist spirit," he said in a 1943 lecture, "they will gladly follow on to new assignments and to new attacks." Lüth had no apologies for his ardor or his words. Fortunately, men like him were few.[13]

The more common attitude toward Hitler and National Socialism was a mixture of admiration and revulsion: admiration for the accomplishments of the New Order, the strengthening of the Kriegsmarine, the recovery of German territory, the elimination of unemployment, and the redemption of German pride; revulsion for Hitler himself, who was regarded in the military as common and loud, and for his methods, which could be ignored only up to a point before they flew in one's face, as happened with Jürgen Oesten the day after Kristallnacht. The revulsion did not prevent them from fighting for a National Socialist Germany, but it was the duty of a military officer to fight. Ideological disagreements, even if they seemed irreconcilable, did not excuse insubordination. Furthermore, it was the duty of every citizen to defend his country. In 1939 Germany was under attack, never mind that her own leaders had brought it upon her. "It did not seem honest," wrote Oesten, "to run away while the house was on fire."[14] This was hardly the stuff that had sent people into the streets to break windows and burn books, nor was it classical National Socialism, details of which very few officers in the Wehrmacht had actually grasped. The charitable view is that the U-boat commander was neither malicious nor doctrinaire but that he was as ill-informed, as misled, and as self-denying as anyone in Germany.

Buchheim's statement about Erich Topp is understandable considering his impetuosity and tactlessness, but it is not true. Topp was no more a Nazi than most of his peers. He may appear so because of what he has said and written, and the irony is that nothing he has said or written makes him any worse than most of the officers in the U-Bootwaffe. In his 1991 autobiography, *The Odyssey of a U-Boat Commander,* Topp openly describes an early infatuation with Hitler and National Socialism. "We had believed that Hitler's personal dynamic force as well as that of his government would create a New Order in Europe," he wrote, "and that this second attempt under German leadership—the first one under Napoleon had failed—would be successful."[15] He held onto the idea of Germany as a nation in a crusade for a long time. "Until the end of the war," he wrote in a letter, "we thought that we were fighting for a United Europe and against Communism."[16] He concludes that these beliefs were misguided, that Germany was wrong, and that her fall into disgrace after the war—a fall he compares to the plunge of Icarus into the sea—can be blamed on the hubris of the National Socialist government they had all trusted.

He has not escaped criticism for these admissions. He was a controversial figure long before *Odyssey* was published, most notably as the object of scornful comments from another ace, Karl-Friedrich Merten, a conservative man for whom an admission like Topp's would be unthinkable.[17] His book has been seized upon by some as an example of pure hypocrisy. "[It is] shot through with a fervor for self-justification that is quite hard to understand," wrote Bodo Herzog in a review. "As a decorated U-boat commander, he was 'infected with a fanatical will to destroy, in the sure knowledge that our boats will be decisive.' Has he forgotten?"[18] Horst Bredow, who still tries in conversation to justify pure (as opposed, presumably, to applied) National Socialism, is almost gleeful in pointing out the inconsistencies in a book written by a warrior who has become what he considers a hopeless pacifist.[19] Most of this criticism is unfair. Topp's book does have its faults, of course, not the least of which are its occasional lapses into incomprehensibility, but it is more often interesting, forthright, not without the essential spice of pure gossip, and it has the virtue of being better than anything its critics have produced.

Until 1941 Erich Topp had never doubted his faith in the fundamental direction of the Reich; at least there is no such indication in the memoirs through which his other emotions are splashed like so much spilled ink. He was not alone in this sentiment. Those who doubted in the beginning still doubted, those who believed still believed, and nothing in the Battle of the Atlantic up to that point had changed anyone's mind. The shocking personnel losses of March had no effect, nor did the loss of the *Bismarck* in May. The process that led to Topp's final rejection of the Reich, the party, the ideology he had sworn to defend, and war in general probably began on 22 June 1941, four days after he sank the British steamer *Norfolk,* when he heard on his radio that Germany had invaded the Soviet Union.

Operation Barbarossa, as it was called, had no immediate impact on the war at sea. The Soviet Union had no naval presence in the North Atlantic and no merchant fleet to speak of. Unlike Britain, its existence did not yet depend on the sea, although this would change significantly in the years to come. The U-Bootwaffe was not unaffected by the news of a second front, however, and reactions, based on emotion, experience, inside information, a knowledge of history, or personal prejudice, ranged widely.

Wolfgang Lüth, for example, at sea in U-43, was euphoric when he heard the news because he believed "that everything the Nazis did was ordained by God" and because, as a Balt, he hated the Russians. Karl Daublebsky von Eichhain, also on BdU staff, decided on the same day that the war was no longer winnable.[20]

Victor Oehrn knew about Barbarossa several months before it began because of his position at BdU. He thought that an invasion of the Soviet Union was the logical consequence of the German failure to defeat Britain; he had no objections to it and was sure that the Germans would be seen as liberators rather than conquerors if it were carried out properly.[21] To Jürgen Oesten, making a long, slow return from the South Atlantic, it made no difference one way or another. "I don't recollect our reaction," he wrote. "Basically we were convinced that it was more or less immaterial how many kilometers our troops ran in one direction or another on the European continent, it would not decide the war, as we regarded the supplies across the sea as the deciding factor."[22] To Topp, however, the news was shocking. "Everything that history had exposed as disastrous," he wrote, "for instance in Napoleon's times, now came together: a two-front war and the overextension of our limited resources. The Russian campaign was the beginning of the end."[23]

In fact, the general outlook for Germany at that time was mixed, and Topp's assessment was not widely shared. The first stages of Barbarossa went as well as anyone could have expected. Germany now occupied all of Western Europe from the Ukraine to the Pyrenees, Britain was still isolated and posed no major threat, Festung Europa was secure. These items were well reported, and the country was in reasonable spirits. But the war at sea was not going as well; had this been reported to the public, the national mood might have been more subdued. After the compromise of Enigma, sinkings plummeted, from 300,000 GRT in June to 60,000 in July and 70,000 in August. The loss of the battleship *Bismarck* in May represented a serious material loss and had the long-term effect of tying up a large part of the remaining Kriegsmarine surface fleet in port. Technology was working against the U-boats; British warships were beginning to carry radar, and radio direction-finding equipment was being used to locate U-boats at sea. Rahmlow gave up his boat to the British in August, shortly before Adolf Hitler had an attack of the jitters, took twelve boats out of the North Atlantic, and sent them into the Mediterranean Sea, which he considered "the decisive area for the future conduct of the war."[24] Finally, in the summer of the year, the Americans came.

In September Wolfgang Lüth returned from a two-month war patrol without a single pennant. The patrol was miserable for several reasons: the weather was terrible, his batteries did not work, his canned food went bad, and worst of all, it was the first time he had finished a patrol of any appreciable length without sinking a ship. He made no excuses for his failure. He did not know that his signals were being intercepted or that the enemy was using radar; to him it was a perplexing case of always being in the wrong place at the wrong time. The only sign that this patrol was different than earlier ones were the entries in his war diary in which the standard nautical German phrases contained not torpedo hits or estimated tonnage but strange new words like *Mississippi, San Francisco,* and *Pensacola.*

The United States was officially neutral in the war and would remain so until the end of the year. But the Roosevelt administration had been an unequivocal ally of Britain from the beginning, and Franklin D. Roosevelt, who became a close friend of Winston Churchill, made every effort to support him. In September 1940, for example, the United States turned over to Britain fifty overage destroyers, "four-stackers" built during and after World War I, in return for leases on several British military installations in North America. In March 1941, Roosevelt pushed the Lend-Lease bill through Congress, allowing Britain to have, for the duration of the conflict, as much military hardware as the United States could provide. And in June, in perhaps the most provocative step so far, the United States Navy began to escort Allied convoys.

At first, convoys were escorted only to and from Iceland, the rationale being that since American troops were occupying that country, it became ipso facto an American destination; but in September United States warships became a regular part of the regular transatlantic convoys under the pretense of patrolling a huge "self-defense zone" that stretched from the east coast of North America out to a line halfway across the North Atlantic commonly called the "mid-ocean meeting point," or MOMP. The usual procedure was for an American escort group to take a convoy from Canada to the MOMP. At that point a British group would take over for the perilous second half of the passage from the MOMP into the Western Approaches and the relative safety of the Irish Sea, and the Americans would pick up a second convoy for the trip back to Canada.

Undertaking these escorts was clearly a belligerent act on the part of the United States, especially since the escort vessels used sonar equipment, chased contacts, directed air and surface attacks for the Royal Navy, and even tossed depth charges at likely targets from time to time, but Adolf Hitler did not want to go to war with the United States and U-boat commanders were ordered to refrain from attacking American ships unless they themselves were attacked. This imbalance caused understandable bitterness in the U-Bootwaffe. If the escorts were immune to U-boat attack, then so was the convoy, whether the ships in the convoy were American passenger liners or British ammunition ships, and as the year went on signs of German impatience became obvious. On 4 September a single torpedo from U-652 passed within one hundred yards of the USS *Greer*. Nobody was hurt, but four days later Franklin Roosevelt, in an emotional fireside chat, declared that United States warships would shoot on sight any enemy who would deny his country "freedom of the seas," meaning freedom of American warships to escort Allied convoys. On 17 October, the USS *Kearny* was hit by a torpedo from U-568 while escorting the slow eastbound convoy SC 48. She did not sink, but eleven men died. The next Roosevelt speech, given on Navy Day, has since been compared to a declaration of war in its bellicosity. Indeed, war was upon them at that moment.

ERICH Topp sighted the first units of HX 156 at 0256 on 31 October.[25] He approached the ships from port, silently, as they steamed in rough rank and file like a herd of elephants in a thick fog. It took him a long time to move into what he imagined would be a good firing position, two hours and fifty minutes, but he was almost there when he saw the *Reuben James* in his way. At that point three things happened almost at once. The USS *Tarbell*, a destroyer far out to starboard of the convoy, picked up a contact: almost certainly U-552. The *Reuben James*, ordered by the escort commander to investigate, began to turn away from the convoy. And Erich Topp fired two torpedoes at the *Reuben James*.

> The *Reuben James* was just starting to swing around to port, puffs of black smoke wafting from her stacks, when the first German torpedo hit. The torpedo smashed into her port side, a little forward of her number one funnel, below the bridge, then exploded, ripping a large gash in her side. Water poured in, breaking lines and smashing bulkheads, and the *Reuben James* rocked and shuddered. The blast must have ignited the forward magazine, for then a huge explosion occurred. "With a terrific roar, a column of orange flame" seared the paling sky, then subsided, "leaving a great black pall of smoke licked by moving tongues of orange. All the ship forward of number four stack . . . disappeared."[26]

The United States destroyer *Reuben James* sank about four hundred miles west of Belfast at 0834 (German time) on 31 October 1941, five weeks before the attack by Japan on the United States Pacific Fleet in Pearl Harbor, six weeks before Germany declared war on the United States. More than a hundred men died.

The sinking of the USS *Reuben James,* a charcoal sketch by CDR Griffith Coale, USNR. The loss of the *Reuben James,* which occurred five weeks before Pearl Harbor, was the climax to several months of undeclared naval warfare between Germany and the United States. (National Archives)

ERICH Topp was unaware that the *Reuben James* was an American ship when he sank her.[27] When he did find out on the radio some time afterward, he was understandably shaken up. "As far as international law was concerned, I felt no qualms whatsoever. After all, I had attacked a British convoy screened by warships. Nevertheless, I felt bewildered." When he first heard about Barbarossa, Topp had thought of Napoleon and his ill-fated invasion of Russia in 1812—but Barbarossa was not his doing. When he heard about the *Reuben James,* he remembered World War I and how the resumption of unrestricted submarine warfare by Germany in 1917 led to the entry of the United States into the war. The sinking of the *Reuben James* was his doing, and if war happened as a result of it, he would be responsible. "The tension a man endures when he thinks he is making history, however unintentional, is indeed enormous."[28]

Topp knew that he was wholly justified in sinking the *Reuben James* despite her flag, but he did not realize that in doing so he ran little risk of inciting war or even of disturbing the rocky status quo. For neither side had any intention of going to war over a single destroyer, and Roosevelt in particular had not a shred of justification for asking Congress to do so. According to historians Thomas Bailey and Paul Ryan, "[He] might invoke freedom of the seas until red in the face, but that concept never gave wartime immunity to the escorts of a convoy or to their charges, whether armed or not, whether belligerent or not."[29] Sadly, the loss of the *Reuben James* had little effect on the Battle of the Atlantic; those who seek vengeance, however, may be assured that it had an effect on Erich Topp, all the more profound for being delayed. He was not punished for it, nor did his career suffer. He was not hunted down after the war and charged with a war crime. His postwar rise in the ranks of the Bundesmarine and the offices of the North Atlantic Treaty Organization were not affected. But today he seems haunted by it, so much so that he felt the need to open his autobiography, not with his parents or his youth but with a written memorial to the men of the *Reuben James*. It is a remarkable discussion, one that cannot be imagined as coming from any other commander— Merten, for example, or Kretschmer, or even Oehrn.

War was officially declared before the new year. It did not come about because of Erich Topp, the *Reuben James,* or even the fitful hostilities between the two countries at sea, but because Adolf Hitler willed it. His declaration of war, made on 11 December 1941, was foolhardy but wholly appropriate as the conclusion to a year in which his country's fortunes in the Battle of the Atlantic were rocked by one misfortune after another and the illusion of a German victory at sea slipped further and further away. For Topp the end of the year and the end of the illusion came a bit later, not in the North Atlantic or in the Reichstag but in a closed and shuttered Parisian nightclub.

The Scheherazade, a restaurant and nightclub located at 25 rue de Fontaine in the Pigalle section of Montmartre, was managed by a colorful White Russian immigrant named Vladimir, supposedly a former lieutenant in the Preobrazhensky Guard, who had fled St. Petersburg after the Bolshevik Revolution. Vladimir had made the club into a "beleaguered outpost of Russia," with Russian music played by Russian bands, Russian singers and dancers, and an exotic atmosphere that many of the larger and more impersonal clubs like the Moulin Rouge or the Lido could not provide. The Scheherazade served as a gathering place for the expatriate Russian community in Paris, many of whom found they could not otherwise fit into the city, and as a focal point for the resurgence of nationalistic fervor that accompanied Barbarossa, which they considered a crusade of liberation. It also became the main watering hold for U-Bootwaffe officers in Paris, so central to their social life, wrote Peter Hansen, that "it really deserves a chapter to itself." [30]

Early on Paris was not inhospitable to the German military, but as the war went on and the population grew less friendly and more reserved toward the occupiers, the Scheherazade became "an island in a growing sea of hostility." Everyone seemed to congregate there for entertainment, relaxation, and friendship. After a routine debriefing at BdU headquarters, someone asked Joachim Schepke what he planned to do for the rest of the evening. "I can't breathe," he announced loudly in front of everyone. "I'm going over to the Scheherazade to bury myself under a mountain of girls." Hansen recalls seeing Jürgen Oesten, sitting in one of the Scheherazade's ample leather armchairs, "so smashed with champagne that he could hardly keep his eyes open," next to his friend Jürgen Nissen, commander of U-105, who had passed out and was talking in his sleep. Even the moody Otto Kretschmer could relax at the Scheherazade. "During the periods when Dönitz and Submarine Command were located in Paris, virtually the entire batch of staff officers and visiting commanders rushed to the Scheherazade rather than taking off for Germany and a family leave, much to the chagrin of Karl Dönitz, incidentally, and to the disgust of that sourpuss and lintpicker Eberhard Godt." The place has become a part of U-Bootwaffe history; as Hansen observed, a chapter, or an entire book, could easily be written about it. "The Scheherazade and its people are almost impossible to describe," he remembers wistfully. "One had to experience it, taste its ambience, sense the overwhelming reception one would receive as a long lost friend. It was like entering an oasis after crossing the Sahara."[31]

Engelbert Endrass, commander of U-567, and Erich Topp, his best friend, were two members of the Scheherazade's extended family. Endrass, Günther Prien's first watch officer in Scapa Flow, had long since left U-47. In May 1940 he took command of U-46, and over the next year and a half he sank twenty-four ships for a total of 130,000 GRT. On 14 October 1941, on the second anniversary of the sinking of the *Royal Oak*, he commissioned U-567 at Blohm and Voss in Hamburg. He eventually ended up in St. Nazaire with Topp, a classmate from Crew 34.

Engelbert Endrass and Erich Topp were so thick around the docks and taverns of St. Nazaire that they were known as Castor and Pollux, the Dioscuri of ancient legend. They had been friends since long before the war, but by the end of 1941 they had achieved a closeness that was almost spiritual; they were, it seemed, two men with one soul. Their war patrols were personal contests. Their parties together were marathon sessions in which each man would try to outlast the other in gaiety and celebration, for unlike his former commander Prien, Endrass was an outgoing and gregarious man who liked to enjoy himself. During one wild party after his first war patrol in U-567 he shot a crystal chandelier from a hotel ceiling with a pistol (an infraction for which he was duly hauled before Dönitz). St. Nazaire soon grew too small for the Dioscuri, and together they escaped as often as they could to Paris and the Scheherazade, where both Endrass and Topp had girlfriends—one French, the other, like Vladimir, a White Russian.

Life for them was as good as the war would allow. But it all came to an end on 21 December 1941, when Engelbert Endrass was lost in a convoy battle. He had just sunk the Norwegian steamer *Annavore*. With him went his boat, his crew, and the last few glimmers of the glory that was Scapa Flow.

From time to time Vladimir, on a whim, would close the Scheherazade without warning for private parties. Alerted by BdU staff of Endrass's disappearance, he did so now for a Russian memorial banquet in his memory, and Topp was there to mourn. The friendship between him and Endrass had made his life tolerable in a world gone mad. "Today all that is gone, irrecoverably, forever. 'The flames have died away, and so have the tides, the games.'"[32]

CHAPTER 7

Fighting for an Image

They deem him their worst enemy who tells them the truth.

—Plato, *The Republic*

THE telephone in Karl-Friedrich Merten's office rang at 1815 on the evening of 22 May 1985. He was sure about the time because he wrote it down; he was sure about the content because he had a tape recorder running. The deep bass voice on the other end was agitated and slightly menacing. "Is this Friedrich Merten?"

"This is *Karl*-Friedrich Merten."

"Well, this is Lothar-Günther Buchheim."

Merten groaned. He was just leaving his office when the call came, but he had answered it and now he was sorry. Lothar-Günther Buchheim was the last person he wanted to talk to. "What can I do for you, Herr Buchheim?"

"Are you the U-boat commander who honored me with that article in *Ritterkreuz?*" demanded Buchheim.

"Yes," admitted Merten slowly, "but I wouldn't say that *honored* was the right term." The *Ritterkreuz* article. This would be unpleasant. He checked quickly to make sure the tape recorder was running—who knew what this man might say?

Buchheim was angry but still civil. "I want to know where you got the idea that my book *Jäger im Weltmeer* was a 'thrilling book for children.'"

Merten had said that, and a great many other unkind things about Buchheim and his books, in a recent *Ritterkreuz* review, but it was funny—he was actually reviewing a television program. The remarks about *Jäger im Weltmeer*, an earlier book of Buchheim's, had simply crept in.

"And who told you that the cook in U-96 thought I was a 'frightened rabbit'? He wouldn't know anything about it anyway, since he was always in the kitchen and I was always in the control room."

"It sounded true enough to me . . . and it was common knowledge in the boat. Besides, I have it in writing."

"In that case, you know what I think about you and your *Ritterkreuz* articles? I think you're a *big pile of shit!*"

Good. *Ausgezeichnet.* "Thank you, Herr Buchheim," replied Merten sweetly. "This tape recording will only confirm the impression I have of you from your books and films—you are a master of profanity!" There was a gurgling sound from the receiver and Lothar-Günther Buchheim hung up the phone.[1]

ON the day Erich Topp sank the *Reuben James* and immortalized her crew, Heinz Lehmann-Willenbrock, the commander of U-96, sank the 6,000-GRT Dutch steamer *Bennekom*. Nobody bothered about the *Bennekom* or her men at the time, and ordinarily she would have joined the almost three thousand other merchant ships that died quietly and without fanfare during the Battle of the Atlantic. But a young war correspondent, on board a U-boat for the first time, saw the *Bennekom* go down, and because he did, she will be remembered long after the *Reuben James* is forgotten.

> The projector's running too fast. Pieces of film have been spliced together meaninglessly, at random, and there are a lot of double exposures. Again and again I see clouds from explosions, which remain frozen for a few instants and then collapse, dropping a rain of planks and fragments of iron. I see the black smoke of oil darkening the sky like a gigantic skein of wool. Then the crackling of the blaze, the flame of oil on water—and the struggling black balls in front of it. I'm overwhelmed with horror at what we have done with our torpedoes. Delayed reaction. One stab at the firing lever! I close my eyes to blot out the haunting visions, but I continue to see the sea of flames spreading out over the water and men swimming for their lives.[2]

This passage is the memorial of the *Bennekom* as written by the German author Lothar-Günther Buchheim. It is taken from his first novel, and by far his most famous book, *Das Boot* (The Boat). U-boat commanders as a group have their differences, but few things serve to focus their differences as sharply, and as violently, as the images presented in this book. And though images are often false, they are important. Buchheim's image is so important that some people will fight over it.

The decision to talk about Buchheim now is a tactical one. The impact of his work, notes Michael Hadley, did not become apparent until the early 1970s, the decade in which he began publishing his U-boat books. But the root of his work, the source for all his books, fiction and nonfiction, is found in a relatively brief period in the fall of 1941 when he made a single war patrol in a Frontboot. The dates are significant. Buchheim's opinions of the U-Bootwaffe were formed at that time; had he made the patrol one year earlier or one year later, the tone of his writing might have been entirely different. Furthermore, the frequent conflicts between Buchheim and his detractors have been waged as though it were still 1941. Modern readers will not understand the venom or the intensity involved if they do not first realize that time for these people has stopped. For all of these reasons, it is best to discuss Buchheim here, when a wild vision of war was planted in his mind, rather than later, when that vision burst forth upon a receptive world.

Lothar-Günther Buchheim was born in Weimar, Thuringia, in 1918. He was trained as an artist, first in Dresden, then in Munich, and made his living before the war as an illustrator. During the war he was commissioned a Leutnant zur See in the Kriegsmarine. He served in minesweepers and destroyers and made three war patrols in two different U-boats as a war correspondent (*PK-Berichter*). His career as a writer began during the war when he published a book about the U-Bootwaffe called *Jäger im Weltmeer* (Hunters of the Seven Seas). Even Buchheim admits it was a propaganda piece, but it was sufficiently inspiring that Karl Dönitz wrote its foreword. His career took a different turn after the war. He is not only a writer but a photographer, an excellent watercolor painter, a collector, and a recognized authority on German expressionist art. He has written several books and many articles on such artists as Beckmann, Klimt, and Kandinsky, but he did not write about the U-boats again for almost thirty years after *Jäger im Weltmeer*, not until *The Boat* hit the market like a ton of bricks in 1973.

Buchheim has written several major books, fiction and nonfiction, about the U-Bootwaffe and its men, and he would doubtless like to be remembered for all of them. It was *The Boat* that "made" him, however, and if he had written nothing else in his life, his reputation would be assured on its merits. Michael Hadley has called *The Boat* "undeniably the finest piece of fiction in U-boat literature."[3] It has been published around the world, and its fame only increased with the release of a movie and a television series based on it. Lothar-Günther Buchheim is a successful man because of *The Boat*. Paradoxically, it also made him one of the most reviled writers in the business.

The Boat is the fictional account of a single war patrol made at the height of the Battle of the Atlantic. It is based on the first of Buchheim's three patrols, in late 1941 in U-96. It does not mirror the real patrol in every respect, and parts are clearly made up. This is to be expected because *The Boat* is a work of fiction and can fall back on literary license to explain a sinking that never happened or a maneuver that was never performed, but it seems to baffle some of Buchheim's critics (not surprising, observes Peter Hansen, "since 90 percent of U-boat veterans cannot tell the difference between fact and fiction"). There are some technical errors, but not many, and none obvious enough for the average reader to notice. Parts of *The Boat* are rough, graphic, even shocking, but the sense of atmosphere has been judged by several veteran commanders to be authentic, and as a description of life in a Frontboot in 1941, the book is close to definitive. Buchheim, wrote Erich Topp, "masterfully captured in a literary sense the reality of U-boat warfare as I myself had experienced it."[4]

The story begins at a wild predeparture party in a St. Nazaire tavern during which Buchheim (as the unnamed correspondent) meets the commander of the boat and his officers. The party itself, an unvarnished orgy of champagne, beer, and vomit, has long been a bone of contention among Buchheim's critics, many of whom deny that such affairs happened. The officers are in the thick of it. Buchheim boards the boat the next day and after some initial discomfiture settles down to record in words and on film the actions of the commander and crew for posterity. The patrol is alternately tedious and horrifying. Long periods of waiting for orders from BdU prompt boredom, complaints, and endless argument on the merits of the war effort. These are punctuated by terrifying depth charge attacks, storms, a meeting with another boat at sea—and the sinking of the *Bennekom,* or rather, a fictional account of the sinking as Buchheim saw it.

Toward the end of the patrol, the boat is ordered to sail through the Straits of Gibraltar for Mediterranean operations. Everyone knows such an attempt would be suicidal, but the commander makes the best of a bad situation. The boat is attacked in the straits and forced to the bottom. The crew, under the supervision of a heroic chief engineer, manages to bring the boat to the surface, and she limps back to St. Nazaire. Everyone is alive, at least until the next patrol. But as the boat makes her way slowly back into the huge concrete bunkers, with bands playing and people wav-

Lothar-Günther Buchheim (with camera) on the set of *The Boat*. To his left is Wolfgang Petersen, the director. The two men often quarreled over the making of the film, but next to the raging battles between Buchheim and some of the U-boat veterans he wrote about, their relationship seemed almost jovial. (CINEMA)

ing a bombing raid begins. The boat is sunk just short of her pen. Buchheim survives, but the commander and many of his crew are killed. All the pain, all the sacrifice, all the heroism of the patrol were for nothing, just, Buchheim seems to say, as the war itself was for nothing.

Michael Hadley is correct in his general assessment of *The Boat* as the finest piece of fiction in U-boat literature. This assessment must be qualified, however, by the observation that there has not been much U-boat fiction on the postwar market. Aside from *The Boat*, there is only one book of merit, a 1956 novel called *Haie und Kleine Fische* (Sharks and Little Fish), written by a former U-Bootwaffe officer and member of Crew V/41 named Wolfgang Ott. Overall, *Sharks and Little Fish* is as good as *The Boat*, and in some ways it is better. If it had appeared in a more receptive era it might have been equally successful. Like *The Boat*, it sold well as a book and was eventually made into a movie, but it has not achieved the universal popularity of *The Boat*, and Ott was unable to provoke the continual debate that Buchheim has.[5]

To appreciate the good and bad points of *The Boat*, it might be helpful to compare it with *Sharks*, for there are significant differences. The scope of *Sharks* is wider. *The Boat* documents a single war patrol, but *Sharks* is the story of a young man named Teichmann who is followed through recruit training on the Dänholm, then minesweeper service, before he reaches the U-boats. Ott describes not only the perils of a patrol but the entire experience of life in the U-Bootwaffe from its ignominious beginning to its often gruesome end. He introduces and cultivates his characters in a more leisurely fashion than Buchheim does, and the characters are one of the major differences between the two books. Finally, the fact that Ott did all this in the same amount of space as Buchheim says something about the two writing styles: one terse, the other prolix.

Ott's U-boat commander is a martinet whom everyone dislikes, but he is fair and professional. Buchheim claims to have patterned the commander in *The Boat* after Heinz Lehmann-Willenbrock, the commander of U-96 at the time of his war patrol. If true, the characterization was made to the disadvantage of Lehmann-Willenbrock, a respected officer who received the Knight's Cross with Oak Leaves for his success. The Old Man in the book is moody and cynical. We are told that he is successful, but by the time of his patrol he has become disillusioned and openly critical of the government, the party, the military leadership, even of Dönitz. He plays French phonograph records to taunt his first watch officer, who is obviously a Nazi. Ott's crewmen are interesting and not stupid. The officers engage in intelligent conversation. Teichmann speaks French and reads Greek. He and his shipmates slip easily (and incongruously) into discussions of *Don Carlos, The Magic Flute,* Wagner, and Kant. Buchheim's crew is a motley bunch, and he has drawn some criticism for his cynical portrayal of them. They curse, scratch, pick their noses, trade insults, and talk continually of women and sex. One man has gotten his French girlfriend pregnant. Another has scabies. A third goes crazy during a depth charge siege and has to be dragged away before the Old Man shoots him. Which are the better representations? The truth lies somewhere in between, but Ott's men seem less stereotypical.

The writing styles of the two authors differ dramatically, although reviewers have compared both of them at various times to Joseph Conrad and Norman Mailer. The difference is that Ott is real, Buchheim is surreal. Ott's descriptions, whether of whoring ashore or war afloat, are gory, grubby, sweaty, and depressing (adjectives that describe the atmosphere of U-boat life in general). Buchheim's are fey and mystical, paintings rather than photographs. To Ott, for example, a cloud is a cloud: a hiding place for enemy aircraft, a harbinger of rain. To Buchheim the morning sky is covered with "turquoise batik clouds bound together by fine veins"; at noon "a quiet pastoral scene unfolds, drawn in nacreous, subtle tints—like the inside of an oyster shell"; in the evening, "an African sky. I picture table mountains, giraffes, acacias, gnus, and antelopes."[6] Ott's picture of a man's thoughts during a depth charge attack is crude and terse: "He knew that he was surrounded by his comrades, but he felt very lonely and wretched, like a pig waiting to be stuck. But the comparison didn't appeal to him. Unfortunately, he thought, he wasn't dumb enough for a pig. Just to be thinking something, he cast about for another animal, and hit on a rat drowned in its hole. But they give it a good shaking first, to torture it; and they let it drown nice and slowly, to be sure it knows what's going on."[7] Buchheim's description of a similar event has a magical air about it, as though the attack might have been a scene out of *Fantasia* or perhaps even a bad acid trip: "Even the smallest sound is painful, a touch on a raw wound. As if my nerves had escaped the outer layer of skin and were now exposed. I have only one thought: They're up there. Right overhead. I'm stifling before I slowly, cautiously, fill my lungs with oxygen. Against closed eyelids I see bombs tumbling perpendicularly into the depths trailing sparkling air bubbles, exploding into fire. Around their incandescent cores all the colors of the spectrum flare up in mad combination, leaping and dying again but growing steadily more intense until the whole interior of the sea glows like a blast furnace."[8] It is no wonder that reviewers have zeroed in on his tendency to run away with metaphor. It defeats him. "The weight of his adjectives," wrote Donald Goddard in the *New York Times Book Review,* "tends to glamorize the merely squalid and restore the 'romance' he sets out to debunk."[9] Happily, the film version of *The Boat* stripped out much of Buchheim's more psychedelic prose without detracting from the story line; it is probably no accident that he is not pleased with the film's director, Wolfgang Petersen.

Both *Sharks* and *The Boat* were successful in their time, but *Sharks* did not last. One reason, according to Hadley, was timing. *Sharks* appeared on the shelves during a time when German writers were very concerned with what he called "the redemption of a myth." Most books about the U-Bootwaffe emphasized the loyalty, the sacrifice, and above all, the blamelessness of the service; Ott, in presenting a very negative image of the U-Bootwaffe, did not follow this trend and his success was limited. He continued to write, but he soon switched to other subject matter, and he had to stop attending his class reunions because of the abuse he was getting.[10] *The Boat,* in contrast, was published during a time when the war experience was being examined with a more critical eye. Buchheim's image of war, no more and no less horrific than Ott's, was more acceptable to the reading public.

The other reason is Buchheim himself. He is a walking billboard for his books. He is loud and vain. He can be rude, unpleasant, and utterly tactless. He is quick to judge and quick to anger; over the years he has picked several fights with people who he thinks are out to get him. He even went so far as to fight with the director of the film (he thought that Petersen was making his character, the correspondent, into a "pitiful creature").[11] His friends defend him as a herald of truth while admitting that they are sometimes embarrassed by his behavior. His enemies consider him dangerous, delusional, and a borderline mental case. It is hard for anyone who has met him, talked with him on the telephone, or even corresponded with him to remain neutral about Lothar-Günther Buchheim. Such behavior is appalling, of course, but any publisher will tell you that it sells a lot of books.

Ultimately, *The Boat* became phenomenally successful. It was a best-selling book. It was made into a very popular film that was distributed worldwide and eventually released into the video rental market, and it became a West German television program. Buchheim's characters are not universally recognized, but more people would see them because they ended up on television and movie screens all over the world. The book's influence extended beyond the usual circle of U-boat enthusiasts. The portrayal of the Old Man as a subversive burnout by German actor Jürgen Prochnow has canceled out most earlier screen images, from the courtly Curt Jürgens in *The Enemy Below* to the homicidal Helmut Griem in *The McKenzie Break*. The orgiastic behavior of Buchheim's officers the night before they left on patrol would be remembered, as would the crude language of his crew and their continual obsession with sex. And, more important, all of these things would be remembered by the next generation of students and the future writers of history.

Although *The Boat* was generally well received by the public and the critics, it did not impress all of the U-Bootwaffe veterans who read the book, saw the movie, or watched its adaptation for German television. Some liked it very much. Erich Topp became one of Buchheim's most enthusiastic supporters. Jürgen Oesten was favorable: "I think that the book is essentially quite good with some very good parts, considering that an amateur writer just went on a rather short North Atlantic trip as a non-paying customer. It is a good example that a man who is not first-class himself can still write something sensible." Others did not like *The Boat* but contented themselves with grumbling about Buchheim's factual mistakes and his profanity. The bar scene seems to have been especially objectionable. "Buchheim describes the sea and the atmosphere inside a U-boat very well," ventured Reinhard Reche, "but he overemphasizes sometimes [the] rude talk among sailors. Relatives reading *The Boat* were rather shocked therefore." Some are wholly negative but remain calm. "For me," wrote Otto Kretschmer, "Buchheim is no genuine source, because he has never seen or experienced the enemy. . . . What Buchheim writes is his own fantasy, without any real background whatsoever. It is a pity that nobody knows these circumstances except a few submariners in my country." For Karl-Friedrich Merten, however, *The Boat* started a personal battle that would drag on for a decade.[12]

EVENTS ensured that Karl-Friedrich Merten was always positive about his past, which is why any unpleasant portrayal of the past was disagreeable to him. He was born in Posen in 1905 and entered the Reichsmarine as a member of Crew 26. He was a cadet officer on the training ship *Schleswig-Holstein* when the war began and the leader of a platoon sent to capture the Danish ferry ports of Nyborg and Korsør during Operation Weserübung. He did not join the U-Bootwaffe until June 1940, but his seniority and experience allowed him to bypass normal U-boat training, and he became a *Konfirmand,* a commander in training, aboard U-38 in October 1940 without first having served as a watch officer. The commander of U-38, Heinrich Liebe, must have been uncomfortable because Merten was senior to him, but fortunately Merten did not remain on U-38 for any length of time. After only a few months in the U-Bootwaffe (possibly a record at the time), he was given his own boat, U-68, in February 1941.

Merten would make only five war patrols with U-68. He left the front in 1942 before the Battle of the Atlantic degenerated into a bloodbath. His view of the battle, therefore, was based on a period that was not as unpleasant as Buchheim often described in his books. His patrols earned him the number four slot on the final tonnage list, but very few of the ships he sank were in convoy. Three of his patrols took place in the relatively placid South Atlantic Ocean. His subsequent positions on shore cushioned him from battle, and he probably never realized how bad things at sea became toward the end of the war. One of Merten's stock arguments against Buchheim (or anyone who wrote like Buchheim) was that the situation in reality was not as bad as it was described in the book or in the movie, and for him this was true.

Merten was a strict man whose sense of humor rarely surfaced and whose political views can charitably be described as retrograde. In his lifetime he was at continual odds with anyone who said or wrote anything

Karl-Friedrich Merten. This photograph, an unusual full-length shot, is not the portrait labeled "rambo-zambo" by Merten's adversary Lothar-Günther Buchheim, and Merten's timid countenance hides a fierce resolve to defend what he believed was the true image of the U-boat commander. (Ruth Merten)

less than adulatory about the U-Bootwaffe or its leadership. "I do not like Merten," admitted Jürgen Oesten. "He suffers under a sort of self-inflicted hero-worship. [He] overestimates himself. There are some people [like him], politically right-wing, who hesitate to admit internally that Germany lost the war." [13] Yet Merten was an excellent officer and a good commander who took great pains to care for his crew. He knew that his success, indeed his life, depended on them, and he did all he could for them. His affection was returned. In 1991, toward the end of his life, Merten and his former crew toured Horst Bredow's archives. "The love they had in their eyes for him was remarkable to see," Bredow commented.[14]

To understand Karl-Friedrich Merten it is necessary to know something of the various factions that exist in the U-Bootwaffe community, for it is as riven as any involuntary collection of men on earth. Most members, like Oesten or Reche, tolerate criticism without complaint or bitterness. Others, like Topp, often criticize themselves. But Merten was one of a small group of veterans who refuse to accept criticism of the U-Bootwaffe in any form and who will, if necessary, act to suppress it. Peter Hansen calls this group the "steel helmets" (*Stahlhelm*) and characterizes them as being composed of the most extreme right-wing U-Bootwaffe officers, those who are "still bitter and dream of final victory like they did until the middle of April 1945." [15]

Any book, article, interview, film, or television show that casts dispersion on the U-Bootwaffe is anathema to this group. *Sharks and Little Fish,* for example, which did nothing to improve the reputation of the U-Bootwaffe, was an early target. In 1984 the historian Peter Padfield published an exhaustive and most unflattering biography of Karl Dönitz called *Dönitz, The Last Führer.* The book is hated, its author despised. When Merten first saw it, he wrote to all his English-speaking friends to warn them that he had never read a book "so full of hate, so emotionally insulting, so falsifying the facts, so persistently repeating war-propaganda lies, and so poisonous for the indispensable consensus between our peoples in Europe!" [16] Erich Topp's *Odyssey of a U-Boat Commander* met similar criticism, though somewhat muted in deference to his war record, and so did Herbert Werner's *Iron Coffins.*

Horst Bredow has printed his own *Index,* not of forbidden books, for that would be too long, but of acceptable books. There are about thirty titles on the list, but none of Buchheim's appear because they contain all the elements that make a book unacceptable to the Stahlhelm faction, and they are written by a man this faction considers completely unsuited for writing anything about the U-boats (all Stahlhelm criticism of Buchheim rests on these twin pillars).[17] The unacceptable elements include his bizarre writing style, his casual approach to technical accuracy, his disrespectful tone when discussing the U-Bootwaffe or its leadership, and his ultimate pessimism. They are present in all his books, all of which have been derided by Stahlhelm veterans.

The Stahlhelm group, like Horst Bredow deep in his archives, has a simple agenda: to protect the image of the U-boat commander at all costs. They know that the media ultimately determine that image and that books are the most enduring segment of the media. They believe that if a negative image is not forcefully contradicted at once, people will start to believe it. They are, in a sense, still fighting. Merten was typical. Like other members of the group, he was distrustful of those who did not share his point of view. He disliked people such as Topp (with whom he also had a running debate) and Werner. He loathed Peter Padfield. But the one he hated most was Lothar-Günther Buchheim. Like embittered spouses united by their quarreling, he and Buchheim sniped, scratched, and bit for years, sometimes privately, often in public, to the point of embarrassment and in spite of recommendations from colleagues and veterans' organizations that they end the battle.

Merten may have heard of Buchheim during the war, but he almost certainly came to dislike him when *The Boat* was first published in 1973. His attitude was not unlike that of many veterans. The book was a fairy tale, all make-believe. "The Buchheim patrol with Lehmann-Willenbrock was completely without incident," he wrote, "no battles, no depth charge attacks, and no longer than 38 days. Everything was a fantasy."[18] He dismissed Buchheim as an outsider who had no business writing about U-boats. He was disdainful of those, like Topp, who encouraged Buchheim, and he was frankly bewildered to think that Heinz Lehmann-Willenbrock, a Seekadett in his division on the cruiser *Karlsruhe* in 1935 and an acquaintance after the war, would support Buchheim in his writing. Perhaps, he thought, Lehmann-Willenbrock recognized in the Old Man his personal memorial. "Of course," he concluded rather uncharitably, "it became very difficult for him to separate himself from this unhealthy friendship afterwards."[19] Oddly, he did not consider the film as bad as the book. "Without several scenes, for example, on the beginning this festivity, which never existed, with those drunkenness and women invented to negotiate the moral and some disgusting other scenes the film has had a good reputation." [20] But even this faint praise is aimed primarily at Wolfgang Petersen, the director of *The Boat*.

Merten may have thought Buchheim's popularity was a fad and would eventually disappear; this had happened to Herbert Werner and *Iron Coffins* in 1969. The success of *The Boat* and the temperament of its author made this unlikely, though, and indeed Buchheim continued to write. In the years after *The Boat*, he published three more books about the U-boats, each with all the same elements that had so dismayed the *Stahlhelm* and each making him more famous and more self-assured in his role as an expert on the U-boats. *The Boat* was followed in 1976 by *U-Boot Krieg* (U-boat War). In 1985 came *Die U-Boot-Fahrer* (The U-boat Sailor) and in 1988 *Zu Tode Gesiegt* (Victoried to Death). All three are largely picture books, collections of Buchheim's wartime photographs with running commentary. Like *The Boat*, all make extremely negative statements about the U-Bootwaffe, its leadership, the bankruptcy of wartime Germany, and war in general. They are known as Buchheim's "U-boat Trilogy."

It was not a book, however, but a television show that caused Karl-Friedrich Merten to leap out of his slippers and into his armor. In early 1985 a three-art adaptation of *The Boat* was run on German television. Many observers, including some U-boat veterans, thought it better than the movie (which had been made at the same time), for it was longer and emphasized the boredom and tedious periods of forced inaction that often occurred on patrol. Merten did not. He wrote a review of the program in the German veterans' magazine *Ritterkreuz*, which began with two paragraphs about Buchheim's unsuitability as an author. The rest of the review pointed out mistakes in the script: the crew made too much noise; too much water came down through the bridge hatch; the boat would not ride out a storm on the surface; the boat could not dive as deep as was shown; the crew of the tender in Spain was exaggerated; and so on. Buchheim's crew was possessed with "an almost hysterical anxiety syndrome, part apathetic, part unstable, and abnormally euphoric with fatigue." No wonder, he pointed out, that the program was so popular in Britain! Finally, he referred to a particularly memorable scene: "I am certain that no commander ever had to enforce his orders with a pistol." [21]

Shortly after *The Boat* was broadcast, Buchheim brought out a television documentary he called *Zu Tode Gesiegt: Der Untergang der U-Boote* (Victoried to Death: The Defeat of the U-boats). The program was graphic and provocative. As Hadley described it, "He engages his viewers with few historical or technical facts, opting instead to incite the emotions and to prompt reflection on a single idea: U-boats past and present are obscene."[22] Merten wrote a scathing review of *Zu Tode Gesiegt,* of which perhaps one-third dealt with factual errors in the program and two-thirds with Buchheim's failings as an author. *Zu Tode Gesiegt,* Merten stated, was an "incoherent, erratic, half-true summary of [Buchheim's own] perceptions, distorted and which in certain cases tended toward the psychopathic." He scolded Buchheim for passing himself off as an "expert" on the U-boat war and as a "working member" of a U-boat crew. He reminded his readers of Buchheim's limited experience on patrol and repeated unflattering remarks made about him by other crewmen in U-96. He implied not only that Buchheim was a psychopath but that he was a coward and a liar. No wonder, then, that Buchheim called Merten shortly after this review appeared in *Ritterkreuz,* argued with him, and finally told him he was a "pile of shit." Merten, in response, immediately typed a transcript of the call, titled it "Lothar-Günther Buchheim feels dismayed," and sent copies to his correspondents.[23]

In late 1985 Buchheim published *Die U-Boot-Fahrer.* Like *U-Boot Krieg* in 1976, it was mainly photographs of U-boats with a deliberately grim and depressing commentary. Merten leaped to the attack. "Buchheim—Buchheim—Buchheim," he began his review in *Ritterkreuz,* "and no end to it! . . . Haven't we real U-boat sailors up until now endured his fantasies, his nervous anxieties, his calculated offenses, more or less with equanimity and sympathetic indulgence?" It was very similar to the review of *Zu Tode Gesiegt* one year earlier. The merits of the book were dealt with only briefly and in general terms. The real target was Buchheim. As in the first review, Merten hammered away at Buchheim's qualifications as a writer. He was less insulting than before, and he avoided the psychopath label, but he did not hesitate to describe what he thought was Buchheim's hypocrisy. The book was "contrary, illogical, contradictory, and without any persuasive line of reasoning." It was an "antiwar" book, even though Buchheim was obviously fascinated with the U-Bootwaffe. Buchheim was loudly "unmilitary," but he held a secret wonder for the virtues of military service. It was a "song of hatred," a "distortion of reality," a "sower of distrust between crew and officers, particularly commanders," and a "mindless slander of [Grand Admiral Dönitz]." Nevertheless, "[Buchheim] wants desperately to be a part of this organization he thinks so insidious."[24]

The final comment contains the root of Merten's dislike for Buchheim, for it was Buchheim's attempts to claim membership in the U-Bootwaffe that drove Merten to distraction. In many of his U-boat books Buchheim includes himself as a member of the crew, often using the pronoun *wir*, "we," rather than *sie*, "they." In Merten's judgment, Buchheim's success as a writer hangs on this simple word. "[Buchheim's] *wir* is the cause for his existence. It connects him with 'Navy,' with 'U-Bootwaffe,' and with 'ship's company' and 'officer's mess.'" In both reviews, therefore, Merten struggles to strip the word from him; to point out that Buchheim was a passenger in a U-boat, not a member of the crew; that he was an ill-suited passenger who, in the words of Horst Bredow, "when everything was calm, analyzed [*gezwiebelt*] the crew, and when things got dangerous huddled in the control room, a picture of misery"; that the crew couldn't stand him; and that the leadership disowned him.[25]

The feud continued for years. The two seemed ready to fight about anything. The broadcast on German television of a new documentary about the Battle of the Atlantic, . . . *Gegen England,* set off another skirmish in 1987. Both men disliked the program but for different reasons. Soon they were arguing about it: "The public squabble reduced itself to questions of image and of perceptions. Merten tossed out an old wartime photo of PK-man Buchheim lolling about on the bridge of a U-boat in a most unmilitary pose and had it published in newspapers. Such a man, he snorted, could not be a comrade who really understood the trade. Buchheim responded by publishing an official wartime portrait of the war-hero Merten with what Buchheim described as his 'rambo-zambo look.'"[26] Only toward the end of the decade did the fireworks die. *Zu Tode Gesiegt* was released as a book in 1988. Buchheim did not publish any more U-boat books, instead working for the next several years on a novel. Merten's health declined. But still neither adversary had anything good to say about the other, and Merten was a bitter man for the last years of his life. Unlike Erich Topp, Herbert Werner, and many of his fellow commanders, he had been completely unable to admit that men, and nations, sin from time to time. He had wasted too much time in the past. In 1991 he tried to explain his ardor, and in doing so he showed a tiny twinge of regret. "Maybe we are too sensitive about the [misrepresentation] of the U-boat life," he wrote plaintively, "having lost nearly three quarters of our comrades, but it makes a difference to us who is the author of any story of submarines."[27]

So much controversy swirls around Lothar-Günther Buchheim that it is hard to determine what about him is good and what is bad. He is an unpleasant person in many ways, but so are some of his critics. His writing is not pretty, but as a good journalist he writes in a descriptive and captivating style. His books are never boring. Some U-Bootwaffe veterans have accused him of lying to suit himself. Others, equally qualified to judge, admire his accuracy and defend him. His books provide as good a description as any of life in the U-Bootwaffe at the height of the Battle of the Atlantic. Some have criticized him for pretending to be someone he is not: a soldier and a comrade. True, he was not, as Oesten puts it, "a paying customer," but he endured three war patrols and risked his life as surely as anyone on board. Obviously, he will not be silent; if anything, the harder he is pushed, the harder he will push back. "Buchheim," writes Topp, "is one of the few who never stray from their path. He hates compromises. He will not deviate one inch from what he has experienced as the truth."[28]

One fact speaks louder than any other in Lothar-Günther Buchheim's favor: he has done more to increase public awareness of the U-boats than any other writer. Even Horst Bredow, who is not an admirer of Buchheim, has had to pay him a backhanded compliment: "He meant to avenge himself with his book and his film, but he failed—both book and film have generated more good publicity for us than bad!"[29] Hansen, who knows his difficult friend as well as anyone, summed up the entire case very simply when he wrote: "Books previously published [about the U-Bootwaffe] usually had a few thousand copies printed and were bought by 'insiders' mainly, not the general public. But *The Boat* sold millions and was the very first book that broke into the general public mass market, [including] the younger generation. . . . Before that the U-boat [was] a dark deep secret for these millions of people. This is Buchheim's true and most important impact."[30] It is not the worse of epitaphs.

CHAPTER 8

The Test of Gold

Fire is the test of gold; adversity, of strong men.

—Seneca, *On Providence*

IS IT possible for a man to go mad with pain?"

"I haven't yet seen it happen." The surgeon glared at his patient. "Anyway, you haven't to think like that," he scolded. "You're damned lucky to be alive." The patient sighed as he looked down at the foot of his hospital bed. He knew the surgeon was right. He should have died. He had wanted to die.

The desert was cold at night, much colder than one would have expected. He had lain alone in the sand for hours after the shooting. He had lost a lot of blood, and he was beginning to feel lightheaded, as though he had been drinking. His left arm was useless. He could feel nothing below his waist. He knew he was going to die. "But I am not afraid to die," he thought to himself. "I am going the way that many of my comrades in this and previous wars have gone. I am in good company. God has willed it." The first line of the *Our Father* kept going through his head: *Dein Wille geschehe.* Thy will be done.

He was found after darkness had fallen. A soldier bent over him, only to take his watch and vanish into the night; then a group stood around him, shadowy figures, like angels. They were silent until Victor Oehrn, still conscious, finally asked them: "Who are you?"

"We're Australians," replied one of them. "Are we good fighters?" [1]

THE climactic event in *The Boat* occurs when the boat tries, and fails, to enter the Mediterranean Sea through the Straits of Gibraltar. That part, at least, has a solid historical basis. In September 1941 a combined German and Italian force under the command of Erwin Rommel was poised to attack the Libyan port of Tobruk. Because of heavy losses to supporting convoys, his attack had to be postponed, first to October, then to November, at which time the British Eighth Army attacked Rommel instead. In October, after a strong cable from Admiral Eberhard Weichhold, the senior Kriegsmarine officer in Rome, Adolf Hitler ordered several U-boats pulled out of the North Atlantic and sent into the Mediterranean Sea. It was an unwise move, opposed by Dönitz, but it was very typical of the man who freely described himself as a "coward at sea." Its only effect was to give the Royal Navy a needed rest, for there were now three times as many boats at sea as there had been two years earlier, and in spite of the loss of the aces in March, the compromise of Enigma, and the clashes with the United States Navy, they were still winning the war in the convoy lanes.

It did mean that the U-Bootwaffe now maintained a significant presence in the Mediterranean Sea, and it resulted in the creation of a new U-boat command: Führer der U-Boote, Italien, or FdU-Italy. The officer in this position would be responsible for the operations, maintenance, and administration of all U-boats between Gibraltar and Suez. Protocol dictated that this officer be a Kapitän zur See with previous experience as a flotilla commander. Certain political, diplomatic, and social duties that only such a senior officer could handle came with the position. Karl Dönitz, however, who had no time for protocol or politics, appointed his own deputy for operations, thirty-four-year-old Korvettenkapitän (lieutenant commander) Victor Oehrn, to the post, and Oehrn, delighted, packed his bags and left for Rome at once.

Some time later Karl Dönitz would tell Oehrn that he had not approved of the transfer of U-boats into the Mediterranean and that no good had come of it. Most naval historians would concur. When Oehrn arrived in Rome in late November 1941 there were ten boats in the Mediterranean, hardly enough for a flotilla, let alone a major command. It is true that those few boats scored some of the greatest individual successes in the U-boat war. On 13 November 1941 the aircraft carrier HMS *Ark Royal* was sunk just east of Gibraltar by U-81 commander Friedrich Guggenberger. Twelve days later, the 31,000-ton battleship HMS *Barham* was sunk off the coast of Egypt by Hans-Diedrich von Tiesenhausen, commander of U-331. In December U-557 commander Ottokar Paulssen sank the light cruiser HMS *Galatea* as she was coming into Alexandria. But these attacks, as glittering as they were, did not make an offensive, and in the long run Dönitz's forebodings proved correct. Many of the boats going into the Mediterranean were lost trying to pass through the Straits of Gibraltar. Allied convoys supporting the British Army in North Africa were not seriously disrupted. And, of course, any boat taken into the Mediterranean was no longer available in the North Atlantic, which, as both Dönitz and Oehrn knew, was the real center of the undersea war.

Hence Oehrn's duties as FdU-Italy were not as overwhelming as he had expected. He reported to the Supermarina (the headquarters of the Royal Italian Navy) as soon as he arrived to begin setting up his base of operations, but it was a small operation with a very small staff. The limited number of boats and the size of the theater meant that wolfpacks were impracticable—most boats operated alone with minimal direction from Rome. There was a communications center in the Supermarina, but signals came in only at night when it was safe for the boats to surface and transmit. Soon Oehrn had a deputy, Georg Schewe, commander of U-105, and even less to do himself.

Away from the supercharged environment of BdU staff, in a position that required less than his total attention, and based in a city that was one of the most beautiful and historic in the world, Victor Oehrn would begin to enjoy himself. He soon learned that the monkish atmosphere of Kerneval did not exist in Rome. The first time he was invited out to dinner with Weichhold, for example, he politely protested that he did not have the time. For that misstep he received a friendly lecture: in Rome, Oehrn, you are not just a U-boat officer. You are a diplomat, a representative of your government, and a model for fellow countrymen in this city. Perhaps your role does require an active social calendar and a lifestyle unsuited for wartime, but it is best to enjoy life today. You might be transferred tomorrow. You might die the next day.

As the days went by, he came to share this point of view. He attended the parties and the receptions. He went to lunches and dinners. He made friends and renewed acquaintances, for he had been to Rome as a student. Most important, he began to explore Rome; not just the city outside his window on the fourth floor of the hotel or the one outside his office in the Supermarina, but the city designed by its builders to be the center of the world. His guides were the best. One was a professor at the Kaiser Wilhelm Institute, another a Jesuit priest. Shortly after he arrived in Rome, he was introduced to a young woman named Renate von Winterfeld, a secretary in Admiral Weichhold's office. They began to see each other regularly, and Renate loved to plan tours of the city for them.

Rome during the war was a strange place. Her streets were alternately swept with mobs of people celebrating one Axis victory or another or empty because of stringent fuel rationing. Restaurants and hotels were open, and as they ate Victor and Renate could easily have rubbed elbows with Jewish refugees, Croat freedom fighters, or Spanish pilgrims. Papal audiences competed with fascist street rallies. Rumors flew like locusts. The city was a hive of espionage, especially inside the walls of the Vatican; diplomats from many countries at war with Germany and Italy lived there and were allowed to come and go. This ongoing sense of history enraptured Victor Oehrn. He did not see the squalid wartime Rome. He saw only the Eternal City, and his words after forty years still reflect the awe of those days: "What will, what strength, what clarity of purpose, speaks to us now from these ruins, still standing in spite of all the destructive forces that have since passed through?" If he had to stay in one place until the end of the war, he probably could not have chosen a better place than Rome or a better position than FdU-Italy. "I was living," he wrote, "in Eden." [2]

But no one can live in Eden for long. The Kriegsmarine was controlled by men of a different era, men who could not, or would not, be as blithe as Dönitz in their actions. Erich Raeder, Dönitz's superior, was a conservative man, and he found he could not accept such a discrepancy as the appointment of a junior officer like Victor Oehrn to the position of FdU-Italy. In early 1942 he overrode Dönitz's decision and rejected Oehrn's assignment. Another officer, Leopold Kreisch, the former captain of the heavy cruiser *Lützow,* was sent to take his place, and Oehrn was ignominiously bumped down a notch to become Kreisch's A1. Kreisch would not be ready to take over for several months, and Oehrn would continue to hold the fort in Rome, but it was a humiliating change of assignment, and a lesser post than the one he had held at BdU. After considering his options, he decided to request sea duty as soon as possible.

Then Dönitz called. "I want you to know that this wasn't my decision," he said to the disconsolate Oehrn, "but I can't make a cabinet matter out of it. There is a war on, and I have to follow orders just like you do. I want you to promise me that you'll stay in Rome and do the best you can." At this, Oehrn wrote later, all thoughts of a request for transfer left his mind, and in a move that would change his life profoundly, he promised Dönitz that he would stay. [3]

Dönitz was entirely correct when he told Victor Oehrn that he had a war to fight and had no time for inside politics. When he put down the telephone, he went immediately back to a war that had changed completely since the last time the two had seen each other. Oehrn was appointed to the position of FdU-Italy on 28 November 1941. He was replaced by Kreisch in February 1942. During that short interval several critical events happened: the air attack by the Japanese on the United States Pacific Fleet at Pearl Harbor, Adolf Hitler's declaration of war on the United States four days later, and the launching of a major U-boat offensive by Germany against the country that had for so long taunted her from under a neutral flag.

It was the last of these events that was now occupying most of Karl Dönitz's time. After the declaration of war he went to Raeder at once with an ambitious plan to send twelve large type IX boats to positions along the eastern seaboard of the United States. He called the plan *Paukenschlag*, Drumbeat, because the sudden strike it described would reverberate around the country with the percussive effect of ships exploding, one after another. Time, he stressed, was of the essence. He knew from intelligence sources that the United States was not prepared for such an offensive, but he knew also that she would surely react quickly and that the window of opportunity for his boats was small. Unfortunately, several of the type IX boats he wanted to send west were tied up in the same senseless Gibraltar operations as U-96 had been. The Kriegsmarine refused to release them even after Dönitz declared that his smaller type VII boats were more than suited to Gibraltar operations. Only six boats, all of which were in French Atlantic ports at that time, would be allowed to go to America, and one of those would eventually be scratched from the operation for mechanical reasons.

If Oehrn sensed any irritation in Dönitz's voice during the telephone call, it was because Dönitz had delivered the prospect of a German naval victory of immense proportion to his superiors on a silver platter and they had given him only five boats with which to accomplish it. Drumbeat heralded a period of abandoned slaughter that can best be characterized as the Happy Times all over again. Over the next six months, almost four hundred Allied and neutral merchant ships were sunk in waters patrolled and protected by the United States Navy. "Overall," states Michael Gannon, the author of *Operation Drumbeat,* "the numbers represent one of the greatest maritime disasters in history and the American nation's worst-ever defeat at sea. For Germany this was the most successful sustained

U-boat campaign in the whole course of the war."[4] But since the number of boats involved in the campaign was never as high as it could have been (the parsimony shown in December lasted throughout), these results must have made Dönitz as bitter as they made him happy.

Victor Oehrn had been at BdU until the end of November. If he had stayed there, he would have been in the thick of the planning, then the execution, of Operation Drumbeat. But the war had gone on without him. On the sidelines, in charge of a campaign that was neither important nor profitable, he was fighting only personal battles. In spite of his promise to Dönitz that he would remain in his new position and support his successor, Leopold Kreisch, to the best of his ability, the relationship between the two was strained.

To understand how hard his demotion hit Victor Oehrn, it is necessary to realize what a proud man he was. It was a quiet pride, neither arrogant nor destructive, but it drove much of what he did, said, and believed. He was proud of his heritage, his abilities, and the trust he had been given. It was pride that prompted him to claim the credit he thought he deserved for Scapa Flow and made him reluctant to wear the award he was given for it. It was pride that forced him to take U-37 out of Wilhelmshaven after only five days in command, the time he had given to Dönitz. His pride made Raeder's decision very difficult to accept and would make it impossible for him to get along with the man who took his place. Kreisch, in training for his new job, came to Rome only twice while Oehrn was running the show in the Supermarina, but during their short meetings he treated Oehrn like a junior aide, Oehrn treated him like an equal, and neither man bent an inch. At dinner one night Kreisch made an obvious display of waiting for Oehrn to help him with his coat. Oehrn refused. "You can't do that with him, Herr Kapitän," Kreisch was warned by another officer, which cannot have improved the relationship.

Fortunately, this awkward tango of wills did not last for long. The siege of Tobruk that was one of the principal reasons for redeployment of U-boats in the Mediterranean had been broken back in November, coincidentally on the same day that Oehrn had been appointed FdU-Italy. Now, in May 1942, Erwin Rommel was preparing to attack the fortress again. Kreisch had still not arrived, and Oehrn decided to move his center of operations from Rome to Libya so he could supervise U-boat attacks on the expected convoy of evacuation ships from Tobruk Harbor. It was to be a short visit—ten days—and he had to do little more than pack his suitcase. But there was something he did not want to postpone until his return.

It had soon become clear to Oehrn that Renate von Winterfeld, who had been taking him around Rome, was special. When they were introduced, he was given the impression that Renate was married, so he treated her with the respect one gave to the wife of a fellow serviceman, even to the point of addressing her as *Gnädige Frau*. Renate evidently enjoyed this, and she did not tell him otherwise for three months. After that they became inseparable. "I felt," he wrote afterward, "that something new had entered my life. In war, abroad, the women were all over us. But not her. I didn't see anyone else after I met her." On the evening before Oehrn was to leave Rome, he invited Renate out to dinner at the Casino Valadier on Monte Pincio. They became engaged that night but kept it a secret. When he returned, they decided, he would fly to Potsdam to ask Renate's mother for her permission (Renate's father had died several years earlier). It was a perfect evening, marred by only a small mishap. Renate had given him a tiny present to remember her by: a bear made out of sugar. When he got back to his room at the hotel, he found he had lost it.

He flew from Rome to Derna, in Libya, the next day, on a Ju88 bomber with Field Marshal Albert Kesselring and his staff. Kesselring, who held the position of *Oberbefehlshaber Süd* (commander in chief, south) was technically Rommel's superior and was in Africa for the ostensible purpose of supervising him. Actually, however, he had little to do and less to say, and as the ten days Oehrn had planned for stretched into weeks, then a month, Kesselring sat in his tent and worried. Neither he nor Oehrn was directly involved in the siege of Tobruk, but they were close enough to hear the sound of the fighting and the deathly silence that followed when the fortress was surrendered. It was after this battle that Oehrn saw more of the enemy in one place than any of his comrades in the U-Bootwaffe would ever see in their lives: "33,000 English, Australian, New Zealand, and Indian soldiers, magnificent and in the prime of life, all milling aimlessly on the high plateau [over Tobruk] among uncounted aircraft and weapons of every kind." All of them were the unbelieving prisoners of the Afrika Korps.

During the heady days after Tobruk, Victor Oehrn lost any possible claim he had to the position and the aura of FdU-Italy. Admiral Weichhold relieved him of all duties in Rome, transferred him to Kesselring's staff, and told him to "await further instructions." There seemed to be no logical reason for Weichhold's action (Karl Dönitz would not have wasted a good U-Bootwaffe officer in such a position). The only possible explanation is that Weichhold acted in the general frenzy of enthusiasm that developed when Tobruk was captured and Rommel aimed his army toward Cairo. He wanted to help, but he had no divisions to give Rommel, no tanks, and no fuel. All he had was one staff officer—one of those mysterious U-boat people—for whom there was less work than expected.

Oehrn's return to Rome and the woman he loved was indefinitely postponed. Rommel was moving east. Kesselring was following Rommel, and Oehrn had no choice but to follow Kesselring. He was in a lonely position, a great letdown after his days at BdU and in Rome. He was completely out of his element as a naval officer. He had become, he supposed, a kind of naval liaison, but he had no official duties, no staff except for a small radio detachment, and no mission. To salvage his pride and to keep himself occupied, he lapsed into the role he knew best: that of staff officer. He became very close to his new commander, Kesselring, attended his staff meetings, dined with him frequently, shared in his discussions, and was party to much of what went on between Kesselring and Rommel.

Rommel was moving fast—too fast, said Kesselring gloomily, for his own good. "We're heading toward a catastrophe," Oehrn heard him say more than once. "It's the same thing that happened on the way to Moscow." German supply lines to Rommel were dangerously stretched; the Luftwaffe could not support him; the enemy was becoming stronger as his own supply lines shortened. Kesselring thought Rommel was out of his depth; he was impetuous, stubborn, lacking in strategic vision. Oehrn, however, was captivated by Rommel, whom he had never seen. He compared him to his own commander in chief, Karl Dönitz: "Like Dönitz with his U-boat crews, Rommel was able to awaken a spirit of willingness in those he led: a spirit that could overcome any misfortune in order to achieve success. Dönitz was respected and loved by everyone under his command; Rommel was feared by his officers, but held in almost mythical reverence by his men." Being with Rommel on the march was to be alive; it was exciting, intoxicating: "I was overcome with youth and ignorance," he wrote. "I forgot my criticisms. They were useless and of no interest to anyone here." Rommel was taking huge risks, no doubt, but Oehrn was used to gambling: a U-boat commander gambled every time he went to sea.

Rommel chased the Eighth Army all the way from Tobruk to the Egyptian border, while Kesselring followed, and Oehrn and his little band of radiomen, trailing along behind Kesselring, sent glowing updates of Rommel's progress back to BdU. The chase lasted until the end of June 1942, when the Eighth Army stopped running at El Alamein and Rommel's lightning advance toward Egypt stalled like a car hitting a wall. The British had chosen to hold this line, bounded by the sea and by a huge, impassable salt marsh called the Qattara Depression, and they did. Both sides were exhausted. Rommel was almost out of fuel. He was perilously far from his supply bases. The road back to Tobruk (the Rommelweg) was strewn with broken-down tanks and vehicles left unrepaired because of a lack of spare parts. Ammunition was short and provisions were low. Oehrn's impression was that the Afrika Korps had reached the Alamein line with the last ounce of its strength: now, with the prize in sight, it was too tired and too hungry to grasp it.

Rommel and the Afrika Korps were to stay just short of El Alamein from July until October, a period of almost complete inactivity punctuated by air strikes and skirmishes but no major offensive. Any prospect of advancing to Cairo and the east had evaporated, but many people at Wehrmacht headquarters in faraway East Prussia could not see it and were fully confident that Rommel, after a prudent wait to regroup, would sweep over the Alamein line into Egypt. In July Weichhold finally gave Victor Oehrn the instructions he had been waiting for. They were extremely vague. "Rommel is planning an attack across the Nile," he said. "Your job is to assist him." Oehrn said he could not imagine how a single U-boat officer could help Rommel do anything. "That's not for you to say," responded the admiral sternly. "One has to do a certain amount of improvisation in war. You'll be given all the support you need. There's a torpedo boat squadron in Tobruk you can have." In retrospect, it was an amazing order. The Kriegsmarine had given a lone BdU staff officer a torpedo boat squadron six hundred miles away and sent him off to help Rommel cross the Nile. It seemed frivolous, even faintly ridiculous, but Weichhold was not smiling.

So Victor Oehrn set off into the desert to find Rommel. Before he left, he put on his best uniform, desert khaki with blue garrison cap, and all his decorations "so Rommel would know who he was dealing with." He found a car and driver, status symbols no staff officer would be seen without. He left Kesselring's camp on 13 July 1942. Neither he nor his driver knew where they were going so they drove in the general direction of the front, which was marked by artillery flashes and tracer shells.

They were lost almost at once (not surprising for a U-Bootwaffe officer in the middle of the desert), and finally Oehrn told the driver to stop. He got out of the car and climbed up a small hill, intending to look for a landmark. He reached the top and saw helmets on the other side—strange round helmets. He spun around, an awful feeling in his stomach, but did not take a single step before shots were fired. The first hit the car. The second hit him in the left shoulder. Three more hit the same shoulder, one after the other, shattering it. His driver threw up his hands and surrendered. Oehrn, his left arm swinging uselessly, tried to run into the desert, but a fifth shot hit his leg and knocked him into the sand.

Victor Oehrn never found Rommel but he had found the front.

THE wounds Oehrn sustained on 13 July 1942 at an unknown forward point on the El Alamein line were critical; they would have killed him had he not been captured when he was. He had a shattered left shoulder, a splintered left leg, and multiple internal injuries. He was dehydrated, bleeding heavily, and in shock. He had managed with effort to remain lucid until after his capture, but as he bumped along in a field ambulance back to the British hospital in Alexandria, sixty miles east, he slipped in and out of consciousness, and when he arrived, he was taken into surgery immediately. He woke up the next day in a recovery ward, wracked with pain and encased in plaster, one cast on his leg and another completely encircling his chest and left arm—a most unlikely, but very real, prisoner of war.

Despite Oehrn's best efforts to remain alert, the rest of that day and most the next few weeks passed in a blur of pain and delirium. The sun rose and set, people came and went, examinations were made and dressings changed, and Oehrn seemed to float as on a cloud. "Renate asked me how long I was in Alexandria," he wrote. "I don't know. Months, no doubt. And though certain events stand out, the rest seems lost in the shadows." The next date he remembers with precision is 28 August 1942, the day his surgeon, a man named Marsden, told him he was going to recover. "We had our moments," he said, "but I think you'll live." "In that case," replied Oehrn, in plaster up to his eyebrows and his left leg in a splint, "I shall have to attempt an escape." Both the German U-boat officer and the Royal Army doctor smiled; they had been through much together since their first meeting in the operating room.

Marsden was one of two doctors Oehrn credits for his recovery. When they first met in the operating room, he wrote, he knew that they were very different men. As time went on, however, they became friendly enough to talk and even exchange jokes, and Marsden forced him to pull himself together when he began to talk about going mad with pain. He was very upset when Marsden was whisked away one day "without even saying goodbye" (he did manage to track him down after the war in Birmingham). His other doctor was a man named Levin, a German Jew who had emigrated to Britain before the war. Because he was a native speaker, Levin had been assigned to care specifically for the German POW patients in Alexandria, and after Oehrn had recovered enough to be placed in a general ward, Levin cared for him.

Like most German POWs at that time, Oehrn was assumed to be a Nazi who disliked Jews. Once, after a transfusion, he became concerned about the sickly color of his eyes and casually asked Marsden what type of blood he was getting. "Don't worry," was the reply. "It's good Aryan blood." But Levin did not seem concerned about Oehrn, and Oehrn, to his credit, did not reject Levin. The two men talked for hours, often about religion, and Oehrn found that he could grasp the tenets of Judaism better than he had ever understood Christianity. "I was never able to accept the idea of God as a man and I could never understand the Trinity. Only in the painting of the Creation in the Sistine Chapel did I recognize the God I had always imagined." Levin, who professed Judaism in defiance of the government Oehrn had been sworn to defend, became Oehrn's friend. "Levin's friendship renewed my strength. I have him to thank for that."

Marsden and Levin were not the only men with whom Oehrn talked. As a captured Kriegsmarine officer, he was required viewing for all military personnel in the area: curious officers, chatty noncoms, even private soldiers. He maintained the utmost civility with all of his visitors and always tried to appear clean, well-groomed, and well-spoken, but he also never forgot that they were the enemy. He could not use his arms and legs to fight them so he used his voice, and because he knew he could not win an argument with insults or mockery, he tried persuasion. His favorite theme was that Germany and the Western Allies shared a common cause; how ridiculous it was, he would often say, for you and us to be fighting each other when our real enemy is the Soviet Union and Bolshevism. No doubt he believed this. He knew more about the Russians than most of his visitors. Unfortunately, he knew very little about what was happening in his own country, and this weakened his position considerably. When anyone mentioned concentration camps, for example, or the treatment of Jews, he dismissed it as propaganda, "lies that neither my friends, nor my superiors, nor my subordinates, would ever accept."

So persuasive was Oehrn in arguing with his visitors that his room eventually became off limits to all but hospital staff and officials. Punjabi guards were posted outside his door to prevent unauthorized visits, but they too would talk with Oehrn, bemoaning British imperialism and assuring him of their own furtive support for Germany. Then we are on the same side, ventured Oehrn (rather disingenuously because he often said the same thing to the British). "True enough," said one of the more pragmatic Punjabis. "But the English are in power. When you are on the Indian border I will be on your side, but for now I have to stay on theirs."

In all of his conversations Oehrn took care never to say more than he had to about military affairs. In wartime people who by virtue of rank or responsibility are privy to information whose compromise would represent grave disadvantage for their own side try at all costs to avoid being captured. Such men have sometimes killed themselves rather than be captured.[5] Oehrn considered himself such a person and acted accordingly. Some time after his capture, for example, Marsden told him that his bones would have to be reset. Anaesthetic could not be used, and it would be very painful. Would he like some tea with rum to take the edge off? No thank you, replied Oehrn, not because he was opposed to rum but because he was afraid he would say something to betray the U-Bootwaffe.

Whether Oehrn actually did possess dangerous information is debatable. He had been away from BdU for eight months when he was captured and so was probably not as valuable a captive as he may have thought. Nonetheless, one would have thought that someone in the Admiralty would have been interested to know that the man who ran BdU Operations for two years was now in their midst. No one seemed to be, and there is doubt as to whether the Admiralty even knew where Victor Oehrn was in the summer of 1942.

Folders were kept in London on all active U-boat officers, including Oehrn, and newly captured prisoners were often shocked to see how much of their personal lives they contained. Oehrn's folder, however, may not have been kept up to date after he left BdU. The British probably knew that he had been assigned to Rome, but his movement from Rome to North Africa may have gone unnoticed. The Eighth Army, of course, had his name and rank immediately, but the instantaneous communication of data we now take for granted did not exist in 1942, and the correct desk at the Admiralty might not have been told for some time. Captured U-boat officers were taken at once and without exception to Britain for interrogation at the London District Cage in Kensington and then to POW camps in Britain or North America. If the news of Oehrn's capture had been passed from Egypt to the Admiralty, therefore, he might have been whisked, broken bones and all, to London as soon as possible. At the very least he would have been visited by a team of interrogators in Egypt. Neither of these things happened. Either the Admiralty chose to ignore the presence of Karl Dönitz's deputy chief of staff for operations in a British field hospital or it did not know he was there.

By this time Oehrn had been moved from the hospital in Alexandria. After passing through a series of camps, he ended up in Camp 306, a so-called hospital cage near the Bitter Seas on the Suez Canal. Instead of British doctors and nurses, he had German ones; instead of English voices, he heard the voices of German soldiers. He was out of danger, but he was still on his back and would remain that way for nine months. His chest and left arm were encased in a single huge plaster cast. His leg was lashed to a splint. He could not move the fingers on his left hand. He was in constant pain, the physical pain of bullet wounds and broken bones and the mental anguish brought on by loneliness and despair. His future was lost in a swirl of confusion. He had no idea where he would be in a month or a year. He knew of the POW camps in Britain and Canada, but he had heard that prisoners were being shipped to Australia. He still might face formal questioning. Rumors of methods used at the Allied interrogation center in Mahdi (just up the road) were flying: solitary confinement, sleep deprivation, and physical and mental torture were used to break the prisoners—or so he had heard.

Above everything else, he missed Renate, all the more because he knew that they could never be together again. They were, as far as he knew, still engaged, but one had to be realistic. He probably would be in captivity for the rest of the war, and in any case he was not the man she had seen on the terrace of the Casino Valadier. He would return a cripple. As soon as he was allowed to, he sent two postcards: one to his sister in Germany, the other to Renate in Rome. He told Renate that he was alive and a prisoner and that she might consider herself released from any obligation to marry him. Both postcards were later returned to him. He had not filled them in properly: in capital letters with ink. He completed two more and sent them. He did not expect responses any time soon.

He could not have known that Renate, in Rome, was trying desperately to find out what had happened to him. She had little success using the normal channels because the Kriegsmarine seemed to have no better idea of his whereabouts than did the Admiralty. "He went to Africa, you know," said Kapitän zur See Albert Loycke, Weichhold's chief of staff, most unhelpfully, when she went to see him, "where the Australians are. The sand has probably covered him up by now." She received precious little help from Loycke or anyone else in Weichhold's office. But Renate von Winterfeld proved to be more resourceful than most women. She loved Victor Oehrn. She was sure he was still alive. If the Kriegsmarine could not find him, she decided, she would find him herself, and this time she did not waste time with the Germans.[6]

And so it was that a Catholic priest walked into Oehrn's room one day. He had never seen the priest in his life. He had not requested one because he was not a Catholic. But the priest seemed to know him. "Are you Victor Oehrn?" he asked.[7]

Oehrn said that he was. "In that case," said the priest, "I bring you greetings from Fraulein Renate von Winterfeld in Rome. If you would like to send her a reply, I will deliver it for you. If you cannot write, you may dictate your reply to me." He stood and waited for Oehrn's response.

Oehrn was astounded. He could not comprehend what he had just seen and heard. Like the majority of Wehrmacht officers, he was Evangelical Lutheran, and he had been taught since childhood to avoid Catholicism like the plague (*mit Feuerzange anfassen*). Admittedly, this attitude had begun to change in Rome, where the visible manifestations of the church were everywhere. The priest he met there, a German Jesuit (and convert from Lutheranism) named Hulsen, had worked as hard to explain Catholicism to Oehrn as Levin had done to explain Judaism, and like Levin, he had succeeded to an extent in changing Oehrn's original impression. But the church had never made an impression on him until that day on the Bitter Seas when it found him for Renate. "I was only a grain of sand in the Egyptian desert, but she took the time for me in any case. She did something in this awful war for two young people that revealed, in my opinion, an essential part of her inmost substance." That essential idea—that an organization so large and powerful could care for "a grain of sand in the desert"—impressed Oehrn. After the priest left with his letter to Renate, he resolved to do everything in his power to recover fully. Renate loved him so much that she found him in the desert, so much that she wanted to marry him not knowing if or when he would ever return. He would return that love, he decided, by returning to her, alive and healthy, no matter what he had to do or how long it took. The visit of this unnamed priest became the turning point in his captivity.[8]

He began to pray regularly, but not the prayers he had learned in childhood and not necessarily formal prayer, for formal religion held no attraction for him. Judaism was out of the question, of course, despite his many conversations with Levin. He respected it as he had respected the Islam of his childhood: from a distance. Nor did he make any move toward Catholicism, although under the circumstances it would not have been surprising if he had. God, as the church saw Him, did not appeal to Oehrn. Prayer, as the church knew it, did not suit him. It would be more correct to say that Victor Oehrn fashioned his faith from what he knew of others, defined his own image of God, and clung tenaciously to both of them throughout his captivity: "I spent every evening in prayer. I always remembered the prayers my mother taught me, but my own prayer was different and always as follows: 'I ask God, the Lord who created everything, to give me the strength to endure every pain, every difficulty, and I ask for the great good fortune to be able to stand once again before Re, and not to disappoint her.' That was all. I said it every evening."

In April 1943 his casts came off and he began to exercise. His joints, frozen at first, began to free up like branches in a spring thaw: first his fingers, then his arm, then his shoulder and his leg. Toward the end of spring he began to walk. Soon he felt well enough to begin exploring the hospital cage, and very soon after that he began to think of escape. To be truthful, there was not much to think about. He was still very stiff and sore, and he moved slowly. Even if he succeeded in crawling under the wire and out into the hostile territory of occupied Egypt, the British Army had a price on the head of each escapee and the local citizenry would have had no hesitation in turning him over for it. The safety of his own front line, so close when he was captured, no longer existed; the last remnants of the Afrika Korps had surrendered in May. Ironically, there was an easy way out, but he felt prevented by honor from taking it. The camp commander had offered him the use of a jeep for day trips into the neighboring towns of Ismailah or Genaifa, asking only for Oehrn's word of honor that he would not try to escape. Oehrn was impressed, but he refused the offer.

Then one day he heard from the camp doctor that an exchange of prisoners was being contemplated. Of course, he was told, only the very badly wounded and perhaps the mental cases would be exchanged; everyone else would probably be sent to Canada or Australia. But he also knew that many men on both sides had turned the machinery of repatriation to their own benefit, including his own commander in chief, Karl Dönitz (who had feigned madness to gain early release from a British POW camp after World War I). It was worth a try.

Ironically, however, the recovery for which he had worked and prayed so long had been remarkable, and he had been told by his doctor that the chances of success were now between 1 and 2 percent. He could think of only one way to improve upon those odds. With only the knowledge of the doctor and the sickroom attendant (who ate most of his rations), he began to starve himself to death. Within weeks he looked gaunt, and by the time the repatriation committee finally arrived, he was failing fast. "Everything about me looked as I had hoped. Pale, emaciated, bandages still on my shoulders, a stricken young man who did not have the strength to deal with his injuries." If the committee had not arrived when it did, he thinks, he would have had to break off his fast to save his life.

The committee examined Oehrn closely. Notes were taken and mumbled discussions took place. They moved to the next case without a word to him. Whether the ruse worked he did not know, nor would he know until it happened (typically these exchanges were conducted suddenly and secretly). At about this time he remembered something that had happened to him two years earlier in Paris. It seemed a lifetime ago now. He was in a nightclub called the Don Juan one evening when a gypsy approached him and offered to tell him his fortune. Not wanting to waste his money, he refused. She came back several times during the evening, and each time he declined. Finally, just before dawn, the woman said she would tell Oehrn's future for nothing, and what she told him was so unbelievable that he discounted it as rubbish. "You will go back to war," she said, "and you will be critically wounded. Within two years you will be back, and you will marry and have two children." Everything the woman told him, he reflected idly, had come true so far, and it had been one year since his capture. Would he be back in another year?

All his suffering seemed worthwhile when, one morning, Victor Oehrn's name appeared on a list of prisoners ordered to prepare for a move. A cursory examination of the list told him that, indeed, this was the group of severely injured prisoners that were to be repatriated. Elated, he began to make his final calls on friends and acquaintances, but his elation turned to bitter disappointment when, almost immediately after the group was told to assemble for transport, he was pulled from the ranks and told to wait behind. Apparently he did not look so bad after all (an impression he probably encouraged by walking around the compound without his stick). Another prisoner was selected to take his place, and the group left the camp without him. A medical examination was ordered, and as he tried, pathetically, to look once more like a dying man, he became more restless and despairing than ever. He was also confused. He had not been returned to the compound. Perhaps they did not know what to do with him. Perhaps there was a penalty for deceiving the committee. Perhaps it was an administrative mixup.

At last, in late afternoon, a jeep pulled up and he was told to get in. "Where am I going?" he asked the driver. The driver was not allowed to tell him, and as soon as he heard that, a terrible light flashed on inside his brain. "Then I will tell you. You are taking me to Mahdi."

He was indeed taken to the Allied interrogation center at Mahdi—the place he had dreaded for months. Happily, it was not what he had expected. He was still a prisoner behind a wire. He was put in a cell and offered a cellmate, but he refused, suspecting (probably correctly) that anyone in a cell with him would be an informer. He was closely watched. He began to play the invalid again, even alone in his cell. One day he hobbled around the wire and sat down, as if in pain, at a certain spot. The next day he did the same, and as he approached the spot he saw a stool. He was still uncertain about his future. He did not know, because nobody told him, if he was going home to Germany or onto the next boat for Fremantle.

The interrogations were not as unpleasant as he had expected. When he arrived, he was greeted by a commander in the United States Navy who knew all about him. His interrogation sessions, which lasted for several weeks, took the form of casual discussions between equals. No effort was made to force information from him, and he shared very little of value voluntarily. When asked about U-boat operations, Oehrn refused to answer. He was surprised to hear more than a few questions about the German resistance movements. He had the overall impression that the American (whom he declines to name) was probing him to determine his state of mind after a year in captivity, and he was determined to show that neither his patriotism nor his resolve was diminished.

Once again Oehrn's perceptions had been changed. The American was his enemy, but as time went on, the two men became unlikely friends who trusted each other and talked frankly. After each man had established his ground and Oehrn had shown his unwillingness to compromise, their regular encounters were almost enjoyable. It was from the American, in fact, in the early autumn of 1943, that Victor Oehrn finally received the word he had been waiting for: he would be returning to Germany. But the American seemed subdued as he conveyed the news. "I want to tell you

Victor Oehrn. This portrait was made in January 1944 after Oehrn's return from British captivity. It shows a man still ravaged by the effects of multiple gunshot injuries, sixteen months as a prisoner of war, and several weeks of voluntary starvation. (Victor Oehrn)

something," he said, "not as an American officer, but as a friend. I have spoken to hundreds of German prisoners, and things in Germany are not as you think they are." Oehrn told him he was wrong, that Germany and the Western Allies shared a common cause and that the Allies were mistaken to attack Germany in the West while she was fighting communism in the East. "You have told me that I am returning to a country I will not recognize," he concluded, "but I am looking forward to going home, and whether things in Germany are good or bad, she is my country and she needs me."

The American smiled sadly. Oehrn was not the first man to leave his office without believing him; he would have to find out the hard way. He stood and extended his hand. "You will be sent home now, Kapitän Oehrn. You will be told many different things along the way, even that you are not going home to Germany, but do not believe them. You are going home. I tell you this now so you will know later that I have never lied to you." They parted with a handshake.

The American officer had not lied to Victor Oehrn. On 3 November 1943, after sixteen months in various British hospitals and POW camps and a tortuous route through Port Said and Barcelona, he landed a free man in Marseilles. Two weeks later he reported for duty at BdU Operations at Lager Koralle in Berlin.

In December he married Renate von Winterfeld.

Every Day a Sunday

We were all infected with the Nazi bacillus, and since we were, it is unthinkable that the war could have turned out any differently. The leadership knew this and it fit in with their plans. Lüth was also a Nazi. He could not have been anything else. But he was a good leader of men, who cared for his crew, who looked after his people and always had an ear for their problems. The suffering and death of the men in the ships he sank was just one of those things. . . . What else could he have done? Could he have saved any of them after all?

—Theodor Petersen

NEXT!

Triton, King of the Seas, belched loudly as another man was dragged to the foot of his throne. Like the prisoners before him, he was dressed like a beggar and covered from head to foot in diesel oil. The king yawned and began to pick his nose ostentatiously. "Name?"

"Schmidt, your Majesty."

"Well, what do you want?" Triton leaned forward to see better. "You are a wretched little thing, aren't you?" The crowd around the rickety throne laughed hysterically, and Triton, a huge smile on his face, nodded and held up one filthy hand for silence. "*Guards!* Give this man a whack for impertinence."

Two men stepped forward. Schmidt bent over and was smacked soundly on his bottom with a pine plank. Triton sighed, his eyes closed, his wig askew, his finger still in his nose. "What was that you wanted again?"

"Holy Baptism, your Majesty."

Triton frowned and waved his hand limply. "Take him away. Work on him for a while and then we'll see." The crowd went wild. Poor Schmidt was dragged off for another round of public humiliation, physical abuse, and chemical poisoning. He was smiling as he went. For King Triton was only a shipmate named Grobelny in a false beard. His court was the weather deck of a gigantic U-boat. And Walter Schmidt was having fun.

Wolfgang Lüth, the commander of U-181, laughed and clapped along with the rest of the crew, but as Schmidt was led away and the next man brought before the king, he separated from the crowd, walked over to the railing, lit a cigar, and gazed out at a horizon as empty and as blue as his Führer's eyes. It was 16 October 1942. U-181 was on the equator, five hundred nautical miles southwest of Freetown and headed south at seven knots toward the Cape of Good Hope. The sun was out. The weather deck was too hot for bare feet. The temperature in the engine room was approximately 140° Fahrenheit. The ceremony going on behind him made it all the more difficult to believe that nine months earlier the ice on his last boat was so thick that hammers had to be used to knock it off.

LÜTH had been a U-boat commander for almost three years in October 1942. His performance during those years, if not the stuff of legend, had been better than adequate, and he had matured in the job. His first boat was U-9, a type II Einbaum commissioned in 1935 and the namesake of Otto Weddigen's old SM U-9. In four patrols he sank three ships, the first two in a farcical manner. His second patrol, a mining operation, was saved by the luck usually associated with fools. During Operation Weserübung he had been assigned to a position outside Bergen, where he was thoroughly bored, and shortly after the invasion he had fired four defective magnetic torpedoes at the Polish destroyer *Grom*, all of which missed or misfired. A picture of Lüth slouched against the tower of U-9 during this time shows a scruffy and thoroughly dissolute young man with a bad attitude.

After U-9 came command of U-138. It was at this time, June 1940, that Lüth became irritated at having to leave the front for her commissioning, but ultimately he won the Knight's Cross as her commander. Curiously, after almost three months spent commissioning and shaking down his new boat, Lüth was allowed to make only two war patrols, both of them in the Western Approaches during the wild month of October 1940, before he had to leave for command of a third boat, the larger type IXB boat U-43. Within three months one of his watch officers allowed her to sink in Lorient harbor. Another man might have been cashiered, but Lüth was eventually forgiven, and over the next twelve months he chased the *Bismarck* in U-43, cheered Operation Barbarossa, saw the untouchable Americans in his crosshairs, and sank twenty-two ships in five patrols.

Five days before Victor Oehrn left Wilhelmshaven for the North Atlantic in May 1940, Lüth had departed the same harbor in U-9 for the English Channel. They would be the only two German U-boat commanders at sea for most of the month, and they made a striking contrast. They were as different as day and night. Oehrn was a handsome man, not dashing but handsome in the saturnine way of a sleek and well-fed burgher. His appearance on the bridge of U-37 in May 1940, every hair in place, calls to mind the image of a successful businessman looking only slightly out of place lashed to the wing of a small airplane. Wolfgang Lüth was a plain-looking man (although he looked less so after a shave and wearing a pressed uniform), bald, with a pointed head, a large nose, and a gap between his two front teeth wide enough to push a pencil through. Oehrn was urbane, a diplomat, a thinker. Lüth had neither diplomacy nor tact, he was remarkably crude, and he was pushy, prying, and utterly prudish regarding other people's personal lives. He was not a sentimental man.

More to the point, there was a critical difference in the way the two men went about their work. Oehrn was tentative; torn between the desire to succeed and the need to temper his destruction with charity. He sank ships because he had to. Lüth was as cold-blooded about his work as any predatory animal. On 9 May 1940, for example, he sank the French submarine *Doris* off the Dutch coast. When the *Doris* blew up and bits and pieces of her crew rained down on U-9's bridge, he was unmoved. "'Poor fellows!' said [my watch officer], 'they were only U-boat sailors like us.' But war drives feelings like this into the background. It is either you or me. If we hadn't sunk them they would have sunk us or one of our comrades."[1] This attitude was not uncommon, but Lüth held it more firmly than most of his fellow commanders. "He had no idea of the suffering he caused," said his friend Theodor Petersen sadly, "when he sank ships."[2]

As his career progressed and his numbers mounted, Lüth's behavior became worse. He developed a reputation as a political man. He was one of the few officers in the U-Bootwaffe who openly admired National Socialism, and he took every opportunity that arose to say something favorable about the government or the party. His mean streak became more pronounced. As Theodor Petersen said, he had no idea of the misery he caused every time he let loose a torpedo. In April 1941 he shot the

Wolfgang Lüth, "a good leader of men, who cared for his crew." He looked over them like a stern but well-intentioned German father, from the day they reported aboard his U-boat to the last day of the war. (Author's collection)

French sailing ship *Notre Dame du Chatelet* to matchsticks and killed several men, not because she was a threat to anyone but because he wanted some target practice and he was smarting from the tongue-lashing Karl Dönitz had given him for scuttling his own boat in Lorient. "Not something I would have done," murmured Karl-Friedrich Merten, who had once let a similar ship sail. Lüth's prudish sense of morality was very annoying. He nagged his men to get married and have children; if they were married, he nagged them to be faithful and have even more children for the good of the Reich. He restricted them to the boat so they could not visit bordellos, he followed his officers around to make sure they did not cheat on their wives, he banned pinups and "unhealthy" reading material from his boats, and he never drank. It is not easy to imagine Lüth relaxing in the Scheherazade. Petersen dragged him into the Lido once, and he was "shocked" to learn that there were nude women inside. Clearly, his behavior was odd, and many people thought it approached eccentricity. "Wolfgang Lüth," said Lothar-Günther Buchheim, "was the craziest man I ever knew." [3]

Few commanders with such character flaws could have survived. There is no doubt that some were fervent Nazis, some were morally straitlaced, some were bullies, some were even psychopaths. But none of the top commanders, the aces, carried all the baggage Lüth carried, and yet he survived and prospered in the U-Bootwaffe. By the time he left the front, he was second only to Otto Kretschmer in tonnage sunk, and his career, which lasted from the first day of the war to the last, was arguably more impressive and more rewarding than that of any commander in the service. Such hardly seems fair, or even fitting, until one realizes that Wolfgang Lüth's faults were like so much chaff compared to his one great virtue. This virtue, which made him a superb military officer and a tolerable human being as well, was his sublime ability to lead men.

The topic of leadership is appropriate for this discussion, even though it is hard to describe and harder to quantify. "It may be regarded as a quality," wrote Jürgen Oesten, "which you have or have not (it is maybe luck). It is useful in any profession where human beings are involved. It means that you have authority automatically." [4] Victor Oehrn takes a less clinical view. "Leadership," he wrote, "is the greatest gift a man can receive." [5] Both Oesten and Oehrn seem to believe that leaders are born, not made. Wolfgang Lüth tended toward the opposite belief: that leadership qualities can be taught. It is an old debate, and the Kriegsmarine went both ways. It tried to select officer candidates with leadership potential, then did its best to teach them good leadership skills.

Formal instruction in leadership principles took two forms. Classroom training at the Marineschule made heavy use of case studies from World War I in which a leadership problem was presented and alternative solutions discussed. The primary textbook was the turgid *Leitfaden* of Siegfried Sorge, "a dry and pretty boring book, to say the least," wrote Peter Hansen. "I never managed to go beyond the first twenty pages." [6] Practical training began in earnest on board the training cruisers and lasted in one form or another until an officer took command of his own boat. For Karl-Friedrich Merten, both forms were useful, and he discussed their merits enthusiastically. For Jürgen Oesten the classroom training did not make a lasting impression, and he thought the only practical training that mattered came after an officer entered the U-Bootwaffe. "I do not recollect any 'leadership training' as such," he wrote in response to a question. "In my opinion, the actual training [normally occurred] during the period of service as watch officer or second in command. The better the commanding officer the better will be the training." [7] Whole families of good commanders could be created this way, he pointed out, down to the third or fourth generation.

There must have been sufficient opportunities for leadership training because most U-boat commanders were adequate leaders and many were exemplary. In fact, one has to admit that the quality Oesten described existed at a very high level throughout the U-Bootwaffe; there is no other way to explain its performance as a military organization. Unfortunately, those who were judged to be good leaders are very often the ones who have the most trouble describing how they led. Reinhard Reche, for example, describes his philosophy of leadership as "self-control and success," admirable in simplicity and brevity but hardly instructive. [8]

Certain characteristics of good leadership are mentioned repeatedly. A leader must be courageous. He must be capable. "[U-boat commanders] have to be good," observes Jürgen Oesten, "because there is no hiding place. If they are not efficient and qualified they have to be replaced at once." He must be firm but considerate. He should be, to some extent, a decent man, for people usually demand more of their leaders than of themselves, and his example, wrote Karl-Friedrich Merten, is his "most important asset [in] personnel leadership." It helps if a leader is successful in battle. "If a man is a success," noted Wolfgang Lüth, "his men will follow him even if he is a fool." Finally, and most important, a leader must care for those he leads. "Be always available for the men and on constant watch for their welfare," said Erich Topp. "Respect the man, and have a heart for him. Give him the feeling that he is an integrated member of the 'crew,' for only a crew being a 'band of brothers' will have success." [9]

It is this final aspect, the responsibility of a commander to his crew, that formed the leadership style of Wolfgang Lüth. It drove him as a leader. We know this because Lüth took the most time and trouble to explain his idea of U-boat leadership, and he authored the single most important first-person document on the subject, a lecture he delivered to a convention of Kriegsmarine officers meeting in Weimar in December 1943. This lecture, which Lüth entitled "Problems of Leadership in a Submarine," was an immediate and sustained success, first as a teaching tool for the Kriegs-marine, then as a legitimate source of information for historians. It is the best-written description of the mind games that so often went on inside a U-boat. It is one of the most candid and unexpurgated statements of personal opinion from a commander in wartime.

"Problems of Leadership" is not a very well-written document. If any-one else had tried to run a boat as Lüth describes, he would probably have failed. Structurally it is a mess. It rambles; it skips from one subject to another; it contains material that is irrelevant, provocative, and blatantly political. It is a classic example of speech as a "stream of consciousness," where the speaker says whatever occurs to him. To borrow from an old saw, if Cicero had presented this lecture, he would have shot himself—if he had owned a gun. There are problems in substance as well as style. Most of the examples Lüth uses are taken from long patrols in the South Atlantic and Indian Oceans. The Indian Ocean, in particular, though sometimes dangerous, was by and large a quiet, almost leisurely, theater in which boredom, not bombs, was the main threat. "[If] I may quote a man who was on all the three boats I had during the war," wrote Jürgen Oesten, "'compared with North Atlantic convoy work . . . travelling in the Indian Ocean was like a holiday.'" [10] For that reason, the applica-bility of Lüth's style to U-Bootwaffe operations was tenuous, and many of the commanders who heard or read "Problems" were disappointed or amused by it.

Few U-boat commanders operated in southern waters during the war. The center of operations for the U-Bootwaffe, the *Schwerpunkt,* to use a word Dönitz loved, was always in the North Atlantic. Those who did go to southern waters included several of Dönitz's best commanders. Karl-Friedrich Merten, Jürgen Oesten, and Wolfgang Lüth all crossed the equa-tor at one time or another. Merten was the first, sinking three ships in the approaches to Freetown in September 1941, and he was also one of the first commanders to operate in the waters around Cape Town in 1942. Oesten, after two years in various shore positions, took command of U-861 in September 1943 and made two marathon patrols, the first from France to Penang on the Malaya Peninsula in 1944, the second from Penang to Norway in 1945. Among the other commanders who went south were Georg Lassen, the seventh-ranking ace of the war; Werner Hartmann, who had to give his boat to Victor Oehrn in 1940; Ernst Sobe, one of Dönitz's twelve apostles, who died off the West African coast in

October 1942 after sinking his first ship; and Heinz Eck, the only man in the U-Bootwaffe executed for a war crime.

In April 1942 Lüth was relieved as commander of U-43 by his first watch officer, Hans-Joachim Schwantke, and sent to Stettin to commission the gigantic type IXD2 U-cruiser U-181. For a commander to be given a fourth boat was unusual. Most second-generation commanders, like their predecessors the years before, were getting shore commands or staff positions instead, and some, like Endrass, were dead. For Lüth the assignment was an incredible stroke of luck. U-181 would make him famous. Over the next eighteen months he made two war patrols: the first, four months long, in the waters around Cape Town and Lourenco Marques; the second, almost seven months long, as far north as Tromelin and Mauritius. During these patrols he sank as many ships as most aces did in a career, and he won the highest awards the Reich had to offer. When he returned from the second patrol he found himself a media hero as Günther Prien had been back in 1939, and it was because of his performance as commander of U-181 that he enjoyed a subsequent career on shore unequaled by any other wartime U-Bootwaffe officer.

Both of Lüth's patrols in U-181 had certain similar characteristics. First, they were long. A routine operation at the Cape of Good Hope required two six-week passages, and to make the trip worthwhile, a period of at least a month was considered the minimum time "on station." During Lüth's second patrol, an at-sea refueling stretched his time on station to four months. These patrols were also monotonous. The huge convoys that lumbered back and forth across the Atlantic simply did not exist in the Indian Ocean. Most ships were found, and sunk, individually, and days or weeks might go by between them. Attacks by enemy warships were rare; air attacks were less likely than in the North Atlantic. But a patrol that was long and boring was no less dangerous for a boat. It led to complacency, laziness, irritability, and bad health. Lüth's leadership style, therefore, revolved around the single idea that everything possible must be done to make the patrol seem shorter and less boring. Leadership was a constant search for ways to keep the crew entertained.

"Problems of Leadership," which is about ten thousand words long and would have taken over an hour to read, is divided into five uneven sections. In each section Lüth discusses one of the factors he thought necessary for good leadership in a U-boat: discipline, success, shipboard routine, the example of the officers, and "real spiritual leadership for the men, together with a genuine concern for their personal welfare." It is as good an outline as any for such a lecture, even if Lüth adheres to it only casually. (Erich Topp used a similar outline for his lecture, "Philosophy of a Submarine," which he presented after the war to an audience quite different from Lüth's.) These major sections are preceded by a salutation to Karl Dönitz, the senior officer present, and a short introduction, in which Lüth describes daily life in a U-boat at sea, and followed by a final exhortation that is as provocative as it is inspiring.

Lüth devotes a great deal of attention to the first factor, discipline, which is surprising because neither Merten nor Oesten will admit to having any disciplinary problems. "Of course," wrote Merten, "there have not been many commanders with analogous lengths of patrols [as Lüth's], but as far as my extended patrol is concerned [his last, to Cape Town, in 1942] . . . I cannot remember any disciplinary difficulties with either officers or crew members."[11] Oesten was more direct than Merten. "No disciplinary problems," he stated flatly. "I am that arrogant to believe that it was sufficient punishment if I took a poor view of a mistake someone may have made."[12] Lüth apparently did have problems, and not just petty ones. Theft and insubordination are mentioned, for example, both serious offenses for which the usual penalties involved time in the brig.

His initial premise is beyond reproach: on a long war patrol, orthodox punishments are meaningless. Two weeks in the brig, awarded for some unspecified infraction a month into a patrol and scheduled to commence as soon as the boat returns, would be silly. "In the meantime we experience success and danger together in which the man proves his worth. We return home feeling triumphant at having accomplished something. Am I to lock the man up then for an offense committed months ago? I consider this unwise." The logical step for a commander to take is to apply immediate punishment as best he can, which Lüth did. But some of Lüth's ideas about punishment, or indeed crime, seem odd. One example he uses is straightforward. Impertinence to a superior usually called for three days in the brig; Lüth's punishment at sea was three days sleeping on the deckplates. Another is out of proportion. He instituted what he called "china muster," a weekly inspection of the boat's crockery, and if he decided that too much had been broken, he forced the mess attendant (a position that usually rotated through the crew roster) to "eat out of a can for three days." To most commanders, the loss of crockery was the least of their concerns. The job of mess attendant was a thankless one, and to punish a man for breaking dishes was ridiculous; after a good depth charge attack, everyone would have to eat out of cans, including the commander himself. A quizzical glance may also be given to Lüth's practice of keeping "fruit, chocolate, and similar things" locked up. "Fruit as a reward for a job well done or withheld as punishment for greediness is a good means for education on a long trip." It is also part of a good diet and a means of preventing disease.[13]

"If [a man] is offending the regulations on board, he must be punished," wrote Erich Topp, "but after that the offense must be wiped out and harmony restored."[14] Lüth echoed this view: "In almost every case the object of punishment is to educate the man, not to destroy him." As if to reinforce this belief, Lüth usually ended the description of a punishment by saying that the miscreant turned out well in the end. One crewman, for example, a lookout, put the boat at risk by failing to spot an approaching bomber. "I did not punish him," said Lüth. "The looks he got from his comrades when the depth charges started to explode were punishment enough. . . . He is now an excellent man." Another crewman was a "chronic grumbler," which could become most annoying in the close quarters of a U-boat. Lüth called the crew together, berated the man, threatened him with being sent to the Russian front, and gave him two weeks extra duty. "He continued to do his work so well that he now wears the Iron Cross, and I have recommended him to my successor as a combat helmsman."

To the second factor, success, Lüth gave short shrift, saying only that "success is easy to take; it raises morale. My efforts on board, however, are directed toward keeping up the crew's morale when things are not going well." Anyone will follow a successful fool, he is saying, but men will follow a good leader even if he is not successful. This is true, and there are plenty of examples. Perhaps the reason why Lüth did not go into this any further is that he never had the opportunity to lead men "when things were not going well." On only one of his sixteen patrols as a commander did he return without at least one pennant; during his two patrols in U-181 he sank twelve and ten ships respectively. Using his own logic, he could not help being a good leader.

No warship, unless she is in the midst of battle, can be efficient for long without an established routine. Daily life on board requires it. In a U-boat it was even more important that a routine be followed because, as Lüth observed, there was no natural order to U-boat life: "There is no constant change between day and night, for the lights have to burn all the time within the boat. There are no Sundays and no weekdays, and there is no regular change of seasons. Therefore life is monotonous and without rhythm." An artificial order was preserved in U-181 by the existence of regular mealtimes, daily meetings, special schedules for Sundays and holidays, and periodic military evolutions such as color ceremonies and seabag inspections. The lights were always dimmed for supper. Music was played in the evenings from 2000 to 2030. The off-duty crew was allowed to sleep in on Sundays, but when they turned out they had to change into clean shirts (if they had any), and when they sat down to dinner they were served from a special Sunday menu.

"The spirit of the crew," wrote Erich Topp, "is dependent to a great extent on the example which is set by the officers," and Lüth takes pains to describe how his officers were expected to behave.[15] His standards, however, had less to do with setting an example for the crew than with how Lüth himself thought an officer should act. Most commanders did not care how their officers behaved among themselves or what they did when they were off duty as long as they behaved themselves in front of the men. This was Merten's attitude. On patrol his officers "had to be accustomed not to let themselves go, either in outward appearance, or in clothing or habits."[16] Nobody was allowed in the wardroom, for example, unless he wore a shirt. On shore they could do what they liked, as long as they didn't miss a sailing. Lüth, in contrast, was utterly censorious with his officers at sea and in port, and he expected their conduct to be blameless at all times.

The last section of "Problems of Leadership," on "real spiritual leadership for the men, together with a genuine concern for their personal welfare," drew the longest discussion from Lüth and the most interest from others who have read and quoted the lecture. It touches on every aspect of a crewman's welfare, including his physical health, his mental state, and his moral condition. The first item discussed in this section, physical health and hygiene, was an obsession with Lüth:

> It is every submariner's duty to stay healthy. It is better to have a boil treated immediately than to wait until it has become big for fear of being called a sissy. A healthy way of life is necessary on board. I not only order every man to wear his woolen waistband, but I also repeat the order every evening at dusk over the radio. I do not permit drinking ice water in the tropics. I have forbidden young hands to smoke on an empty stomach, and I see to it that the mid-watch coffee is not made quite as strong as is usual in the Navy. . . . I have also had cases of gonorrhea and even syphilis on board which, however, could be cured by the doctor. Three days before shoving off I stop all shore leave without previous notice, so that the men will not make a last quick visit to the whorehouse.

His concern for health took two forms. The first was diet. Lüth was convinced that every health problem on board a U-boat was rooted in irregularity, and he took a lively interest in what his men ate, what they drank, and when they went to the toilet. The second was sex. Lüth did not disapprove of sexual relations between married partners (in fact, he encouraged them), but anything of a sexual nature in the confines of a U-boat, whether spoken, written, or displayed, he considered both mentally debilitating and physically dangerous. "I never had to deal with sexual problems on board," he boasted, "not even during the mission which lasted seven and one half months." All reading material was censored, pinups banned, and anything that might have "appealed to a man's lower instincts" was thrown overboard. Lüth admitted to having cases of venereal disease on board, but it was not because he hadn't done his best to prevent it.

Merten was not as maniacal as Lüth, and he did not go to the same lengths to ensure the health of his crew. To him, the most important thing for a sailor was to be clean, something that was not easy, or really necessary, in a U-boat. Most crews became filthy at a uniform rate, and nobody noticed it; but once a man did bathe, he soon realized that everyone around him smelled like a garbage can. Thus if one man bathed, everyone had to bathe. Merten is very proud of his solution: "We had mounted a pipe with four shower roses between the two aft antennas and connected it to the upper deck seawater connection." It remained a permanent fixture during the entire time Merten's boat was below the twentieth parallel. Every evening at dusk the entire crew, led by their officers and checked off on a clipboard by the *Obersteuermann* (first mate), would troop up to the weather deck with soap and towel to take a shower. "Two men at a time were allowed on the upper deck to take a shower and to clean themselves with the excellent sea water soap, then provided. Of course during the showering period the watch on the bridge was extended by either myself or the IWO, so that the boat was no more endangered than during gun practice or weapons cleaning. Naturally all the officers and the commander also took part in this refreshing and hygienic measure." [17] None of Lüth's worrying about his men's eating habits, bowels, clothing, or sexual habits seems to have done them any more good than Merten's regime of daily showers. "We had on U-68 on all our cruises under my command not a single disease due to dirt or infection," he brags, "neither diesel oil scabies, nor *furunculosis* [commonly called the red dog] nor German measles appeared, and surprisingly also no catarrhal diseases." [18]

Oesten did nothing in this area. Health and hygiene were not problems for him. There were, he claims, normally no infections on the boat because "the germs do not like the pressure differential." He did have a case of ear infection, which the ship's doctor cured in a very basic way: "Special chisels were prepared in the engine room for cutting the bone and scraping away what had to go." About cleanliness he says only that "the salt water soap was very good," which leads one to assume that formal shower parties led by the boat's officers did not take place in U-861; in fact, Oesten gives the clear impression of believing that both Lüth and Merten made a lot of heavy weather out of their patrols.[19]

Having seen to the physical needs of his crew, Lüth took even more time and trouble to see to their mental, emotional, and recreational needs. He knew the danger of a crewman with nothing to do. The man would become bored, dispirited, and irritable, and he would lose the fighting edge that was necessary for survival in wartime. The mind must be kept active, the soul pure: "The officers must be inventive in order to keep up the men's enthusiasm, particularly on such long trips. I do not arrange everything that should be done during the off-duty hours myself, but call the officers together and tell them: 'See to it that we get something organized again. Perhaps we could do this or that, this way or that way,' and I add some suggestions but remain in the background and let the men do the rest." It is this part of Lüth's lecture that has intrigued his readers, for it is here that his genius for leadership becomes most evident. Many commanders were able to find ways to keep their crews busy on long patrols. That Lüth was able to find or invent so many things (despite his words, it was he who usually led the way in doing "this or that") was remarkable, equivalent, say, to entertaining half a dozen people on a stalled elevator for a week or driving a busload of first graders nonstop from coast to coast. It was, he said, a case of making "every day a Sunday."

Examples of Lüth's perspicacity in finding things for the crew to occupy their time included all the normal diversions: music, books, classes, a boat's newspaper. Every night a *Wunschkonzert* (request concert) was held (the term was borrowed from a popular German radio program), during which records were played on the boat's phonograph. When classical music was featured, impresario Lüth would take the microphone to present background information. "The crew really did listen with a little more appreciation after that." Sentimental songs were kept to a minimum because they "often do not fit into a system which is to make the men tough." Jazz and other decadent Western music were not allowed. Books were available for everyone and magazines were passed out according to a schedule; crewmen were encouraged to discuss them among themselves and with the boat's officers. Classes were held on any subject someone was willing to teach: "the Atlantic, its climate and fauna, about the Gulf Stream, flying fishes, and the trade winds . . . flags and insignias, plotting

Lüth sitting in relative leisure on the bridge of U-181. This was not a luxury most commanders in the North Atlantic could afford, nor was this their usual apparel, but Lüth was in the Indian Ocean at the time, far away from the war and more worried about boredom than enemy attack. (Author's collection)

and chart reading." The boat's newspaper, which consisted of news from the wireless, shipboard gossip, contest results, poetry, the latest tonnage totals, and interesting trivia about the places they were passing, was printed and distributed daily.

One of Lüth's favorite leadership tools was competition. He made a contest out of anything, no matter how dull or how odd it was. After the boat's doctor, Lothar Engel, had presented his de riguere lecture on hygiene and venereal disease, Lüth arranged a poetry contest on the same subjects. The winning entries were predictably vulgar. He had a tall tales contest, in which contestants tried to outdo each other in telling lies. He held a shipboard Olympic Games, a drawing contest, chess and card tournaments, and a singing contest that was broadcast (with commentary) over the address system. He encouraged a sense of competition with the few other boats in the Indian Ocean by printing each boat's tonnage totals in the newspaper.

He had a talent for taking advantage of the unexpected. One could only manufacture so many things to do within the hull of a U-boat, even a boat that was eighty-eight meters long with three deck guns and her own refrigerator. Thus it became very important to adapt external events to fit the need. A sinking was always best for interrupting the tedium, and Lüth liked to turn them into special events. During a chase he would summon crewmen onto the bridge to look at the ship through binoculars and identify it. During an attack he would keep the crew informed of torpedo firing, target angle, expected run time, hit or miss. After sinking the Panamanian steamer *Amaryllis* in December 1942, he allowed his crew to haul an entire sheep aboard; fresh meat was rare on a long cruise and the sheep was chopped up and roasted with enthusiasm. (Sometimes this kind of thing could backfire. In September 1942, after much pleading from the crew, Karl-Friedrich Merten pulled several large boxes from the wreckage of the British ship *Trevilley* and pried them open to find a load of waterproof trousers and hats.)

He was a strong believer in celebrating holidays and birthdays. Any holiday, no matter how obscure, was the occasion for a party. The most important of these, of course, was Christmas. On Christmas Eve the officers' mess was dissolved; the entire crew ate together, presents were distributed, and songs were sung around a Christmas tree made out of green toilet paper. But Easter was also cause for celebration, and so were Mother's Day and Father's Day. Lüth made a lot of these last two because he had such strong views on the value of family and the responsibilities of parenthood (by the time he returned from his last patrol he had three children). Birthdays were celebrated in U-181 with songs, parties, cakes, and cognac. The day the boat crossed the equator, Lüth held a wild crossing ceremony preceded by weeks of publicity and commemorated with hand-lettered certificates. Finally, U-181 was one of the few boats in the U-Bootwaffe that observed the Führer's birthday.

"Problems in Leadership" contains a high level of political content. There are several statements in praise of National Socialism, Adolf Hitler, and the Third Reich, which do nothing for the lecture and indeed detract from it. They are there either because Lüth wanted to placate his audience (which included a number of senior party functionaries) or because he genuinely wanted to show what a good National Socialist he was. The latter seems more likely; after all, he was a returning hero accepting his laurels, not a suspect in front of a people's court, and in any case there was a higher degree of truckling than would usually have been expected in the former case. Even Dönitz, a master at playing politics for his own needs, must have cringed at the following: "The men must know what they are fighting for and must be eager to risk their lives for it. It is necessary to get rid of a certain passive philosophy in some of the men. On Sunday I sometimes dive and hold muster underwater to tell them something about the Reich, and the centuries-old struggle for it, and about the greatest men of our history. On the Führer's birthday I tell them something about his life and about my visit to Führer Headquarters. Another time I tell them about racial and population problems, all from the viewpoint of the struggle for the realization of the Reich." For what it is worth, nobody in Lüth's crew can remember these lectures. They probably never occurred, which is all the more reason to suspect that he used his lecture to demonstrate his fervor for National Socialism as well as his talents as a leader. He wraps himself around a sociological axle during a simple discussion on the use of reading material as a leadership tool (a valid concept that should have taken two or three lines at the most):

> We had on board the volume of the 1933 issues of the illustrated news magazine *Die Wochenschau,* a very good paper, which still showed in its first number of January 1933 many pictures of Jews. The crew was at that time on the average only ten years old, and had never experienced anything like that. Then came the day of the assumption of power, the Reichstag fire, the day of Potsdam, the superhighways, the Reich Labor Service, etc. The men were surprised about many of these pictures, because they could not imagine that there had been times in Germany when all these things to which we are now accustomed were still being fought for.

And he cannot resist a plug for the New Order in his discussion of the boat's officers. "You can't let them hang the picture of the Führer on the left side of the bulkhead . . . and a picture of a girl from a box of candy on the left," he said, "that shows bad taste. The same is true if they like to listen to American and British jazz. Whether they like it or not has nothing to do with the matter. They simply must not like it, just as a German man must not like a Jewess." This last statement is ridiculous on its face, and it is made even more ridiculous by the fact that Lothar Engel, the doctor, was famous for his collection of jazz records, and the crew often played them in the torpedo rooms while Lüth was safely away on the bridge.

In the closing paragraph of "Problems of Leadership" Lüth stated, clearly and simply, a very simple truth: a commander's first obligation, his first thought, his first love, must be his crew. He blows the opportunity completely, wasting it on one last gratuitous wheeze of Nazi ideology. The result is a curious welding together of his greatest virtue, the virtue that led him to present the lecture in the first place and made him famous despite himself, and his greatest vice. Like most bad welds, it is not pretty: "It is the duty of every captain to have faith in his men; he must want to have faith in them, even if they have disappointed him at one time or another. For beyond this we know for a fact that our young men are thirsting for action with unqualified devotion. This is an important advantage over the Anglo-Americans. If our men are led into action united in the National Socialist spirit with revolutionary ardor, then they will always follow gladly onto new assignments and to new attacks. We must only show them respect and we must like them."

Reaction to "Problems of Leadership" was mixed. Five minutes after the lecture was over, the general consensus was that Lüth had missed badly. The U-Bootwaffe was fighting for its life. Poetry contests and broken crockery seemed frivolous and irrelevant. The ubiquitous Peter Hansen, who was in the audience, thought it was an awful lecture, "very far-fetched, totally unrealistic for the North Atlantic, and too patronizing towards officers and crews, treating them more like orphans than grown-ups." Hansen was not alone.

While there was a lot of "official" hot air and wind made by Karl Dönitz and his entourage in Berlin and Bernau regarding this much-discussed leadership [lecture], almost everyone who attended the presentation was . . . perplexed rather than wildly enthusiastic. Only yes-men like [FdU-West Kapitän zur See] Hans Rudolf Rösing were putting up a noisy show about it. Every front officer I talked to or whom I encountered on a one-to-one basis . . . thought it was daft, a lot of baloney [and] totally ridiculous—pure propaganda mostly. In fact, until the OKM and U-Boat Command cliques started to clap and holler there was a stunned silence and listeners seemed embarrassed at worst and slightly amused at best.[20]

Despite Hansen's observation, Lüth's lecture enjoyed initial acclaim. It was helped no doubt by enthusiasm at the higher levels of Kriegsmarine command, the "OKM and U-boat command cliques," and by his own ascendancy from U-boat commander to national hero to, eventually, the youngest Kapitän zur See in the Kriegsmarine and the last commandant of the Marineschule Mürwik. For a time it was used as an official text in the training of new officers.

After the war, "Problems of Leadership" followed its author into semi-obscurity. It was translated into English by the Office of Naval Intelligence in 1946, but it first became known to the general public outside of Germany when it was published in a book called *U-Boats at War* by Harald Busch (who felt the need to strip it of all references to Hitler or politics). Writers who have used parts of the lecture since then include Douglas Botting in *The U-Boats,* Richard Compton-Hall in *The Underwater War,* and Bodo Herzog and Günter Schomaekers in *Ritter der Tiefe/Graue Wölfe.* Only Compton-Hall made any attempt to analyze "Problems," observing tentatively that "Lüth was a devoted Nazi . . . but, that apart, his brand of leadership would have been admirable in any navy." Lüth's most eloquent critic may have been Lothar-Günther Buchheim in *The Boat.* Most readers do not know, because Buchheim does not tell them, that Lüth's lecture is the favorite reading material of the first watch officer, a fervent Nazi whom everyone else in the boat detests.[21]

The reactions of U-boat commanders to Lüth's lecture, like their reactions to Buchheim's books, prove only that they are a fickle bunch. "I think the leadership methods described in [the lecture] proved right," wrote Reinhard Reche. "There is certainly not a correct [or an] incorrect leadership [style]," wrote Erich Topp, "but Lüth [was] operating under quite different conditions and he perhaps [was] more devoted to National Socialism than I [was]." Karl-Friedrich Merten, who first read the lecture in 1991, was disappointed. Some of what Lüth had to say, he wrote, "embarrassed me very much." In one passage, for example, Lüth said that everyone had to learn to "hate his enemy without reservation." Such a sentiment was not acceptable to Merten, who thought it "repugnant and not the general feeling of educated officers." He took issue with Lüth's lectures on National Socialism, which he found "disturbing." He was genuinely surprised that Lüth, of all people, had ever felt the need to punish a man.[22]

He found the general content no better. "I was amazed by the pedantry and particularities [that seemed to be Lüth's] leading qualities," he wrote. "I never heard [about this] before, not even a rumor about this style of U-boat command." The most striking feature of Lüth's lecture would seem to be his strong support for National Socialism, but Merten fought for a different view. Just before he read the German text of "Problems of Leadership" he wrote: "In my opinion [Lüth] was not the man to write anything he would not stand for and there is no reason for him to accommodate a publically wellcomed [sic] opinion of the time." Afterward he changed his mind: "As a matter of fact, [it was] not your Nazi-like observations of Lüth that really impressed me, since I believe I have found the correct interpretation of his lecture, but all the other stuff he filled in this lecture to impress his present superiors."[23]

Ironically, one of the more positive reactions to "Problems of Leadership" came from a prominent American submarine commander, Edward L. Beach. "My general impression of the lecture is that it was right on target," he stated. "Making allowances for the differences in submarines and our own submariner experiences during the war, [his practices] would have applied perfectly well to us." He agreed that some of Lüth's methods were pedantic, "but so were mine, in a similar situation." Others he considered genuinely innovative and only wished that he had thought of them himself. As a prize in one of his competitions, for example, Lüth would stand a man's watch for him. "This had a double effect that no submariner would miss, but which others might: the skipper could stand any watch in the ship. . . . I don't know if I would have had the self-confidence to do that." Would Lüth's style have worked in one of Beach's boats? Probably not, "because both the boat and the crew would have been different. But he was smart enough that he would have thought up appropriate things for the same objective and they would have worked about as well."[24]

Lüth never intended for "Problems of Leadership" to be used as a leadership model, and he never pretended that the methods he outlined in the lecture would work for anyone but himself. "I have mentioned here a number of general examples," he said toward the end. "They are meant merely to serve as suggestions and can either be followed or changed according to temperament." There is little doubt that they worked for him. He brought four different crews safely home from patrol sixteen times. When U-181 returned to Bordeaux in October 1943 amid a media hurricane, his last crew hoisted forty-eight pennants on her periscope housing, one for each of the ships he had sunk in his career. His total of 227,000 GRT made him the second-ranking ace of the war (in any navy). When he staggered off the gangplank he was awarded the Knight's Cross with Oak Leaves, Swords, and Diamonds, the highest combat decoration normally available in the Wehrmacht. He left his crew, now minor celebrities themselves, shortly afterward, but in a sense he never left them. Over the next eighteen months he tried to stay in touch with as many of them as he could, and they would search him out for help. One man needed an apartment for his family; Lüth found him one. Another, a new commander himself, wanted Lüth to speak to his crew; Lüth took time away from a frantic schedule to do so.

"Problems of Leadership" should be recognized for what it is: an imperfect but illuminating glimpse into the practice of good leadership at the U-boat command level. It is the best glimpse we have, even though it is badly written, politically skewed, and easily mocked. To get a better idea of the qualities that made Lüth special, one is well advised to skip it and listen instead to his men; their bond with him has lasted over fifty years and transcends death. "Kapitän Lüth was a man to depend on," wrote Franz Persch, one of the crewmen on that last long patrol, "and I can say with great pride that his entire crew stood beside him and, as one would say in German, would go through fire for him." "There are no men like him anymore," sobbed Walter Schmidt.[25]

CHAPTER 10

A Bunch of Arabs

From about 1942 onwards, I can't remember anyone who loved U-boats. One tolerated them at best; nobody was enthusiastic about them anymore. . . . [We were] fatalistic, neither eager nor afraid. . . . More like a bunch of Arabs, really, than Germans.

—Peter Hansen

STOP the music, please." As Wolfgang Lüth held up his hand for silence, the smoke from the cigar between his fingers curled lazily toward the ceiling of an utterly silent room. The babble of conversation, hitherto loud and punctuated with laughter, had stopped. The clatter of glasses faded away. Cigarettes hung in midair. All eyes were upon him, and he paused, as if to appreciate the effect of his simple request. "Meine Herren, I have the latest personnel assignments from BdU." He took a puff on the cigar and flipped through the handful of telegrams he had in his hand. Idly he selected one and looked at it. He smiled. And as he held it up, a roomful of officers in dress blues and slicked-back haircuts watched him as though he were a small child with a loaded gun. He looked round the room, then gently removed the cigar from his mouth. "Unfortunately I've only got one combat assignment here," he said, "It's for Oberleutnant zur See Werner." He extended the telegram and smiled. The gap in his front teeth was visible at the back of the room. There was a shuffle, then one officer slowly separated himself from the silent blue mass and stepped forward to accept his new orders. "Congratulations, Werner," said Lüth. "As of 1 April you are the new commander of U-415." [1]

WOLFGANG Lüth's career as a U-boat commander was over. When he returned to Bordeaux in a burst of flashbulbs from his record patrol to the

Indian Ocean, he had been relieved from sea duty at once. Dönitz had too much invested in him to risk another war patrol. He was a hero, like Prien and Kretschmer; he would not be wasted as they had been. In November 1943 he gave U-181 to *Fregattenkapitän* (commander) Kurt Freiwald, an Oberkommando der Marine (OKM) staff officer with no wartime command experience. In December he presented his landmark lecture in Weimar, and in January 1944 he was sent to Gotenhafen to take command of the Twenty-second U-Flotilla, a training unit through which all new U-boat commanders had to pass before they took over their boats. Although it may seem odd that an officer like Lüth would be sent so far behind the lines, it was not unusual. Erich Topp, for example, had been in charge of the Twenty-seventh U-Flotilla in Gotenhafen since September 1942. Karl-Friedrich Merten had been ordered to the neighboring flotilla in Memel the following April. The reasoning was that the best front-line commanders would make the best training flotilla commanders, especially at that point in the war, when student officers very aware of their chances at sea were in greatest need of inspiration.

The exchange between the veteran Lüth and the young Herbert Werner in early 1944 represented a significant transition for the U-Bootwaffe. As Lüth, the war hero and *Brillantenträger,* shook hands with Werner, an officer who had not even been in uniform when the war started, the symbolism was thicker than oil on ice. Two years earlier, the first generation of U-boat commanders had given way to a second. Now the second generation was yielding to a third, or rather, to a group of men so diverse in their backgrounds, their training, and their experience that they are characterized less by similarities to each other than by differences from their predecessors. There was irony as well as symbolism in the encounter. One could not easily have found two men in the U-Bootwaffe more different in temperament or attitude than Wolfgang Lüth and Herbert Werner.

The third generation of U-boat commanders can be defined roughly as those who were neither in command of boats nor serving as commissioned officers in the Kriegsmarine when the war began. Any attempt to narrow this definition fails, although several generalizations can be made about the group as a whole. The third generation was much larger than the first or the second. There were few famous names among its members, fewer aces, no heroes like Prien, no legends like Kretschmer. They included a large number of staff officers, reserve officers, and former enlisted men, and the few good commanders were sprinkled among many who were unready, unfortunate, or unqualified. The third generation

Herbert Werner. The experiences of Werner, who became a commander fairly late in the war, formed the basis for a book that charted emotions as well as events. (Herbert Werner)

was younger, made fewer attacks, sank fewer ships, spent less time on the surface, and enjoyed a shorter life expectancy than its predecessors. Most of the commanders who died in the war belonged to the third generation.

Herbert Werner was a third-generation commander, and his background was as representative as any. He joined the Kriegsmarine three months after the war began as a member of Crew XII/39. He endured the Dänholm, just as every officer candidate had done, and sailed on both the *Gorch Fock* and *Horst Wessel*. In May 1940, after the invasion of France, he was sent to the Netherlands to assist in creating the Thirty-fourth Minesweeping Flotilla in Den Helder with tugboats gathered from the ports of Amsterdam and Rotterdam, the "Mickey Mouse Flotilla," so named because of its insignia, designed by Werner, which depicted Mickey Mouse cutting a mine cable with a huge pair of scissors. Still officially a Seekadett, he became the captain of one of these vessels. He participated in the exercises for Operation Sealion, the invasion of Britain, towing one of the large landing craft and instructing the soldiers on how to debark from it, and he shot down several British bombers that had flown in low over the North Sea to drop their excess bombs after air raids in Germany.

Finally, in December 1940, after a career as a Seekadett that can best be described as full, Werner was sent to the Marineschule Mürwik. He graduated in April 1941 and, along with 80 percent of Crew XII/39, entered the U-Bootwaffe still a Fähnrich. His first boat was U-557, commanded by Ottokar Paulssen.[2]

The idea of marching four out of every five Marineschule graduates straight into the U-Bootwaffe—before they were commissioned and without regard for their own wishes—was fairly new. The U-boat training Dönitz had decreed for the first and second generations was formal, exhaustive, and unhurried. Before Lüth joined the U-Bootwaffe in 1937, for example, he had already spent three years as a Seekadett and a Fähnrich and one year as a junior officer on a light cruiser. Before he reported to his first boat as a watch officer he had been through eighteen months of U-boat training. Yet there was something to be said for a prospective U-boat officer having to spend time in a boat as a Fähnrich before he was commissioned. Wrote Gottfried König, another member of Crew XII/39, "For me, a young Fähnrich without any experience in U-boats, it was a very educational time, especially since the commander took such a personal interest in my training. . . . I had to spend the first patrol as a seaman in the bow compartment, standing watches as a lookout and in the engine room, alongside the torpedoes and in the radio room. During the second patrol I acted as a junior officer and I was trained in the duties of a watch officer by the commander, the officers, and the chief engineer."[3]

In November 1941, after three rather intense patrols, Herbert Werner was detached from U-557 and sent to Pillau for U-boat training, and in the spring of 1942, only thirteen months after he had left the Marineschule and only weeks after he had been promoted to Leutnant zur See, he became first watch officer of the newly commissioned U-612.[4] To put someone as second in command of a boat so soon and with such little experience would have been inconceivable in 1939, but the first man in the position became ill and Werner was the only available replacement with combat experience. In this he did somewhat better than his classmate König, who had just been assigned as second watch officer in Wolfgang Lüth's new boat, U-181. The two men had accumulated the same amount of combat experience over the preceding twelve months, but König had served as a Fähnrich in Lüth's U-43 and Lüth was sufficiently impressed to ask for him when he got his new boat. He had both the seniority and the pull to do so, and as Jürgen Oesten said, "You stick to the people you know, as you have tested them already."[5]

Gottfried König and Theodor Petersen. Like Werner, neither man achieved command until later in the war. Petersen made it to the front, König did not. Without his knowledge Wolfgang Lüth had arranged for König to be sent to a training boat in the Baltic Sea. (Theodor Petersen)

As rushed and fragmented as the training for Crew XII/39 appears to have been, it was much more thorough than what some members of the third generation ever got. Along with Gottfried König, Lüth had also brought Theodor Petersen with him from U-43 to be his first watch officer. A merchant seaman before the war, Petersen entered the Reichsmarine in 1934, served in a variety of positions at sea and ashore, and was promoted to Obersteuermann in December 1939. He entered the U-Bootwaffe in February 1940 and joined the crew of U-138, of which Lüth was the prospective commander, in May. He then served under Lüth for two patrols in U-138 and five in U-43, in the process becoming, he likes to think, more of a friend to him than a subordinate. Finally, in January 1942, with only a fraction of the training Lüth had received, Petersen was promoted to Leutnant zur See. It was a temporary promotion and he was well aware of it (he was a *Kriegsoffizier,* a war officer), but it too would have been unthinkable ten years, perhaps even five years, earlier.

Both König and Petersen have interesting tales to tell. But neither they nor anyone else spoke for their generation as eloquently as Herbert Werner. Werner's story is that of a man whose spirit fought for years against the truth and finally lost. He reported to U-612 in May 1942. Over the next eighteen months he served as second in command of two boats, endured the bloody and ferocious Battle of the Atlantic, and watched, uncomprehending, as it ended. In the spring of 1942, U-Bootwaffe fortunes were high and his prospects were good. When he shook hands with Wolfgang Lüth two years later, the U-boats were fighting a lost cause and he had few prospects save a speedy death at sea. Sometime in between these two events, the Battle of the Atlantic collapsed like the Möhne Dam, but Werner did not see the collapse when it happened, nor did he believe it when it became too obvious to ignore. His description of the period can be found in *Iron Coffins,* his autobiography. It is an emotional roller coaster, but there is little indication in its pages that he ever gave up hope. Every bad day was followed by a good day; every worrisome blot of reality was papered over with a flower.

Iron Coffins, like *The Boat,* has been simultaneously praised as a classic and condemned as a historical delusion. "The best book in most respects on the market," wrote Peter Hansen, but Michael Hadley calls it "one of the worst distortions of the postwar period," and Horst Bredow pronounces it "full of mistakes and errors—it is not a historical source."[6] Both sides can be defended. *Iron Coffins* is shot through with factual errors because it was written long after the war ended and Werner relied too heavily on his memory, but he himself does not consider this a problem. "The few memory lapses are immaterial," he wrote derisively, "and do not mar the book or the message I was putting forward. . . . Remember, I was there—while my few critics were wetting their pants."[7] It is not the best attitude, but fortunately the facts can be verified elsewhere. Werner's style of writing, however, is unique, and although, as Bredow observes, *Iron Coffins* is not a good historical source, it is the best personal account of the sights, sounds, and atmosphere of the last years of Hitler's U-Bootwaffe.[8]

The book begins, not with Werner's youth or military training but with his graduation from an abbreviated course of instruction at the Marineschule in April 1941. The first several chapters have to do with his time as a watch officer in U-557. Life was good for the U-boats in those days, and he enjoyed working for Paulssen, who sank five ships while he was on board. When he joined the commissioning crew of U-612, commanded by Paul Siegmann, in spring 1942 his mood was cheerful and optimistic:

> While U-612 and her crew were preparing for battle our armies drove ever deeper into enemy territory. Leningrad had been surrounded. . . . Sevastopol in the Crimea had capitulated; our fast-moving divisions had reached the Caucasus. . . . In North Africa, Rommel had led his Afrika Korps to vic-

tory after victory over the Tommies. . . . In the North Atlantic our U-boats ravaged Britain's convoys with increasing ferocity. . . . Operations were extended to America's east coast against little or no opposition. From Nantucket to Hatteras, from Florida to the Windward Islands, our torpedoes shattered the silence of peaceful commerce. . . . The golden age of U-boat war had arrived.

The paragraph quoted above reflects perceptions in the summer of 1942. The German offensive in the Soviet Union seemed to be going well, and Rommel was perched on the Alamein line, from which Victor Oehrn sent glowing status reports to BdU on a daily basis. Operation Drumbeat, the U-boat offensive along the eastern seaboard of North America, was cooling off. The United States Navy, after having for months refused to learn from Britain's mistakes, finally instituted a convoy system along the east coast and sinkings dropped at once. But Dönitz had merely moved the U-boats back from the coast into the mid-Atlantic, where the battle was as fierce as ever. The month of June 1942 had been the most successful of the war so far, and July opened with the destruction of convoy PQ 17 in the Arctic Ocean, in which sixteen merchant ships were chased down by U-boats and aircraft and sunk after the convoy was ordered to scatter.

The sinusoidal temperament of *Iron Coffins* becomes apparent at this point, however, for although Werner began the summer with good spirits, he soon lost them. In August, U-612 collided with another boat. She sank immediately, killing two men. The other boat, U-444, was deemed to be at fault, but Werner had to absorb some of the blame for not ensuring that all of his men had escaped alive. After the sinking, Siegmann's crew was assigned to another boat, U-230, which was scheduled for commissioning in October. Unfortunately, the entire process of Baubelehrung and trials would have to begin again. Werner would be away from the front for the entire second half of 1942, and he would miss the height of the Battle of the Atlantic, when U-boats sank more ships, on average and in total, than in any comparable period of the war.

In June 1942, 131 Allied and neutral ships of about 615,000 GRT were sunk. These were the highest numbers for any month of the war so far, much higher than the average for the six months since Operation Drumbeat started and at least double the average for late 1940, the halcyon days of the Happy Times. The numbers fell slightly in July, probably because the U-boats were moved away from the eastern seaboard and back into the North Atlantic, but the average tonnage lost to U-boat attack from July through September was nevertheless almost 500,000 GRT. In

October the total crept back up to 585,000 GRT, and the zenith of the U-Bootwaffe in World War II was reached a month later. Almost three-quarters of a million tons of shipping were lost in November 1942; 118 ships were sunk. Most were merchantmen, a few were warships, and one was a 14,000-ton aircraft carrier. Most went down in the North Atlantic convoy lanes, some as far north as Bear Island in the Arctic Ocean, others as far south as the Mozambique Channel. It was welcome news in Germany's fourth year of war: "The hunger blockade that the U-boats had established around England seemed to be near its ultimate objective," wrote Werner in *Iron Coffins*. "The ghost of starvation and of a lost war was marching across the United Kingdom and knocking at the door of No. 10 Downing Street."

November 1942 was the deadliest month, and the numbers looked very good indeed. But they do not tell the whole story. In October 1940 there were 26 boats at sea; in November 1942 there were 180. More boats led to more sinkings, of course, but it is significant that seven times as many boats could not sink even twice as many ships. It is also significant that 28 out of the 118 ships sunk in November 1942 (totaling 160,000 GRT) went down in the Indian Ocean, an area of easy success not available to the U-Bootwaffe in 1940. The sinkings of October 1940 were distributed among eighteen commanders; those of November 1942 among fifty-five. Most telling was the ratio of tonnage sunk to U-boats lost. In October 1940 this ratio was three boats for every million GRT of shipping. By November 1942 it had risen to about seventeen boats per million GRT, or one U-boat for every nine enemy ships. Another fact that skewed the numbers in Germany's favor was that BdU had modified its Enigma machines in February, and Allied code-breakers in Bletchley Park did not catch up until December. All message traffic was secure for most of the year.

Finally, a critical milestone had just been passed that made all these numbers meaningless. At some point in the fall of 1942—the exact day is hard to determine—the number of Allied merchant ships built exceeded the number sunk. In other words, the number of ships was now rising and would continue to rise until the end of the war. The "tonnage war" was the basis for Karl Dönitz's entire strategy. If his U-boats could sink more merchant tonnage than the enemy produced, Britain would eventually sue for peace—or starve to death. This strategy had almost won the war for Germany in 1917. It was for this reason that Dönitz was willing if necessary to deploy his boats anywhere in the world: a ship was a ship, wherever it was sunk. It was why his boats did not make warships their primary targets: a cruiser or a destroyer could carry no oil, food, or tanks. Therefore, when net tonnage at sea began to rise, rather than fall, it meant that Dönitz's strategy had failed and that any chance the U-boats had of bringing about a German victory—however small—had vanished. Erich Topp wrote in *Odyssey* that the war ended, not at Pearl Harbor or Stalingrad but when this invisible line was crossed in 1942.[9]

Siegmann and Werner were out of the picture for most of this stage of the battle. The loss of U-612 was followed by extended leave for the entire crew, then Baubelehrung for U-230. After the boat's commissioning in October came the usual routine of exercises, drills, and moves from one Baltic port to another, lasting well into December. On Christmas Eve, U-230 was sent back into the yards for the installation of another gun. Herbert Werner spent the next day eating a "skimpy" holiday meal and listening to gloomy news broadcasts about the war situation. The Ministry of Propaganda was just getting around to admitting that November had been a bad month for Germany. The U-boats had not been able to stop a major Allied landing in French North Africa in which more than one hundred thousand British and American troops took part. The Red Army had begun a powerful counterattack in the Caucasus with the city of Stalingrad as its primary objective. The German Sixth Army was in danger of being cut off and encircled. The British Eighth Army had recaptured Tobruk in November and was moving west. "But the temporary difficulties of our conquering armies," he wrote, "were easier to accept than the glowing accounts of U-boat triumphs in which we did not share."

Clearly he did not believe that Germany was in serious trouble at this point, even after he was caught in a bad air raid during a quick visit to Berlin in January. When U-230 finally left Kiel on her first war patrol some weeks later, somewhat forlornly, in a blinding snowstorm and without a brass band, his only thoughts were of the opportunities ahead. "Nothing mattered but that we were sailing. We were convinced that victory was only months away and that we had to hurry to sink our share of enemy vessels." It was the troubling echo of an earlier attitude: the war will be over by Christmas and I must rush to win my medals. It is curious that Werner would have thought this way, especially when many officers in the U-Bootwaffe had already made up their minds that the war was lost, but it demonstrates that his spirits, for some reason, were up again.

ERIC Rust, in his study of Crew 34, identifies two points in the war at which the crew's expectations of victory changed, and it is reasonable to assume that these points were the same for the entire Kriegsmarine officer corps. Most officers, he found, felt by the end of 1941 that Germany could not win the war.[10] One of the reasons for this doubt was the invasion of the Soviet Union in June 1941. "Until the opening of the second front (against Russia)," wrote Karl Daublebsky von Eichhain, "I had hoped for an acceptable ending."[11] A second was the appearance of another enemy, a huge country with unlimited resources and a suddenly fierce resolve, in December. "I realized that Germany could not win," wrote Reinhard

Reinhard Reche, one of many commanders who were beginning to face the reality of a bad situation. When Germany declared war on the United States, he wrote, it became clear to him that she could never win. (Reinhard Reche)

Reche, "when, in addition to the Russians, Hitler declared war on the USA on 11th Dec. '41." He goes on to say plaintively that "I had recently commissioned U-255 for our desperate task."[12] Other reasons no doubt included the stubborn disinclination of Britain to surrender, the failure of the German surface fleet, and the losses the U-Bootwaffe had suffered in the spring of 1941.

Of course, the prospect of not winning was different than the prospect of losing. "There were too many imponderables for Germans to fall into complete despair," observed Rust, "possible dissent or war weariness among the Allies; promise of new weapons; Hitler's death or removal; reasonable peace offers or mediation; military reversals, etc."[13] There was still the possibility of a negotiated peace, in which Germany might at least escape with her self-respect and perhaps some additional territory as well. This was Dönitz's "best-case" scenario on the first day of the war, and for those who had tired of National Socialism, it was not an altogether unpleasant idea. "Fairly early on in the war," wrote König, "—I don't remember the exact time—I came to believe with many of my comrades that it would be bad if Hitler won the war, but worse if he lost. We liked to think about a negotiated peace, one that would bring NS power to an end and make possible a new political future without a wholesale surrender and destruction of Germany."[14]

Eighteen months later, however, it had become clear (barring a cataclysmic falling-out between the Soviet Union and the West) that there was no chance of coming to terms: an Allied demand for unconditional surrender issued from Casablanca in January ruled out any such possibility. As a result of the news of disastrous setbacks on all fronts, the deteriorating situation at home, and what they could see for themselves at the front, many Kriegsmarine officers were going through a sequence of classic symptoms that would result in the reluctant acceptance that Germany was actually going to *lose*. It was a profound realization, especially for a professional naval officer fighting a war in which the very survival of his country was at stake, and not everyone reached it at the same time. Neither Erich Topp nor Karl-Friedrich Merten had yet arrived. Victor Oehrn, flat on his back in Egypt, refused to believe any of the dispiriting reports he was hearing from visitors and argued Germany's case strenuously to anyone who would listen. Wolfgang Lüth seemed immune to such ponderings.

Jürgen Oesten made up his mind in January 1943. On the last day of that month the battle for Stalingrad finally ended in a humiliating German defeat. The loss of Stalingrad signified the end of German expansion in the East; her armies would now begin to withdraw, slowly but inexorably, from the Soviet Union, from Poland, across the Oder, and into the streets of Berlin. The defeat had no direct bearing on the war at sea, but when it was announced, it had a predictably negative effect on morale everywhere. Oesten was serving on the staff of *Admiral Nordmeer* (flag officer, Polar Coast) during the final stages of the battle. "One of the admirals in charge was [Hubert] Schmundt, extremely intelligent, a bit soft maybe, cultivated, and full of wisdom. Our staff incorporated an army and an air force officer and, as normal in a good staff, things were called by their names. When the Russians took Stalingrad this admiral stated that herewith the war is lost." [15]

For a junior officer to echo Schmundt's words in public would have been extremely unwise, and Oesten, Reche, and Daublebsky all kept their counsel. But the general level of cynicism aboard the boats was rising, and many commanders were voicing similar sentiments in the privacy of their wardrooms. Usually this took the form of discussion or idle complaint. Seldom did it approach the level of conspiracy or seditious behavior, if only because sedition was a line most were unwilling to cross for reasons of honor. It was rare, for example, that an officer would do something as rash as Oskar Kusch, the new commander of U-154. Shortly after taking over in February 1943, Kusch tossed the obligatory wardroom portrait of Adolf Hitler into the trash can and announced that henceforth idol worship would not be tolerated on his boat. It was an act his subordinates would not forget.

Herbert Werner had not progressed very far down this road in January 1943, at least it does not seem so from his recollections. But he had little time in the first three months of 1943 to reflect on the fall of Stalingrad, the course of the war at sea, or anything other than the intensely personal objective of staying alive. The first eight months of 1943, as he describes them in *Iron Coffins*, seemed to be one long hideous patrol. Actually there were three patrols, but each one was the same: filthy weather, continual air attacks and depth charge sieges, missed opportunities and precious little success, all played to the unnerving accompaniment of intercepted U-boat distress calls as one boat after another was bombed, shelled, or blown up around the beleaguered U-230. The Battle of the Atlantic was coming to a close, and Herbert Werner was there at the end.

On the morning of 6 March, one month into the boat's first patrol, Siegmann received word of a large convoy to his south. He turned toward it at once. Fourteen hours later, a lookout in U-230's bridge sighted a destroyer on the left flank of the slow eastbound convoy SC 121, and by early the next morning U-230 was off the beam of the British freighter *Egyptian*. Werner pulled the firing lever. "The vessel split in front of her bridge. Then the convoy began signalling furiously. Star shells spurted into the clouds [and] flashed briefly into the sky." Siegmann was forced to withdraw, but at 0925 he found what looked like a tanker. Again, Werner fired, and just before U-230 was driven below by two destroyers he saw a second explosion. After Siegmann broke off the attack on SC 121 and turned for home, a signal was made claiming, among other things, that he had sunk both ships.[16]

Paul Siegmann was optimistic. The *Egyptian* was the only ship he sank all year. When convoy SC 121 finally entered the Western Approaches, however, twelve of her ships had been lost from various other attacks, and by the time U-230 reached Brest, March was well on its way to becoming the third most successful month of the war for the U-boats. The next eastbound convoy, HX 228, lost seven ships and one escort, and the two after that, SC 122 and HX 229, together lost twenty-one ships in a frenzied fight that lasted three days and stretched across hundreds of miles of ocean. A total of 105 ships were lost in March 1943. So complete was the devastation in the convoy lanes during the month that many believed the Battle of the Atlantic was over and Britain had lost. Many writers are apt at this point to use the words of Stephen Roskill, the official historian of the Royal Navy and the author of *The War at Sea,* who said that "the Germans never came so near to disrupting communications between the New World and the Old as in the first 20 days of March 1943."[17] But his was a glum assessment. "Here too British understatement had painted the gloomiest colours," wrote Peter Cremer, an officer temporarily attached to Dönitz's staff after having been badly wounded as commander of U-333 the previous autumn. "In reality the situation was by no means so bad. The turning point was just coming."[18]

March 1943, despite its frightening numbers, would turn out to be a blip in an otherwise smooth downward curve. The U-Bootwaffe had been in decline for some time, a decline that would prove irreversible and for which there were several reasons. A new class of smaller aircraft carrier, the escort carrier, began to appear in the North Atlantic, closing the air gaps and providing continuous air support for convoys. The invention of centimetric (EHF) radar allowed the construction of radar sets that were not only smaller and more accurate but much harder for their targets to detect. Installed in aircraft, these sets made surfaced U-boats visible from great distances, and U-boat lookouts often did not see or hear their attackers until they were being bombed. Powerful direction-finding stations, based on shore and in ships, were able to plot U-boat locations from their radio signals. New ASW weapons were invented: the hedgehog, the Leigh Light, the homing torpedo, the smart bomb. Finally, the impact of the Enigma compromise cannot be understated (one of the principal reasons for the temporary rise in sinkings for March was that BdU had changed code books again that month and Bletchley Park was blind for ten days).

No single factor was decisive. Taken together they were overwhelming, and they began to make a difference almost immediately after Werner returned from his first war patrol in late March. When he began his second patrol at the end of April, the tactical situation in the North Atlantic had changed significantly to Germany's disadvantage: air cover was complete, convoys were unapproachable, and time spent on the surface was a dangerous proposition that claimed one boat after another. March 1943 had been one of the most successful months of the war, and the Allies were in despair. May 1943 would be one of the worst, and the despair was Germany's. "Black May," it would be called, "the Stalingrad at Sea," the "Month of the Lost U-Boats." U-230 was fortunate; bereft of success and the victim of multiple attacks from the air, she nevertheless managed to limp into Brest at the end of the month without serious damage. Forty-one boats did not return, among them U-954, commanded by Odo Löwe and carrying Leutnant zur See Peter Dönitz as a watch officer.

Five days later, Karl Dönitz withdrew all boats from the North Atlantic convoy lanes. The Battle of the Atlantic ended that day, and the U-boat was never again a serious threat to Allied shipping or to any military operation upon which the Allies chose to embark.

This was not made clear to everyone at the time, of course, and Werner did not see through the explanation offered to him and his comrades by BdU: that the retreat was a "temporary" tactic and that the battle would be resumed as soon as countermeasures were available. The story had some credence because such countermeasures were being produced. The *Schnorchel,* a tube that enabled a boat's diesel engines to run while submerged, began to appear on U-boat towers in late 1943. Various devices for detecting Allied radar were installed, beginning with the Metox in 1942 for VHF radar, then the Naxos in 1943 for the hated EHF radar. Some U-boats were given so many additional guns that they looked more like destroyers than submarines. Others were given radar sets of their own. All this equipment, however, was basically reactive in nature. It was meant to help the U-boats keep up rather than get ahead. The weapons that might have provided a real edge in the fighting, those everyone was beginning to call the "miracle weapons," were some distance off. And it was still easier to build a new radar or install a new gun than it was to train a U-boat commander and his crew.[19]

Werner had the chance later that summer to see some of these new miracle weapons for himself. After U-230's third war patrol ended in September, she was sent into overhaul to be fitted with more guns, a new radar detector, and some mysterious new torpedoes that required him to travel back to Gotenhafen for more training. There he was shown two unusual demonstrations. The T5 Zaunkönig (Wren) was an acoustic torpedo designed to home on the sound of a propeller. For purposes of testing, its warhead had been replaced with a nose that glowed green in the dark, and Werner was enthralled by the sight of this verdant speck chasing in giant loops and graceful swirls after its target warship. The Lage-Unabhängige Torpedo (LUT) could be manually programmed to follow a preset course, regardless of range, bearing, or target angle. It was especially useful in situations, increasingly common, where a boat could not come close enough to a target for a conventional firing solution. After seeing the T5 and the LUT and exercising with them for three days, Werner was once more optimistic about the future: "For the first time in months," he wrote, "I believed that we were beginning to get the weapons to survive and to risk our lives intelligently. We might yet be around to see the turn of the tide."

Werner returned to Brest in late September 1943, the fifth September of the war. Allied forces had crossed the Straits of Messina from Sicily to the mainland, and a new Italian government had just agreed to an armistice. The German army had abandoned Smolensk and Poltava. Wolfgang Lüth was preparing to cross the equator on his way home from the Indian Ocean, and in Egypt Victor Oehrn was waiting patiently to be repatriated. German cities were devastated; Werner was shocked at the widespread destruction in Frankfurt when he visited his parents there that month. Twelve ships were sunk in September 1943. Ten U-boats were lost. But this was also the month in which U-230 was to come out of the yards with her new weaponry, and this seemed to have pushed any glimmer of impending doom from Werner's mind and inspired him to echo the thoughts he had had on the test ranges of Gotenhafen: "These fast-shooting guns, the wonder-working torpedoes, and the newly installed

radar detector gave us a fair chance to return to old glory—and to port."
Once again he managed to be optimistic. Once again his hopes were
dashed. The fourth war patrol was no better than the previous three. Neither the new torpedoes nor the new guns had any effect, nothing was
achieved, and several times the boat came within a split second of
destruction.

The next patrol, Werner's fifth in U-230, was to be a risky dash from
Brest through the Straits of Gibraltar to southern France. It would be very
similar to the patrol Lothar-Günther Buchheim described in *The Boat,*
with considerable danger and few returns. Surprisingly, it went without
serious incident, and in December 1943 the boat glided quietly into Toulon Harbor. Soon afterward Paul Siegmann called Herbert Werner into
his stateroom, congratulated him, and told him that he had received
orders to leave the boat for training as a commanding officer.

The year 1943 had been terrible for the U-Bootwaffe, all the worse
when one considers the heights from which it had fallen. In 1943 the
Battle of the Atlantic had been lost, the U-boats had been driven from the
convoy lanes, and control of the seas had passed to the enemy for good.
And as the year limped to its painful close, the oscillation of Herbert Werner's spirit began to increase in both frequency and intensity. In the space
of a few pages in *Iron Coffins* it goes from resignation, to doubt, to cau-
tious optimism, to depression, to hope, to utter despair. When he came to
U-612 in the summer of 1942, the world had been as he described in the
"golden age" passage above, but when he left Toulon for Germany in
December 1943 it had become a much less appealing place: "While I was
carried peacefully through the summery hills and valleys of southern
France, in Russia, Soviet divisions pounded the German lines as an over-
ture to their winter offensive; in Italy at Monte Cassino, the Americans
bombarded our front in an attempt to break through to Rome; and on the
British Isles the engines of a thousand bombers were being readied for the
night's assault of the continent."

As he traveled north through France and into Germany, the bombers
Werner envisioned left England and headed east. When he arrived in
Frankfurt the next day, the city was burning and his parents were living in
an apartment without a back wall. His visit was mercifully brief; within
forty-eight hours he would be on a second train to Neustadt for two weeks
of attack simulator training, and afterward he would be on a third for
Danzig. When he had awakened in his parents' home that first morning,
however, in the room that was his as a boy, he was hit by doubts that he

had hitherto not recorded. When he left the room in 1939, he wrote, the war was to have been over by Christmas. Now his room, his home, and his city had been wrecked by a war that showed no sign of ending. "I suppressed the feelings of pessimism that had been nagging me more and more of late. Soon, soon, we would bring this ugly war to a victorious conclusion."

He allowed this hesitant note of optimism to be reinforced on the Danzig train. During the journey he found himself with a band of infantry officers on their way back to the Russian front. Each believed that German fortunes in the East would soon improve; one cited better weapons, another the superiority of German tactics, a third the German war industry at home. Werner mentioned them all in *Iron Coffins*. For the first time in the book, however, he did not add a personal endorsement of their views, and his own spirits plummeted once again when he reported to the Twenty-second U-Flotilla and Wolfgang Lüth began to introduce him to the other officers in his course. He was depressed to find that only one besides him had served in the U-Bootwaffe and that the rest were a motley collection of Kriegsmarine surface officers, staff officers, reserve officers, and *Kriegsoffiziere* recruited to fill the gaps. "These raw newcomers," he wrote, "who would be entrusted with a U-boat in just a few weeks, stood almost no chance of surviving and neither did their crews."

The course, which lasted four weeks, was an almost uninterrupted series of drills in torpedo attacks, defensive measures, evasion, and emergency procedures. With thirty months of experience as a U-Bootwaffe officer, Werner easily came in at the top of his class. He fully expected to be given a good boat, perhaps even one of the miracle boats he had been hearing so much about. Even after what he had endured, he had no desire to avoid command and no desire to avoid the front. Despite his doubts, he was still moved by honor to defend his country, to win if possible, for against all indications to the contrary, he still believed that Germany might pull it off. He was still struggling to keep himself from tumbling into fatal despair. "As a commander," he wrote, "[I had promised] I would do all I could to help achieve victory." It was ironic, therefore, that he was handed his orders by Wolfgang Lüth, who seemed to be very good at keeping the officers he cared for away from the front and out of danger.

In May 1943 Theodor Petersen got his own boat. It was not what anyone would have called a plum command. After Werner's old boat, U-612, sank in the Baltic Sea, killing two crewmen and forcing him to rethink his rosy outlook on life in the "golden age of U-boat war," she was re-floated, towed into port, cleaned out, polished up, and given to Petersen on 31 May 1943. He was underwhelmed at his new command: boats like U-612 that had been recommissioned after sinking or serious damage were considered *very* bad luck, and he soon learned that U-612 was to be sent to the Twenty-fourth U-Flotilla, a training flotilla commanded by Karl-Friedrich Merten in Memel, rather than to a forward base in France. "I was rather annoyed," he wrote, "because U-612 was not a Frontboot," but he believes today that the assignment saved his life and that it was not as accidental as it seemed at the time. "I believe Lüth had something to do with this. I once complained to him about having to sit around in Memel with the 24th U-Flotilla, and he replied that the situation in the North Atlantic was rather so-so anyway. A *Crew-Kamerad* of his, a Kapitänleut-nant Jeppener, was the man at BdU responsible for assigning officers to boats, and I think the two of them played Providence [*Vorsehung gespielt*] a little bit."[20]

There seems no doubt that Petersen's suspicion was correct. Wolfgang Lüth was notorious for his public confidence in an ultimate German vic-tory, and he took an extremely dim view of defeatism in any form. But he knew that the North Atlantic had become a dangerous place in mid-1943, so dangerous that he was prepared to make sure that his own officers were sent to commands away from the front. It didn't just happen to Petersen. In the winter of 1945, long after König and Lüth had parted company, Lüth pulled the same strings at BdU to get his old watch officer assigned as commander of U-316, a training boat in Danzig. König wrote: "It was not to my liking at the time, but Lüth actually saved my life by doing so, since almost all the operational boats after 1944 were lost at sea. He thought that as a young commander I should spend some time in a train-ing environment; as a result I stayed with U-316 until the end of the war and sank her in the Trave on 2 May 1945."[21]

It was perhaps unfortunate that Werner had never worked for Lüth. As it was, Lüth handed Werner his orders not as a U-boat commander look-ing after a valued subordinate but as a representative of the Führer and the Kriegsmarine who knew that Werner had taken an oath to serve the Führer and that he should be prepared to honor that oath without com-plaint even unto death. Werner accepted the orders in like manner, cheer-fully and without complaint, as a German soldier was supposed to do, even though they were "as good as a death sentence." He was bitterly disappointed with U-415, a two-year-old type VIIC boat out of Brest. He knew from experience that she would be obsolete, underpowered, in need of constant repair, and completely inadequate for frontline duty. In a word, U-415 was a relic. "This honor, this bright new command, was merely a matter of changing vehicles for an early ride to the bottom." The optimism that had sustained him time and again through the year was gone.[22]

THESE men are dead. I am looking at corpses. Wolfgang Lüth stared darkly through the smoke as the last young man went back to his seat. His smile was gone, and he slumped in his chair. *Dead.* But Germany still lives. And as if fortified by that thought, he stiffened, stood up, clapped his hands, and turned to the band. "Music," he shouted, "*Lili Marlene,* if you please!" And as the sad, sweet tune began, he walked into the crowd to say good-bye to his men.

CHAPTER 11

Dragon's Teeth

Our fathers and ourselves sowed dragon's teeth.
Our children know and suffer the armed men.

—Stephen Vincent Benet

ON 30 January 1943, the day before the German surrender at Stalingrad and the tenth anniversary of National Socialist accession to power, Admiral Karl Dönitz succeeded *Grossadmiral* (grand admiral) Erich Raeder as commander in chief of the Kriegsmarine (*Oberbefehlshaber der Marine,* or simply ObdM).

The immediate cause of this change in leadership is well documented. Adolf Hitler had become enraged at the performance of the German surface fleet after an engagement in December 1942 known as the Battle of the Barents Sea. He told Raeder that he wanted the large surface units paid off and their guns used in shore batteries. Raeder promptly resigned and recommended two admirals, Rolf Carls and Dönitz, as possible successors. Hitler chose Dönitz. The promotion meant that Dönitz would become a Grossadmiral, that he would have to move his center of operations from Paris to Berlin, and that he would have to surrender nominal command of the U-Bootwaffe to another officer. It also meant that Dönitz would move away from the officers and men in the U-boats, that he would move closer to Adolf Hitler and National Socialism, and that he would begin to wander from the difficult path of honorable military service in the Third Reich.

One thing Dönitz did not lose in the shuffle was the affection of those he led; in fact, he has never lost it and will not until the last man in the U-Bootwaffe dies. For this reason it is impossible to examine the U-boat commander properly without examining Karl Dönitz and just as impossible to examine Dönitz without incurring the displeasure of several U-boat commanders. Karl-Friedrich Merten, for example, was very sensitive in this regard. Victor Oehrn, like most members of Dönitz's personal staff, was especially close to the man he calls simply, "D.," so close that he felt the need to provide a gentle admonishment when he heard of this chapter. "Do your best to promote truth in history," he wrote in unsteady but unequivocal English. "In my age it is my aim to do what I can to transfer in the public opinion the reality concerning that exceptional man, who is even in Germany very often not seen as he really was. . . . Lots of people think they know D. very well, but really they know not much." [1]

Oehrn's motive is pure. He saw goodness in Karl Dönitz, and he believes that others will see it if Dönitz is described fairly and objectively. It is true that when Dönitz became ObdM he had several virtues which, had he dropped dead at that point, would have marked him as a good as well as a great man. Among them were his personal integrity, his genius as a tactician, his relatively apolitical conduct as a military commander, and his unquestioned ability to lead men—familiar virtues, qualities that had formed the German professional officer for centuries. Erwin Rommel, for example, to whom Oehrn likened Dönitz several times, possessed them all, and history has been kind to him.

Like Rommel, Dönitz was a master tactician but only a passable strategist. The strategy he elected to follow, the principle of tonnage war described earlier, was straightforward and logical under the circumstances, and he executed it well. It failed him only when his boats were redirected to support other ends such as the invasion of Norway or Rommel's advance in North Africa. The specific operations he planned, whether limited, like Scapa Flow, or large, like Operation Drumbeat, were well thought out and usually successful, but even his failures were imaginative. In 1943, for example, he attempted a rescue of several U-Bootwaffe officers who had planned to escape from the Bowmanville POW camp in Ontario and make their way to the sea. The attempt fell through, not because the boat he sent did not arrive at the rendezvous point but because the escapees never showed up. His greater talent, however, lay in the tactics of submarine warfare; he was without argument the most innovative commander in history in using a small number of boats to their greatest advantage. His masterpiece, of course, was the wolfpack. Between 1940 and 1943, U-boats attacking in groups and controlled from shore were responsible for the vast majority of Allied sinkings in the North Atlantic. The night surface attack, first examined in the early

1920s, was perfected by Dönitz during the war, and despite the general impression that Otto Kretschmer invented the maneuver of attacking from within a convoy, Victor Oehrn credits Dönitz with that innovation as well: "Kretschmer was not even a commander when we started drilling with that one." [2]

Dönitz was not a political innocent. One could not become a Grossadmiral without some knowledge of palace intrigue and a measure of ruthlessness; but he managed to avoid the black hole of internal party politics for several years. Peter Padfield believes that Dönitz accepted National Socialism uncritically from 1933 onward but that he was as unwilling to introduce it into the U-Bootwaffe as his men were unwilling to accept such an intrusion. He played political games when it was necessary. He hobnobbed with the party elite because he had to. Otherwise he was as strict in keeping politics out of the U-Bootwaffe as Erich Raeder was in keeping it out of the Kriegsmarine as a whole. From time to time he even challenged Hitler on matters of principle. In September 1942, for example, after a U-boat was bombed while rescuing survivors of a sunken prisoner transport, Hitler issued an order (the *Laconia* order), which stated that henceforth surviving crewmen of sunken ships were to be killed. Dönitz refused point blank to follow it and Hitler backed down.

Not even his fiercest critics will deny that Karl Dönitz was one of the most compelling military leaders of World War II. He would do almost anything for his men. He bailed them out of trouble, protected them from the law, and refused to enforce punishments administered by other branches of the service. He set up rest camps in the French countryside for their use, gave them leave as often as he could, and lent them his staff car for evening trips to Paris. When they were at sea he sent them news from their homes, reported the births of their children, and checked on their families after bombing raids. He was one of a very few men who could comfort or inspire with a word or a touch. According to Oesten: "If [a U-boat] came back, say to Lorient, with a worn out crew, Dönitz normally saw the crew. If there was an oldish chief petty officer, fed up to the brim after more than a dozen trips under awful conditions, with the intention to report as sick, then Dönitz [would ask] him: 'Hey Meier, how many years do we know each other?' The man, standing to attention, answered, pleased as punch, 'eight years, Herr Admiral.' It may sound silly, but this particular man was good for another three trips, he just forgot all his troubles." [3]

Karl Dönitz's virtues served him well in eight years as FdU and BdU, and they did not disappear when he took over the entire Kriegsmarine in

January 1943. He still had them when the war ended in May 1945, and he was able to use them to good effect when he wanted to. But in the corrosive atmosphere through which he had to move as one of the Third Reich's senior military commanders, they began to deteriorate noticeably: his leadership qualities dulled, his skill as a tactician rusted, and his claim to be an officer above politics collapsed into dust.

THE appointment meant that Dönitz had to move his office from Paris to Berlin; first to Charlottenburg, then, in November 1943, to a large compound on the outskirts of the capital called Koralle. Suddenly he was six hundred miles farther away from the U-boat bases and six hundred miles closer to the surreal world of Führer headquarters. It also meant that his responsibilities grew and his staff ballooned; the Kriegsmarine was a much larger concern than the U-Bootwaffe, and it had different problems. As ObdM, Dönitz would have to work with and around Adolf Hitler on a regular basis, briefing him, making demands of him, and even consoling him from time to time. Finally, as a member of Hitler's "inner circle," a psychiatric caseload that included Joseph Goebbels, Hermann Goering, and Heinrich Himmler, he became privy to the horrible secrets of National Socialism. All in all, Berlin was not an environment conducive to virtue or even to a minimal hold on reality; one thinks of *Alice in Wonderland* as written by Bertolt Brecht and illustrated by Georg Grosz.

To be fair to Dönitz, he did try, until the end of the war, to stay close to the men of the U-Bootwaffe. He visited the bases as often as possible. He received the commanders in Berlin as often as he could and talked with them, warning them to spare neither detail nor feelings in telling him what was happening at the front. "I must go to the front," he told his adjutant as he left to spend Christmas 1943 in Paris, "that is where I belong. I must be with the troops. I must ever and always have an ear for my people."[4] But his continual presence in the everyday lives of his men had ended. It was not his fault; it was not something he had planned for or wanted, and from time to time at Koralle he would show flashes of nostalgia for the old days and regret that they had passed. It was the unavoidable consequence of having been promoted to a position that insulated him almost completely from the real world.

This problem was not unusual; on the contrary, it was fairly common among officers who had served at sea in the first years of the war, then went on to staff or training positions. When Herbert Werner went to Gotenhafen in the summer of 1943 to study the new torpedoes, for

Karl Dönitz, commander in chief, first of the U-Bootwaffe, then of the entire Kriegsmarine. (U.S. Naval Institute)

example, he was temporarily assigned to Erich Topp's Twenty-seventh U-Flotilla. Werner considers Topp a good officer, but his flotilla was a "mess" and he got nothing out of the training, primarily because Topp was teaching the tactics of the Happy Times and not those of the bitter endgame Werner was in.[5] Dönitz was in a much more dangerous position than Topp, however, because Topp at least was not responsible for making decisions that affected the survival of the U-Bootwaffe. As BdU, Dönitz insisted on a small staff of relatively junior officers upon whom he relied to tell him the truth. At OKM he had a much larger and more senior staff, some of whom would not or could not follow this rule and whose natural inclination was to tell Dönitz whatever he wanted to hear. "There existed a somewhat unrealistic ambience around Dönitz once he moved to Berlin," wrote Peter Hansen, "both at the Hotel Am Steinplatz [Charlottenburg] and even more so at Camp Koralle in Bernau. His courtiers kept undesirable facts away from him frequently or beautified them considerably. Dönitz never liked outright opposition to his preconceived opinions, despite his often talking otherwise. It upset him greatly and [Chief of Staff] Eberhard Godt gave everyone the chop who was not a good yes-man and ass-kisser."[6]

Victor Oehrn saw this immediately. In April 1944, newly released from Allied captivity and only partially recovered from the wounds he had received in the North African desert, Oehrn limped into Koralle and reported for duty. Dönitz was so appalled with his appearance that he ordered Oehrn to eat breakfast with him every morning so that he would gain weight. The terms of his repatriation required that he not serve outside the borders of pre-1933 Germany so he was assigned to work with Dönitz's A1, Hubert von Wangenheim, and was expected to relieve him in August. Oehrn thought Koralle was a strange place, almost Byzantine, and not at all like Sengwarden or Kerneval. Von Wangenheim, he wrote, "warned me over and over again, during long informational walks where nobody could hear us, that I would have to learn to understand the atmosphere here. I felt that a lot of people didn't say what they really thought." He sensed that von Wangenheim could not wait to get out of the place and go back to the front, where he was to take command of a destroyer flotilla.[7]

One incident sticks in Oehrn's mind for the glimpse it gave him of the Dönitz he had known in Sengwarden. In late 1944 Dönitz called a meeting with his staff to discuss a particularly difficult problem. He wanted to bring the giant battleship *Tirpitz* back home to Germany—or at least closer to Germany—from the Norwegian fjord she had occupied for several years. According to Oehrn, the junior officer present, nobody among them could come up with a sensible idea, but since Dönitz was so adamant, they began to put forth ideas that were neither sensible nor believable. Some of them were "quite *gespenstischillusionär*," he thought, illusory, even eerie, and he finally told Dönitz that it was a ridiculous idea. "One shouldn't give the enemy the triumph of destroying a ship that should by rights cost him many men. It was the last thing Dönitz wanted to hear." Dönitz was furious, and Oehrn had to leave, but thirty minutes later Dönitz called him in his barracks to apologize and extract a promise that he would always tell the truth, even if it was unpleasant. "Because of this incident I understood how completely alone a man is when he is in a position of high responsibility; how much he needs other men who will stand by him without flattery or deception. And I also understood— unfortunately not for the first time—how weak some men are when confronted by a strong will." [8]

It is small things like this encounter that lead Victor Oehrn to defend Karl Dönitz. Such a gesture is the mark of a leader, and, in truth, his ability as a leader was the virtue least compromised as the war went on. Indeed, perhaps the single best example of his skill in this area occurred after he became ObdM. In May 1943 Dönitz was forced to withdraw his boats from the North Atlantic. Tonnage war, in which the simple objective was to damage or sever Allied supply lines by sinking more ships than could be built, was replaced by a holding action, in which the U-boats were to keep as many Allied resources tied up for as long as possible. The first strategy had always been dangerous, but there was some glory in it, rewards for those who did well, and the chance of victory. Now the men of the U-Bootwaffe were being asked to fight and die for a different and altogether less pleasing cause, just as they were coming to the realization that the war was lost anyway. "Dönitz had no doubt that the continuation of the battle would be a veritable bed of nails," wrote Peter Cremer. "The only question was, would the ordinary U-boat man see the necessity of a battle in which great successes would no longer be achieved and only selfless commitment was envisioned? The Grand Admiral spoke about this to the operational flotillas on the Atlantic coast. The U-boat men—and this must be said—backed their commanders in approving the decision to fight on and shared the responsibility." [9]

Karl Dönitz's leadership ability is made clear even in books by writers who do not like him. "In the constant press of activity," wrote Padfield, "Dönitz did not lose sight of his duty to provide personal inspiration for the U-boat service. . . . According to [his adjutant] Hansen-Nootbar his outstanding approach was the foundation for the morale that was preserved through this difficult period of defeat." [10] Many U-boat veterans had such a high opinion of his leadership qualities that they excused any failings he may have had in other areas. "Nobody in this world is perfect," wrote Victor Oehrn, "also D. not. From my point of view it is much more important to know *where* a man is perfect," and Oehrn believes that Dönitz was perfect in the art of inspiring other men. [11]

One has to be careful with absolutes. All too often something contradictory turns up. Dönitz was an excellent leader, and it was probably his inspiration alone that kept the U-Bootwaffe going through the last two years of the war, but he wasn't perfect, especially if one realizes that his celebrated leadership style once killed a man. The man was Oskar Kusch, the commander of U-154, who blithely dumped the Führer's portrait into the trash one day. Kusch did not die in battle, in a training accident, or in a bombing raid. He was executed for sedition when his words and actions became too loud to ignore. Dönitz could easily have prevented it—there is little doubt that he would have done so in 1940 or 1941—but he chose to do nothing, and in doing nothing he never looked less inspiring.

The "Kusch affair" captured perfectly the moral dilemma faced by every member of the U-Bootwaffe, from Dönitz himself down to the least seaman and cook: the paradox of serving honorably a regime that was inherently dishonorable. Books too numerous to mention have been written about this dilemma and the mind-splitting problems it presented. Everyone handled it differently. Kusch, in confronting it, acquitted himself better than most, and it was odd that he did. Logically, he should have been enthusiastic about the Third Reich, for he was a product of the "new Germany." He grew up in Berlin, the seat of the new government. He was fourteen in 1933 when Adolf Hitler became chancellor. No doubt he heard the cheering; he may have seen the smoke rising from the Reichstag. The organization he joined as a boy, the Bundische Jugend, was soon swallowed up by the Hitler Youth. He was exposed to the deceits and subtle influences of the New Order in school, and when he left school he spent his mandatory year in the Reich Labor Service.[12]

But Kusch, like Oesten, was an early skeptic. In 1935 he left the Hitler Youth and soon came under investigation for disloyalty. It is possible that he entered the Kriegsmarine in 1937 to avoid arrest, although his service record does not show any sign of trouble and in fact offers the picture of an above-average officer with several talents. In June 1941, after initial U-boat training, Kusch was assigned to U-103 as a watch officer. During his time on board U-103 he served under three different commanders, each of whom graded him highly. "An excellent young officer," wrote one. "He has matured in the war; his impeccable disposition, his fine attitude and quickness of mind make him a valuable aid to the commander . . . he will be very well qualified to be a U-boat commander." Oskar Kusch was an artist, a devout Christian, and a quiet man who kept to himself; to those who knew him he was pleasant, thoughtful, forthright in his views, and formidable in discussion.

In February 1943, when Kusch first took command of U-154, the Battle of the Atlantic was approaching its end, and his fortunes as a commander reflected that decline. By the end of the year he had made two war patrols: during the first he sank one ship and damaged two others, but during the second he was unable even to approach the enemy, let alone attack. His skepticism increased and became vocal. He began to say what he thought, and he apparently did not care who in the boat heard him. He criticized the actions of the government and the high command and made rude jokes about the party. He began to complain about the boat, a type IXC built to a modified World War I design; she was out of date, obsolescent in the undersea war of 1943. He wondered out loud about the strategy he was trying to execute and even about the leaders he had to follow. He predicted Germany's loss within the year. Ordinarily such criticisms would have gone no further, even if others who heard them did not agree with them. Loyalties within the boat and the service would have prevented anyone from taking the matter further. Kusch, however, had the misfortune of having a first watch officer, Oberleutnant zur See Ulrich Abel, who was disdainful of Kusch personally, consumed with bitterness at having to serve under a man whom he considered his intellectual inferior, and ardent in his enthusiasm for National Socialism. In January 1944, in a detailed report to the Second U-Flotilla commander, Ernst Kals, Abel formally charged his commander with sedition and cowardice.

The charges were ludicrous and should have been dealt with as such. "The 'crime' he was accused of was committed by more or less all of us," observed another commander, Eberhard Wallrodt, "listening to enemy radio stations and talking disparagingly about the bigwigs." Most accounts indicate that there was widespread dismay in the U-Bootwaffe officer corps that Abel had taken such a step. It was not the proper thing, and several officers tried to talk Abel into withdrawing the damning report. He refused, however, and Kals had no alternative but to initiate court-martial proceedings against Kusch. After preliminary investigations, during which the cowardice charge was thrown out, the trial began on 26 January 1944 in Kiel. Abel testified, as did three other officers in U-154; two backed his accusation, the third, a midshipman, was probably pushed into doing so. Kusch tried to put the best light on his actions, but he did not deny them, and he was convicted. Because of the nature of the charge, the president of the court had no choice but to sentence Kusch to death, and he did. At dawn on 12 May 1944 Oskar Kusch was taken from Kiel-Wik Naval Prison to a nearby rifle range. At 0632 he was shot by firing squad. Two minutes later he was declared dead, and immediately after that he was placed in a plain service coffin for burial.[13]

It was a disgraceful episode in the short history of the U-Bootwaffe, and it reflected badly on almost everyone involved. Only Kusch himself rose above the tawdry mess. Aside from Abel, who is generally considered a reptile for having filed the charge, the worst loser was Karl Dönitz. His widely advertised bond with his men seems to have failed completely the day Kusch was accused. He accepted the charges against Kusch as truthful without investigating Abel, his motives, or his veracity. He approved the sentence of death and against the advice of several other officers, including former U-103 commander Werner Winter, declined to commute it. Gustav-Adolf Janssen, Kusch's last commanding officer in U-103, found himself traveling with Dönitz at that time from Lorient to Berlin by automobile; in a macabre replay of the 1940 Christmas encounter between Dönitz and Otto Kretschmer, he spent the entire journey trying in vain to persuade Dönitz to spare Kusch's life. Most puzzling, Dönitz, who was supposed to be so accessible and so solicitous, never met with Kusch from the day he was accused until the day he died. It is incomprehensible that he would abandon one of his own in such a way. "Whatever the political environment may have been," wrote Erich Topp, "it would still have been in place here for Dönitz to speak to his commander at least once and to stand by him. Or was he so naive that he did not know what people were saying in the U-boat messes?"[14]

Most U-Bootwaffe officers did not know the details of the Kusch case while it was going on or even after Kusch was executed. For several reasons it was not widely reported. Those who are now familiar with it fall into predictable camps. Kusch was determined to bring about his own execution, wrote Karl-Friedrich Merten, and not even his best friends could talk him out of it. "I have experienced types like him. He could not be considered as 'normal.' If he was not able to comply with the normal standards of a naval officer he could have found reasons to abandon [his position]. But he felt he must try the decisive point!" Erich Topp, not surprisingly, takes the opposite view: "If we comprehend tradition as being in touch with and continuing lofty intellectual currents, then Sub-Lieutenant Kusch undoubtedly fits into this pattern, whereas Admiral of the Fleet Dönitz does not." For Topp, Oskar Kusch is a true hero of Germany. After the war, as a senior officer in the Bundesmarine, he tried and failed to have Kusch memorialized in the fashion of Stauffenberg or Bonhoeffer. It is a measure of how far Topp himself came, for when asked whether he could have done what Kusch did, he replied with admirable candor that he could not.[15]

"Our fathers and ourselves sowed dragon's teeth." When Oskar Kusch was shot, his father received a terse notification of his son's death, along with a warning not to publish a death notice. It is hard to know exactly how he felt, but ironically Karl Dönitz, the man who had done so little for Kusch's son, did know. Two days after Kusch's execution, a German *Schnellboot* was attacked and sunk in the English Channel. Among the dead who later washed ashore on the coast of France was Oberleutnant zur See Klaus Dönitz, who had been on board as a guest of the captain.[16]

THE Schnellboot in which Klaus Dönitz lost his life was at sea that day to monitor Allied preparations for an expected cross-Channel invasion. Dönitz knew such an invasion was imminent, although he did not know the time or the place. He also knew that any prospect of stopping or even slowing the invasion was illusory. The Allies had complete control of the English Channel, and any boat that came near the invasion force would probably be destroyed. Nevertheless, in an order issued in April from Koralle, he directed that commanders involved in such an invasion attack vigorously, "even if one's own boat is put at risk . . . the U-boat which inflicts losses on the enemy at the landing has fulfilled its highest task and justified its existence, even though it stays there."[17]

The confusion caused by this directive amply illustrates the problems Dönitz was having. U-boats were to attack the landing force with the objective of sinking anything they could find, even landing craft, or, it seemed, to die trying. It was a bad trade. A landing craft carrying fifty men was not worth a U-boat also carrying fifty men, especially if that boat was capable of sinking even one freighter at sea. The order was hard enough to believe on the face of it. "As can be imagined," wrote Peter Cremer, who heard it on La Pallice, "this call was discussed by the crews. More than once I heard, 'Now we are to sacrifice ourselves.' No amount of empty words or undisciplined bearing was going to suppress this view." But he could not imagine that it was to be taken literally, if only because Dönitz could not waste his commanders so blithely if they were to command the new miracle boats he kept promising. After all, he wrote, "what else was a C-in-C to say in those days—what was expected of him?"[18]

Not everyone saw it that way, however. By the time the order had filtered down to the two U-flotillas in Brest, for example, it looked as though it had been through one of BdU's Enigma machines. Kapitän zur See

Hans-Rudolf Rösing, FdU-West, told the commanders in these flotillas that an order had come from Koralle stating that all boats were to "attack and sink invasion fleet with the final objective of destroying enemy ships by ramming." This is the so-called ramming order that has become one of the principal bugaboos in Werner's book. "Deadly silence gripped the room," Werner recalled. "Fifteen captains, all experienced U-boat men, could not believe what they had heard. This was sheer madness." He asked Rösing to repeat himself; were U-boat really to ram enemy vessels, a maneuver that would mean almost certain destruction for the boat and her crew? Rösing confirmed his statement.[19] Werner quotes Karl-Heinz Marbach, another veteran commander present that day, to back him up on this point. Marbach had described the ramming order in Harald Busch's book *U-Boats at War,* and he is as clear as Werner. The order to ram was given to him as well, just before the invasion.[20]

"It is not true," fumed Horst Bredow, "that Grossadmiral Dönitz gave the order to ram (if necessary)—there was only one Chief of a home flotilla who made a speech to the commanders going to the front . . . but never Dönitz! Such an order was never issued!!!"[21] In fact, there is little doubt as to Dönitz's real order, and the source of the confusion can be traced back to Rösing. It was not the job of a group commander like Rösing to issue operational orders; he held only an administrative position. Furthermore, Hans-Rudolf Rösing was not a man given to independent thought; he could only echo the wishes of his superiors, so faithfully that he was known as "his master's voice" after the little dog in the old RCA advertisements. Werner pictures him as a rather flighty and superficial officer with beautiful silver hair who, while La Rochelle was being evacuated in September 1944, jauntily packed tennis rackets and balls as he gave Werner a last set of ridiculous orders to attack enemy shipping in the heavily guarded North Channel. Thus it seems most likely that Rösing received Dönitz's order as Cremer heard it and put his own enthusiastic spin on it for the benefit of the Brest flotillas. The question is academic. It certainly did not matter to Werner. He and fifteen other commanders had been given an order to ram, and they were obliged to follow it. Had it come down to this—had Werner actually had to steam at top speed into the side of a troop transport—he would have been just as dead no matter who gave the order, Rösing or Dönitz or the man in the moon.[22]

The tactical decisions made by Dönitz as BdU were for the most part sound. Those he made as ObdM were less so; they often seem ill-informed, hurried, and clumsy. Many were affected by the initial strategic decision he had made in continuing to send his boats to sea. In mid-1943, for example, German shipyards began fitting boats with huge batteries of antiaircraft guns so that the boats could remain on the surface when attacked from the air and fight it out. For a while they tried to blast their way out of the Bay of Biscay with these guns. The results were disastrous. The gun batteries and the new torpedoes that were being delivered to the boats led Dönitz to resume convoy attacks in September. Time and again wolfpacks were thrown against convoys with heavy escorts and stifling air coverage; time and again the boats were hunted down and the convoys escaped unscathed. In January 1944 Rudeltaktik was given up for good. Henceforth boats operated independently, just as they had done in World War I. Nor were his tactical mistakes restricted to U-Bootwaffe operations. The decision to send the battle cruiser *Scharnhorst* to sea against a Murmansk convoy in December 1943 proved to be a dreadful mistake that resulted in her sinking, and Victor Oehrn barely talked Dönitz out of a similar blunder during the *Tirpitz* discussion in 1944.

OKM reaction to the invasion of Europe, which began early on 6 June 1944, was completely in character. Dönitz, like most theater commanders, was taken by surprise and did not know at first what to do. Some U-boat commanders tell of waiting hours for orders or of receiving orders that were unrealistic or unwise or both. There were not enough boats available to make an effective response, and the few that finally made it into the Channel were ill-equipped for the close-in operations required. The ramming order never came into effect; no boats got close enough to the invasion force for that. Cremer, Werner, and Marbach were able to get under way from their respective bases, and Marbach even fired torpedoes at three different destroyers on D-Day plus 2. But not a single vessel in the landing force was lost or damaged by U-boat attack until 15 June, nine days after the invasion began.[23]

There were several reasons for this loss of tactical effectiveness, and the comedy of errors surrounding the ramming order illustrates some of them. The physical distance between Dönitz and the U-boat bases denied him the tactical information he needed to issue such an order and meant that he could neither correct nor explain the order afterward. His unwillingness to delegate tactical decision making to lower levels forced the order to fall through several levels on its way down to the boats. Thus it was garbled and embellished by subordinate commanders. Finally, Dönitz was by this time allowing his tactical judgment to be affected by other, less rational, considerations.

According to Padfield, Dönitz after 1943 had acquired a fanaticism that he allowed to "override rational calculation." The ramming order was an example. He objected routinely to proposed withdrawals, preferring to hold on in unrealistic expectation of later developments until wholesale surrenders were inevitable. He offered Hitler one cheerful note after the other: new weapons, great success at sea in this battle or that. In indulging this tendency toward optimism in the face of contradicting reality, wrote Padfield, "Dönitz was not fighting with his head, but with his blood, behaving not like a rational commander but as a National Socialist, convinced like Hitler that will-power and fanaticism would make up for numerical or technical inferiority."[24] For many years Dönitz seemed immune to such criticism, certainly among his own men, but also in military and historical circles on both sides. Recently, however, historians have tended increasingly to link him with National Socialism. Peter Padfield leads the attack, but he is not alone, and now even some of Dönitz's former subordinates have grudgingly accepted that he was less than perfect in this area. "Dönitz's apologists hold that he was an unpolitical officer," wrote Erich Topp, "but I am not convinced. . . . His unconditional commitment to Hitler, his decrees and speeches . . . all this induces me to reject this assessment."[25]

In the last two years of the war Dönitz became much more closely aligned with the National Socialist thought of his Führer than he had been as BdU; in his calm and collected way, he was as enthusiastic as anyone in Hitler's entourage. There are any number of reasons for this. For Topp it was a simple case of hubris: "He was intoxicated by the military successes to whose glamor he contributed himself and that blurred his vision."[26] Jürgen Oesten's explanation is more exotic and typical of his character. "There is no doubt that Dönitz succumbed to the mesmerizing influence of Hitler," he wrote. "According to my opinion all people with an even slightly emotional character were in danger [of falling] for Hitler's irrational sauce of emotional influence. I think mathematical brains only, with no emotions at all, were in the position to sustain and to use their own intelligence. . . . If you have a strong transmitter, transmitting a certain frequency, most receivers (emotional) will be swamped by this one frequency and cannot receive any other frequencies. Very few receivers (nonemotional) are in the position to select other frequencies as well and to keep their independence."[27] Padfield theorizes that Hitler, surrounded by sycophantic staff officers who did not tell him the truth, came to rely on Dönitz more and more as an officer of integrity who did not cater to his tantrums and whims. Dönitz returned Hitler's increased trust by allowing his own political enthusiasm a freer rein, even after he became aware of the full import of Hitler's New Order and the crimes it spawned. And Dönitz did know what was happening; for example, he almost certainly attended the fateful convention of October 1943 in which Heinrich Himmler outlined the gruesome specifics of the "final solution," his scheme for exterminating the entire Jewish population of Central Europe. Since he knew about Himmler's plan and did nothing, concluded Topp, his behavior "comes very close to a passive toleration of [these] insane crimes." Few in the U-Bootwaffe would go so far, but Topp, whose aunt was imprisoned in Theresienstadt concentration camp from 1943 to 1945, has a very low tolerance for National Socialism.[28]

The decrees and speeches to which Topp refers are those Dönitz began to issue and make after he became ObdM, many of which were no more than the standard National Socialist drivel wrapped in navy blue. In September 1943 he issued a "Decree Against Criticism and Complaints" in which he stated that "the Führer has laid the basis for the unity of the German people through the National Socialist ideology." Oskar Kusch complained loudly about this decree—it was one of the things that Abel used against him. The order of the day issued from Koralle on New Year's Day 1944 was fairly routine for the period: "The battle for freedom and justice for our people continues," he announced. "It will see us pitted inexorably against our enemy. The Führer shows us the way and the goal. We follow him with body and soul to a great German future. Heil our Führer!" The worst was probably a speech he made in August 1944, in which he stated that he would rather eat dirt than have his grandson "brought up and become poisoned in the Jewish spirit and filth." This particular utterance is even more disturbing when one realizes that it was made almost a year after he listened to Himmler's description of what was actually happening to the Jews in Europe.[29]

Victor Oehrn differs from this view of his commander in chief as a willing participant in Hitler's actions. "Certainly Dönitz was very impressed by Hitler," he wrote, "as were many others inside and outside Germany. [And] he was without doubt an absolutely loyal officer. . . . It would be absurd to accuse him of complicity, however, just because he sought every opportunity to speak with Hitler and to stay in close contact with him." The reason for Dönitz's willingness to deal with Hitler and his seeming acceptance of National Socialism was, according to Oehrn, fairly apparent. He had to do so to protect the interests of the Kriegsmarine: excluding himself from Hitler's presence would have hurt his attempts to get more men and more resources for the service. He remained on a cordial basis with many members of the party—Heinrich Himmler, Martin Bormann, Albert Speer—for the same reason, and if he saw or heard more than he would have liked in the process, it was just one of those things which his virtues more than balanced. "One has to caution against judging men in places of great responsibility by their words. Everything depends upon their deeds—one is best able to judge a man by those." [30]

BY THE middle of July Victor Oehrn had come to the same uncomfortable realization that many of his comrades had already reached: Germany could no longer win the war. The Allied armies were fighting their way southeast toward Paris and west toward the U-boat bases. The Red Army had reached the border of East Prussia. Rome had just fallen and German cities were being incinerated by Allied bombers. He still believed, based on his general knowledge of the political situation and his personal knowledge of the Soviet Union, that a political solution was possible, but even that slim hope was fading. And then, late in the evening of 20 July 1944, he was awakened by an urgent call from Karl Dönitz. Do not come into work today, he was told; stay at home and do not answer the telephone again. There has been some trouble at Rastenburg. [31]

Oehrn did not know then, but a colonel in the German army, a decorated veteran of North Africa who had lost an arm and now worked on OKW staff in Berlin, had just tried to assassinate Adolf Hitler by blowing him and most of his senior staff up with a bomb in a briefcase. Dönitz ordered Oehrn to stay at home because he knew that Berlin, indeed the entire country, would soon erupt into a bloodbath of retribution. The would-be assassin, Claus Schenk von Stauffenberg, would be executed at once, as would several of his co-conspirators. Hundreds of senior Wehrmacht officers would die in the following months for real or imagined complicity in the plot. Erwin Rommel, Oehrn's hero, would be forced to commit suicide for his pitifully small role. There was no reason for Oehrn to risk being caught up in such a purge. After all, Dönitz had no intention of being caught himself.

Dönitz's reaction to the assassination attempt reinforces much of what historians have lately had to say about him, particularly the idea that as ObdM he became unacceptably close to Hitler and National Socialism. As soon as he heard about the bomb, he moved to place himself and the Kriegsmarine firmly and visibly on the side of the stricken Führer. Within hours he was at Rastenburg taking tea with Hitler and his staff. Before the day was out he had sent a signal to the fleet: "Men of the Navy! The treacherous attempt on the life of the Führer fills each and every one of us with holy wrath and bitter rage towards our criminal enemies and their hirelings."[32] A longer signal in the same fulsome vein followed the next day. At least one officer who heard these signals, the contrary-minded Jürgen Oesten, was unimpressed: " On July 20 1944 there was a lot of noise on the radio and wireless due to the fact that Stauffenberg had tried to kill Hitler. We were somewhere in the Indian Ocean. I had to call the crew together in order to explain the situation. I remember that I mentioned that whatever these officers may have done, I was convinced that they had honest motives."[33]

Normally this would have been a suicidal statement even though Oesten was a veteran Kriegsmarine officer, a noted U-boat commander, and a holder of the Knight's Cross. Officers more powerful and more decorated than he were dropping like flies, or hanging, as the case might have been, for less. His uncle Erwin Plank was hanged on January 1945 as a result of post-assassination hysteria. But Oesten was on the outward leg of a war patrol to Malaya that he knew would last at least six months, possibly longer, during which he and his crew would be hermetically sealed in their boat and protected against any reprisals from the party. It would have been interesting to have overheard Oesten "explain the situation" and to see the crew's reaction when he told them that the plotters' motives were honest; the fact that he had sunk a small Brazilian troop ship that very day probably helped his credibility.[34]

In Germany during the first frantic days after the assassination attempt most people, including Dönitz, were tripping over themselves to proclaim their loyalty to Hitler and their outrage at Stauffenberg's treason. In many cases this outrage was entirely genuine, and the prevailing opinion within the U-Bootwaffe officer corps was diametrically opposed to Oesten's personal opinion. The excesses of National Socialism were not fully known in the fleet, nor, as Eric Rust notes, was there any knowledge of an organized resistance to Hitler. The events of 20 July came across as the acts of a madman who would kill Germany's supreme commander, and her only leader, at a time when Germany herself was fighting for survival as a nation. Far from having an "honest motive," Stauffenberg and those who plotted with him could only be considered traitors, deserving of their punishment.

Dönitz's reaction did not stop with speeches and signals. By the end of the week the traditional military salute used in the Kriegsmarine since its birth had been replaced by the *Deutsche Gruss,* resulting, as Herbert Werner wrote, in some odd exchanges "as the traditional salute was quite frequently executed to return somebody's new-style greeting." Officers were given permission to join the party (which had been banned for over a decade). Finally, a new category of naval officer, *National Sozialist Führungs-Offizier,* the NSFO, began to appear in the U-Bootwaffe with responsibility for ensuring loyalty to the party within the boat. Not surprisingly, he was hated by everyone on board, not just because he was in many cases a useless passenger but because his presence was a symbol of distrust. The reaction of Werner's crew when they met their new NSFO in late 1944 was predictable. "They had proved their loyalty and courage with deeds, and they needed no Party preacher to tell them how to fight and die." Werner solved the problem by assigning the new man so many other duties that he had no time to enforce ideological purity.[35]

The atmosphere of suspicion that began to pervade the boats was just as charged in the Kriegsmarine shore establishment. One example more glaring than most involved Wolfgang Lüth, an officer who by mid-1944 was very definitely in the Kriegsmarine's fast track. In July Lüth was moved from the Twenty-second U-Flotilla in Gotenhafen to the Marineschule Mürwik, where he became a division officer, and in August he was promoted to Fregattenkapitän. In September he was promoted again to become the youngest Kapitän zur See in the Kriegsmarine and named commandant, a position traditionally held by a flag officer. (The appointment annoyed several admirals, but so grimly intent was Dönitz on making it that he threatened to promote Lüth again if he had to. It is a measure of his increased power that he was able to do for Lüth in 1944 what he could not do for Oehrn in 1942.)

Wolfgang Lüth was a capable officer and an excellent leader. So were many other officers, including one or two U-boat commanders who were just as qualified for the position. His political credentials, however, were impeccable and may well have clinched the job for him. For despite all that had happened, the loss of the Battle of the Atlantic, the invasion, the assassination attempt, and the tremendous losses, Lüth was still a champion of the merits of National Socialism and incorrigibly cheerful about prospects for a German victory. One day after his appointment, he was informed that the wife of the chief engineer of the Sixth Schnellboot Flotilla had been heard making an unwise remark in the Glücksburg officer housing area. Lüth, who was the senior Kriegsmarine officer in the Flensburg-Glücksburg region, hauled the man into his office and accused him of sedition (*warf mir wehrzersetzende Einstellung vor*). "[He told me] I was responsible for the public opinions of my wife. In addition he would have to consider this episode in connection with the events of 20 July 1944, and if any further remarks, however innocuous, became public, I would have to bear the consequences." [36]

One night in December 1944, after the beginning of the Ardennes offensive, Lüth gathered the Fähnriche of the Marineschule together. Standing in the snow, to the accompaniment of the wind in the beeches and the crackling of signal flares, he delivered a stirring exhortation to victory that impressed even the officers who heard it. [37] But men like him were now scarce. In December a young officer named Heinz Schaeffer took command of the new U-977, a boat that was destined to make him famous. Almost immediately he had to abandon his base in Pillau, for the Red Army was advancing fast into East Prussia. "It was clear that we were defeated," he recorded bitterly in his biography, *U-Boat 977*. "At heart I revolted against the useless prolonging of the war, and I was infuriated at the thought of incompetent cowardly civilians sending boys and old men into action while they themselves broke every promise they had ever made." [38] On the day after Christmas, Herbert Werner looked up from the bridge of his boat and watched listlessly as wave after wave of bombers passed overhead on their way to Hamburg. He had given up all hope in August after barely escaping from the besieged base in Brest; then in September, as though fate were rewarding him for his despair, his parents were killed in a huge air raid on Darmstadt. [39]

As 1944 passed painfully into 1945 and the U-boats sailed and were sunk, Karl Dönitz slipped perceptibly away from the men in the boats and ever closer to Adolf Hitler, placating him and bolstering him with cheerful reports of U-boat successes and optimistic predictions about the future. As he did so, Hitler came to rely more and more on the upright, loyal, and always reliable commander in chief of his navy and less and less on the gloomy and dissipated leaders of his armies, his air forces, and his SS. By the time Dönitz observed his second anniversary as the most powerful man in the Kriegsmarine, he had become perhaps the most powerful man in the Wehrmacht as well, but it had cost him his integrity, his independence, and his honor, and he now had only the love of his men to carry him through the last bitter months of a dying nation.

CHAPTER 12

The Woodcutter

The man who masters himself is delivered from the force that binds all creatures.

—Goethe

29 MARCH 1933. And so we cross over to the Dänholm. One can look upon it as a symbol. On the one side lies the previous life, the first stage; on the other the beginning of a new life." This book began with this diary entry by a young Reichsmarine recruit. Nineteen years old, he had just crossed a narrow ribbon of dirty seawater and his life had changed. The future seemed limitless. It is best ended with the same man, now a weary and suspicious veteran, standing at another crossing and contemplating a different future. Jürgen Oesten, like so many of his comrades, was approaching the end of a war that Germany was bound to lose, and everything in his life was going to change again.[1]

OESTEN brought U-861 into the harbor of Trondheim, Norway, on 19 April 1945, after a three-month passage from Penang in Japanese-occupied Malaya. The patrol he had just completed (actually two patrols separated by an extended layover in Malaya for overhaul and provisioning) had been only a partial success. He had sunk four ships, hardly a total for the record books, but his crew was still alive, and crammed into U-861's hull were containers of opium, rock crystal, rubber in tanks, and 120 metric tons of molybdenum concentrate (whether any of this got from the docks of Trondheim to the factories of Germany is not known, but it is doubtful considering the tenuous condition of the supply lines at that time).

The Reich had less than three weeks to live when Oesten returned, and he stayed with U-861 until its end. There was one close call: Konterad-miral Erich Schulte-Mönting, Admiral Nordmeer, had planned to reassign him as commander of a minesweeping flotilla that was fast disintegrating into mutiny, but Oesten managed to talk him out of it with a large bag of coffee he had brought back with him from Malaya. Was it a bribe? He says no. It was simply a measure of how much things had changed in a year. Priorities had changed. The war was obviously over, and he had sur-vived the worst of it. Better to stay in the relative safety of his own boat, among friends, than to take command of a flotilla of strangers looking for trouble. The imperative of accepting orders without question had been overriden by the more practical notion of using one's common sense to stay alive.[2]

To understand this mind-set, it is necessary to understand what was happening in the last days of the Third Reich. Allied armies had crossed German borders on both sides and were preparing to link up on the Elbe near Torgau. Refugees were flooding into the west. Adolf Hitler and his government were in Berlin, huddled in underground bunkers and insu-lated from reality. The fabric of discipline that had held the U-Bootwaffe, indeed the entire Wehrmacht, together for so long was beginning to unravel. Commanders were moved, and moved again, to serve the needs of a confused leadership. Some sought to avoid orders with an eye toward their own best interests; others began to disobey them; and still others were placed in positions of judgment to track these men down and punish them. Many were swept into captivity. Two took themselves and their boats away from the fight entirely. One, having seen defeat, died tragically soon afterward.

In March Karl-Friedrich Merten was forced to close the Twenty-fourth U-Flotilla in Memel, which he had commanded since April 1943, and to evacuate all flotilla personnel to the west. To his credit, he was also able to evacuate a large number of German military casualties and civilian refugees, who would otherwise have fallen into the hands of the advancing Red Army. He was subsequently assigned to what he will only call "Spe-cial Duties, Führer Headquarters," actually a position as *Erster Beisitzer* on a *Fliegendes Standgericht*, a special flying court, attached to Navy Group West. The primary duty of these special courts, which consisted of a naval judge and two *Beisitzer,* naval advisers, was to try and pass instant judgment on naval personnel accused of cowardice, desertion, and other offenses likely to occur when an enemy force is advancing inexorably and withdrawals are either forbidden or heavily limited. Often the men accused were tried and sentenced by the court in a matter of hours, and their punishments, usually the death sentence, were carried out at once. Merten's record as a member of the *Standgericht* is not available; it would be wrong to lay at his feet a death resulting from anything other than a fair and impartial execution of his duties, although his performance was good enough for him to be promoted in May 1945, just days before the war ended, to the rank of Kapitän zur See over 179 more senior officers.[3]

Gottfried König was lucky enough not to have to appear before a Standgericht in the last week of the war. He had been away from the front since he left U-181 in October 1943 and was commander of the training boat U-316. On 1 May 1945, after the boat experienced a mechanical failure and could not be repaired, he sank her in the mouth of the River Trave and led his crew onto land and into a desperate search for safety in the plains of Schleswig-Holstein. At one point he was stopped and ordered to form an infantry company for a final defense of the Kiel-Flensburg area. "At the last minute," he wrote, "a *Panzerfaust* was pressed into my hands for a final defense against the attacking English forces. I thought it was a crazy idea and refused, and since the English were in Lübeck a few days later I could not be held accountable for it. Of course U-boat sailors are not infantrymen, and could only make a mess of things in land warfare." Like many others, König elected to follow his common sense rather than orders that were clearly absurd.[4]

The destruction of the U-boats continued apace. More than one hundred boats were lost in the first four months of 1945, most of them with their entire crews, for negligible returns in tonnage and no strategic benefit whatsoever. There was one glimmer of hope in 1945. Toward the end of the previous year the first of two new U-boat types were commissioned: the small type XXIII and the large type XXI. Both were revolutionary; the latter in particular was as different from existing U-boats as the jet engine was from the propeller and was comparable in many respects to a modern submarine. Hull design was improved. New electric motors reduced sound signatures, and increased battery capacity raised maximum underwater speed to seventeen knots. Improved fuel economy and better snorkels allowed the type XXI to make an entire patrol without surfacing. They were indeed the miracle boats for which the U-Bootwaffe had been waiting so long; in spring 1945, after years of development and months of testing, they were beginning to arrive at the front, manned by veteran crews and commanded by the most experienced U-boat commanders still available (no matter how long they had been absent from the front). Adalbert Schnee, for example, Karl Dönitz's operations officer since 1942, was given U-2511. Erich Topp, head of testing for the new boats and a staff officer for almost three years, finished the war in command of U-2513. Peter Cremer was moved from U-333 to U-2519.

It would have been interesting to see how these boats fared in battle; had they appeared a year or two earlier, they might have had a real effect (although probably not the desired one of turning the war around). As it was, few of them reached the front. Dozens were sunk in their berths. U-2519 was bombed and damaged beyond repair on 5 April; she remained in commission, but Cremer elected to scuttle her shortly after the surrender. Topp took U-2513 out of Kiel on 1 May and headed for Norway. He heard of Hitler's death as he sneaked through the Skagerrak and was informed of the surrender as soon as he put into Horten. Schnee had managed to initiate an operation patrol on 30 April from Bergen but received the order to cease fire just after he had found the heavy cruiser HMS *Norfolk* in his crosshairs, which he had been able to approach without detection. A later comparison of both logs showed that the *Norfolk* would have been destroyed; instead, Schnee broke off the attack and returned to Bergen. The type XXI miracle boats had not sunk a single ship. Neither they, nor the type XXIII boats, nor any of the other boats lost at sea since January had any effect on the course of a war whose death rattle now echoed in the discharge of a small pistol clutched in the hand of Adolf Hitler.

Before Hitler died, he designated his successor as head of the German state and commander in chief of her rapidly fading armed forces. To almost everyone's surprise, this man was not Heinrich Himmler or Hermann Goering but Karl Dönitz, the Kriegsmarine chief and U-boat admiral. Dönitz, who had by this time become a somewhat fey and gloomy figure, received notification of Hitler's death and of his own inheritance in the tiny Schleswig-Holstein town of Plön, where he had just relocated from Koralle. Shortly after that he moved again, to Flensburg, where the new center of government was set up in the gymnasium of the Marineschule. A new guard unit, Wachtbataillon Dönitz, was created from the crew of Peter Cremer's boat U-2519 to protect it, and Cremer himself was made the commander of Wachtbataillon Dönitz, responsible for security around the gymnasium and the school compound.

One of Dönitz's first acts in his new capacity was to recall his boats. There is some confusion even now about the number of transmissions, their originators, or even the sequence in which they were sent, but there

Wolfgang Lüth's funeral cortege in May 1945. Note the swastika on his casket, the armed guard, and the parade of naval officers more than a week after the armistice. (Author's collection)

is no doubt that on the afternoon of 5 May 1945 Dönitz made a signal to all U-boats that began: "My submariners: six years of submarine warfare lie behind us. You have fought like lions. An oppressive superiority in material has driven us into a corner. From the remaining ground a continuation of the fight is no longer possible." It was signed "Your Grand Admiral." It was a historic order, if perhaps not Nelsonian. "If the English sounds stilted," wrote Dan Van der Vat rather cattily, "the reader need only consult the German to understand why." Nevertheless, its meaning was clear: the U-boats were to cease all offensive action.[5]

WITH this signal World War II ended for the U-Bootwaffe. It had not been an easy battle or a satisfying one. They had indeed fought like lions: sinking twenty-eight hundred ships of fourteen million tons, tying Allied supply lines into knots, causing their enemies to fear, more than once, that the war would be lost because of them, all with scant resources and only grudging support on their own side. But the other side of the ledger was so dismal that one is led to wonder whether it was worth the effort. Almost twelve hundred boats were commissioned in six years, and almost eight hundred were lost. Of the forty thousand men who served in them, almost thirty thousand were killed, most of them after the Battle of the Atlantic was irretrievably lost.

For these reasons the reaction to Dönitz's signal was mixed. Herbert Werner was relieved, if not delighted, to hear it. "This," he wrote in *Iron Coffins*, "was the message that put an end to the suffering. . . . My death in an iron coffin, a verdict of long standing, was finally suspended. The truth was so beautiful that it seemed to be a dream."[6] Not everyone was so enthralled. Heinz Schaeffer, commander of U-977, was incredulous when he picked up Dönitz's recall signal in the English Channel. He did not believe that Dönitz was responsible for it; it was the work of an impostor, or the Grossadmiral had been forced to do it. "I couldn't conceive it possible that our leaders had sunk so far as to send out official orders to surrender."[7] When, the next day, he received another signal from Dönitz stating that all boats still at sea were to hoist a black flag and put into the nearest Allied port, Schaeffer knew the war was lost. The thought of defeat was unbearable. He decided to do something that would take him away from it and from the suffering that would inevitably follow. He disappeared, and nobody could find him. In the surge of events it was assumed that he had been lost. Few mourned.

On 14 May 1945, one week after the German surrender in Rheims, Wolfgang Lüth died. Still the commandant of the Marineschule, he had survived six years of war and sixteen war patrols without as much as a scratch only to be shot dead by one of Cremer's sailors on sentry duty. It was late at night in stormy weather, and Lüth was walking from Dönitz's headquarters in the school gymnasium to his home in the commandant's quarters along a narrow walkway called the Black Path. The sentry, young and nervous, challenged Lüth but heard no response; he fired once. Lüth was struck in the head and killed instantly. Since Lüth was the man who gave the order for the sentries to shoot, and since he kept walking even after the sentry had screamed three times for him to stop and identify himself, it was thought at first that he had committed suicide. This theory was rejected by a board of inquiry, and the shooting was ruled an accident.

Lüth believed in his country, her leadership, and National Socialism until the last days of the war, but he died knowing that Germany was defeated, Hitler was a fraud, and National Socialism was a bankrupt ideology responsible for untold suffering. We cannot know whether he rejected them before he died; Erich Topp believes that he would have done so had he lived. Nevertheless, Karl Dönitz requested, and received, permission from occupation authorities to bury Lüth with the military honors of the Third Reich: an honor guard of Ritterkreuzträger, an armed escort in his cortege, three volleys of rifle fire over his grave—and a swastika ensign on his casket. His story ends at that point. Dönitz never made much of his relationship with the man he buried so ceremoniously and mentions him only briefly in his memoirs. Other histories deny him the credit and the notoriety he deserves for his part in the Battle of the Atlantic. Lüth died, a talented officer, a confusing man, and vanished into time.

As Lüth lay on a bier in the memorial hall of the Marineschule, arguably a victim of the last bullet fired in Europe, other U-Bootwaffe officers more fortunate than he were contemplating an unlikely and often unexpected survival and a new life in an unrecognizable world. The country was devastated and lay in pieces. Of her once proud armies only dregs remained. Her people were exhausted, hungry, and homeless. In some cities, quite literally, there was no stone left upon another. One might say they had brought it on themselves; if so, they were paying for it. The families of U-Bootwaffe veterans suffered as much as anyone, in many cases even more because an abnormal number of their husbands, fathers, and sons had died at sea, and many others were still prisoners, their futures unknown.[8]

More than six thousand U-Bootwaffe officers and men were registered prisoners of war. Most of them were in North America, and there were no immediate plans to send them back home. Hundreds more were interned when they brought their boats into Allied ports after the war. Captivity took on various and fickle forms, and if a man was lucky he might remain free. Peter Cremer should have been arrested in Germany but was sent home after the camp he was supposed to be housed in was found to be full. Gottfried König was not arrested, nor was Hans-Rudolf Rösing or Karl-Friedrich Merten. Victor Oehrn was spared; as it happened, he was in the hospital again for another operation on his damaged hip. And finally, as of 21 May, two weeks after the armistice, Karl Dönitz was free, albeit under close supervision and without any real powers as the German head of state. The Allies put up with him because they needed someone in his position to deal with. He was a useful tool, but he knew his usefulness would not last much longer, and he said as much in a somber conversation at Oehrn's bedside. "Soon they will come to arrest me," he said toward the end. "I will be tried and sentenced, and I won't make it out of here alive [*man wird mich einen Kopf kurzer machen*]."

Oehrn found this very hard to believe. "How can you say that? Why would anyone treat you—a blameless naval officer—in such a way? It won't happen!"

"You are still young," said Dönitz matter-of-factly, "and you can't see it. The victors are in charge. It is a political thing now, and there will be a political trial. I can count on being sentenced to death, and I only hope that I will have the strength to see it through without making a mess of things. Everyone will condemn me in the end; I only hope that my U-boat men will stand by me."

"I can't believe it will be that way," replied Oehrn. "But whatever happens, the U-Bootwaffe will always stand by you. You can be assured of it." Dönitz left then, "completely relaxed and calm," and Oehrn, helpless in his hospital bed, could only reflect on Dönitz, on the U-Bootwaffe, on his own career, which, for someone who had always thought of himself as a staff officer, "a man without a name," had been much more exciting and more fulfilling than he had a right to expect. The magnificent Tatars of the Caucasus. Mecklenburg Bight. The Schnorchelbude and Prien. "Five days, Herr Admiral." Rome. Renate. "I can't make a cabinet matter out of it. There is a war on, and I have to follow orders just like you do." The magnificent Rommel. *Dein Wille geschehe.* "We are Australians. Are we good fighters?" Two grains of sand in the desert. "You will know later that I have never lied to you." He had come such a long way from the Dänholm. And yet he was only thirty-eight.[9]

Two days later, Dönitz joined his men in captivity when he and his cabinet were arrested by representatives of the Supreme Allied Commander in Europe, General Dwight D. Eisenhower. By all accounts, he conducted himself with dignity, and the arrests took place without incident. "Words," he said, "would be superfluous." Six months after that he was on trial at Nuremberg, along with twenty other senior party and Wehrmacht officials, including Hermann Goering and Erich Raeder (Goebbels and Himmler were both dead, suicides like their leader). He was, of course, entirely correct in his predictions to Oehrn. The world wanted his head.

JÜRGEN Oesten, still in command of U-861 but marooned in Trondheim with his crew, could only watch as the events of April and May flashed before him. When the British finally came for him, he surrendered his boat quietly, having no idea what would come next. There was no rhyme or reason to the fates of U-boat crewmen in Norway. Erich Topp, for example, turned U-2513 over to the British in Horten and was unconditionally released several weeks later in Germany. Herbert Werner, in contrast, captured just down the road from Oesten in Bergen, was turned over to the French army, which shipped him with a large number of POWs back to France. After three attempts, he escaped in October 1945, hopped a train back to Germany, and fled into the woods outside Frankfurt.

Oesten was sent neither to Germany nor to France, although he was promised the first option. The British wanted his boat in Northern Ireland, and since they did not have the expertise to do it themselves, they asked Oesten and his crew to take it from Trondheim to Londonderry. Oesten declined; the war was over, he announced, and he wanted to go home. Negotiations began, and a deal was eventually worked out with Oesten and several other commanders in the area: if they would sail their own boats to Northern Ireland, they would be rewarded with early repatriation to Germany. The boats were duly delivered. As Oesten sailed into the harbor, shepherded by British destroyers, he flashed a message: "Thank you for the escort." The reply, "It was a pleasure," was followed with arrest and internment. The agreement had been overruled somewhere up the line. It was an act of bad faith for which Oesten is still bitter, for it meant that he too was a prisoner of war.[10]

Oesten's first stop was a tiny POW camp of two Nissen huts and a barbed wire fence in Lissahally. Theodor Petersen was in one of the huts when he got there. Petersen was commander of U-874 when the war ended, and he surrendered his boat under similar circumstances. The two were sent to London—to the London District Cage (LDC) in Kensington, to be precise—for formal questioning. All U-boat officers captured by the Royal Navy passed through the LDC, which continued to operate for some time after the war ended. The interrogators at the LDC were excellent at their work; they invariably impressed their guests with an encyclopedic knowledge of the U-Bootwaffe and a detailed outline of their own personal lives. Oesten appreciated that Kensington was a dangerous place, but he gave nothing away and "cannot recall anything unpleasant."[11]

At the LDC a prisoner would be classified as to his political persuasion: the usual designation was white for apolitical or anti-Nazi, black for Nazis, gray for those in between. On this basis, he was assigned to a permanent camp for internment, and in due course, after the usual administrative red tape and paper chase in London, Jürgen Oesten and Theodor Petersen were classified and sent to POW Camp 18, Featherstone Park, located on the banks of the South Tyne in Northumberland. There they were put in with several thousand other prisoners, officers and men, to await the pleasure of the king.

Featherstone Park was a large camp. It would eventually house many thousands of German prisoners from every branch of the Wehrmacht. The camp spokesman was a Luftwaffe colonel. There was an army contingent led by several other colonels, a sprinkling of Kriegsmarine surface officers, a horde of U-boat crewmen, and almost seventy commanders. Like many such camps, Featherstone Park was a depressing place. Until the end of the war it was a typical POW camp in which the prisoners were treated as dangerous men. It was divided into three major areas, each identified with one of the color designations described above, but the camp leadership was in the "black" range. It was heavily guarded, and prisoners were allowed out of their huts only for exercise in ranks. Hostility and mutual distrust were the norm. When the war ended, this mood did not improve but merely changed into one of sullen indirection. "Ideologies fell down like a house of cards," wrote Matthew Barry Sullivan, author of the best book on prisoner of war camps in postwar Britain. "There was a parting of the ways between those who wanted to work for the future and those who endlessly mulled over the past." [12]

Theodor Petersen does not appear to have been overly affected by his bad fortune, but Jürgen Oesten was a nervous wreck when he arrived. His condition did not stem from defeat; unlike many in the camp, he was able to deal with the fall of National Socialism and the defeat of Germany. But the experience of war had left him emotionally exhausted; the sound of the guns, now silent, was deafening. He later described his mental state in a letter to an English friend, allegorically rather than literally, by using the image of a confused traveler in a strange land:

> Once upon a time there was an odd-job man, who by chance got to a place in Northumberland to do some wood-cutting. He was a bit clumsy, handled the language roughly . . . and [he was] a bit curious about the situation and the new experience. The war had spit him ashore in this country and he was somehow drifting between two entirely different lives, the one behind and the one ahead. Few things had kept their value. The times that passed had left their marks. To be married to uncertainty for a bit too long a time had made him somehow hard-boiled and less sensitive. There were some undigested sensations and experiences hanging around still. [13]

He was on the brink, and what happened to him in the months after his capture would probably affect him for the rest of his life. His "hard-boiled and less sensitive" veneer might have been very much exacerbated had Featherstone Park continued as Sullivan describes above; indeed, in many camps that did not change for the better, he would probably have become even more insensitive to life and perhaps been permanently scarred by bitterness and distrust. For such has happened to others in his position—men who are even now immersed in the gall of the past.

As Oesten prepared himself for the long Northumbrian winter, the world received its one final jolt of U-boat intrigue. On 17 August 1945 Heinz Schaeffer suddenly reappeared in Buenos Aires. By a remarkable feat of navigation, he had managed to take U-977 and most of her crew all the way from Norway to the River Plate without being detected. The journey had begun the day he received the second signal from Dönitz. Most of the married men were put ashore in Norway, a detour that meant U-977 would have to make a long and hazardous dash past the British Isles to Gibraltar through waters still vigorously patrolled by enemy ships and aircraft. The first sixty-six days of the journey were spent underwater. The crew became ghostly and listless; tempers were frayed; small incidents of theft and insubordination occurred. It is a tribute to Schaeffer that he kept everyone together until U-977 sailed into Argentine waters.

Things did not work out as Schaeffer had planned, however. He was accused after he arrived in Buenos Aires of having smuggled Adolf Hitler out of Europe, and for that reason he was interrogated at length by both Argentine and American authorities. Such a possibility seems patently ridiculous now, but many otherwise sensible people were prepared to believe it in the months and years after the war, and Schaeffer's voyage has since provided a flimsy historical basis for wild tales of Adolf Hitler founding a fourth Reich in South America or Antarctica. For all his troubles, unfortunately, Schaeffer became a prisoner of war, first in Argentina, then in the United States, and the boat he had shepherded all the way to Buenos Aires was destroyed.[14]

Oesten's first winter in Featherstone Park was not as bad as he might have expected. The cheerless air of the previous summer improved markedly during that time so that by the spring it seemed a different place. When Burkard von Müllenheim-Rechberg, the ranking survivor of the sunken battleship *Bismarck*, arrived from Canada in March, he was surprised by what he saw. "When, as a member of a large group, I first glimpsed Camp 18," he recalled, "something unusual was immediately evident. There was no barbed wire; no watchtowers; British guards were nowhere in sight. I saw German prisoners leisurely strolling outside the camp area; completely without British 'supervision'; their simple word of honor sufficed now." Taken inside, he found less a prison than a small German city: a city that bragged a newspaper, two theaters, a university, a library, a working population, and a surprising level of trust and good-will. For von Müllenheim-Rechberg, who had known both good camps and bad in his five years of captivity, Featherstone Park was a new experience.[15]

It was a remarkable transformation, and several factors were involved, but Sullivan gives most of the credit to three men: the camp commandant, a new camp spokesman, and an unusual interpreter whose talents lay far beyond his duties. The commandant, a bluff and practical lieutenant colonel named Vickers, arrived at the camp just before Oesten. A prisoner himself in World War I, he realized at once that the men in Featherstone Park were being handled improperly. The war was over, and the purpose of the camp had changed; he "could see that . . . what his Germans needed was to be trusted, to feel less hemmed in and to have ways of relieving their cramped feelings and muscles." As if to underscore this point, he removed the watchtowers and barbed wire fences surrounding the camp.[16]

Theodor Petersen helped to tear those fences down. When he arrived at Featherstone Park he had seen only the wire, but when the wire was gone he was able to look around him, and he saw, perhaps for the first time, the beauty of the area, the flowers along the Tyne, the deer in the fields. Petersen's image calls to mind a book by C. S. Lewis called *The Last Battle*. In it he describes two soldiers, both of whom believe they are imprisoned in a cage. One soldier will not be told that the cage is an illusion, and so he remains imprisoned; the other opens his eyes, looks around, the cage disappears, and he is free. In fact, he has been free all along. This is what was happening to men in Featherstone Park: for some of them the place was no more than a prison and it stayed that way until the day they left. For others, like Petersen, the prison disappeared when they opened their eyes and looked around.[17]

In January 1946 the interpreter arrived. His name was Herbert Sulzbach, and his background was as interesting as that of anyone described in this book. He was a German Jew, born in Frankfurt and a veteran of the German army in World War I. In 1938 the political climate forced him and his family to flee to Britain, and when the war began he was interned on the Isle of Man. He joined the British Army in 1940, received a commission, and by 1946 had risen to the rank of captain. He became a British subject during the war, but he held an undying love for Germany and never stopped believing in the underlying virtue of his former countrymen. His posting was not accidental; he was not sent to Featherstone Park because of his skill as an interpreter but because of his extraordinary ability to console, to advise, to counsel, and, if necessary, to admonish those who in his judgment had been temporarily misled by National Socialism. As Vickers improved the material lot of the men in Featherstone Park, Sulzbach improved their mental and emotional condition.

Sulzbach achieved an immediate affinity with almost every German in the camp. Such was his ability to comfort and to assure that they lined up outside his tiny office to talk to him. Said one former Featherstone Park prisoner (a farmer) in 1976, "Even now, if it were necessary, I would sell half my cows and drive over half the world just to be able to talk to Herbert."[18] Unfortunately, one of the few men who could not get along with Sulzbach was Jürgen Oesten. "[Sulzbach] did a tremendous lot of good handling POW affairs in a sensitive and fair way," he wrote. "Why did we not like each other? I think he thought me to be arrogant and I did not take his camouflage seriously."[19] Paradoxically, the differences between the two men helped Oesten more than they hurt. They may even have been the key to his survival.

Shortly after Oesten arrived, he was made deputy camp spokesman, but the position did not seem to work out, at least not insofar as he used it to help other prisoners. "As a born man-manager," wrote Sullivan "[Oesten] quickly asserted his force of character and ability at Featherstone Park. He was not, however, widely popular. He tended to bear rather heavily on the younger naval men . . . and he was not behind the new spirit that was being created in the camp."[20] Oesten concedes that he might have been unpopular, but he professes to be unconcerned: "Whether I was popular or not did not worry me overmuch as long as I could achieve more freedom for the camp inmates by cooperation with and suggestions to the British authorities. Of course for some of the die-hard boys who were prisoners [for] many years this was going too fast and I may not have been popular with them."[21] In either case, Oesten's leadership style did not appeal to Sulzbach.

Oesten had accepted defeat, and he felt it his responsibility to convince the men around him to do the same. "Based on an education by broad-minded parents," he wrote, "I was in a position to help many younger prisoners to see the era of Hitler and Co. in the proper proportion and to regard the defeat in its proper value."[22] For him it was a logical process. Once they were shown that the Third Reich was an evil institution, they would realize that Germany's defeat was necessary and perhaps even a good thing. Unfortunately, the human mind does not work that way, and very few German soldiers of any political stripe would have accepted such an argument. Sulzbach had the same goal as Oesten, but his methods were entirely different. Rather than argument or logic, he used persuasion, trust, understanding, and humor. Compared to Oesten's confrontational style of argument, Sulzbach could be disarming as well as direct. "His approach was very personal. It was as though he had his own dowsing technique into a person's true feelings, into his quality as a human being." [23] Not surprisingly, Sulzbach succeeded where Oesten had failed, and Oesten's influence began to fade.

Oesten was also a loner. He had his own agenda from the start, and he went along with the routine only reluctantly. Every prisoner in the camp, for example, had to undergo regular interviews and psychological testing to monitor his progress. Oesten, never interested in National Socialism, jaded by nature, and doubtless annoyed at being a prisoner in the first place, was not impressed by any of this and adopted a supercilious attitude toward the entire procedure. During one such interview he proposed that he be evaluated by three different officers because he could predict ahead of time how he would be evaluated. Unfortunately, he wrote, "The camp authorities did not have sufficient sense of humor." [24] Such an attitude may well have seemed arrogant to Sulzbach or to anyone else who had the misfortune of conducting an interview with Oesten.

This conflict was unfortunate for Oesten, especially in his position as deputy camp spokesman. He would have benefited from Sulzbach's friendship. For soon afterward Sulzbach initiated a shakeup in the camp leadership structure that left Oesten completely out of the picture. Both men considered the camp spokesman all wrong for the position. "He was a dead duck," wrote Oesten, "and the situation was hopeless." [25] But rather than replace him with Oesten, Sulzbach convinced Vickers to bring in a new spokesman from a different camp: an army general named Ferdinand Heim. Vickers, Sulzbach, and Heim would effectively run the camp from that point on, and Oesten no longer played an active role.

In the end he went quietly. He gave up the role of counselor to Sulzbach, who seemed to be having more success than he, and he paid less attention to his position as a camp spokesman. Instead, he threw his efforts into a new responsibility he had been given. One of Vickers's ideas was that prisoners should be able to work outside the camp during the day (an arrangement that had already been tried with great success in North American camps). It allowed the prisoners to get out, and it enabled the local community to benefit from an extraordinary collection of talents which otherwise would have gone to waste. Oesten was made the officer responsible for forming the various work details that walked, rode, or drove out of Featherstone Park's main gate every morning. He supplied laborers to Northumberland farms for the harvest, masons for repairing walls, carpenters, electricians, even a gaggle of shovel bearers for an archaeological dig along the Roman Wall. Officers, ordinarily exempt from manual labor, often volunteered for these jobs. Von Müllenheim-Rechberg, a hereditary baron, took the "greatest pleasure" in draining peat bogs. It was a job Oesten turned out to be very good at, and it seemed to satisfy his need to keep occupied, to focus on something other than his captivity.

It helped that captivity had become a rather abstract concept. It was hardly imprisonment in the classic sense. Military discipline, such as it was, had become the province of the German chain of command rather than the British. There was free communication to points outside the camp; the German cooks in the bakery, for example, could send packages of homemade chocolate bars back home to impoverished families. There were two camp newspapers and unlimited access to outside media. A program of higher education was instituted, with classes in almost every subject imaginable (most of these were later accepted for credit by German universities). There were two theater groups, one for serious theater, the other for lighter fare, and a camp orchestra. Bus tours to various scenic spots in northern England were arranged. Debates, organized and otherwise, raged within the camp: politics, religion, and social affairs were freely discussed.

Oesten could come and go as he pleased. He could use public transport; he could visit businesses in town or deal with local merchants. He was even able to remain outside the gates of Featherstone Park overnight and was a guest for some time at the home of the British archaeologist Eric Birley, who lived not far from the camp (it was to the Birley family that he addressed the letter quoted above). Under the circumstances, it would not have been difficult to escape, and some did, but when Oesten was asked about it later he stated that escape would not have made sense for him. In any case, by the end of 1946, he was a free man in every sense but the strictly legal one, and to leave Featherstone Park for Germany on an "unofficial" basis would have caused more problems than it solved.

Such an atmosphere was based on trust on both sides. It could not have existed in many postwar POW camps. Once Jürgen Oesten was sent away for a "sort of re-education course," and instead of returning at once to Featherstone Park, he was held temporarily at another camp, Lodge

Moor, near Sheffield. He believes this was to test his reaction to Lodge Moor, or perhaps to test the reactions of the Lodge Moor prisoners to him, for it was "rather black and primitive compared to Featherstone Park."[26] Prisoners from POW camps in the United States and Canada were sent to Lodge Moor on their way back to Germany. Their attitudes, he found, were frozen more or less at the point of their capture, and although he tried to convince several of them that things had changed, they were not interested. One of these officers was Otto Kretschmer, who had just arrived at Lodge Moor from Bowmanville POW camp in Ontario, Canada.

Otto Kretschmer had been in various forms of Allied imprisonment for five years and had not played an active role in the Battle of the Atlantic since early 1941. But as a POW he had pursued a war of his own and had become almost as famous for what he did after his capture as for what he did before. When U-570 was given up by Hans-Joachim Rahmlow in August 1941, her officers (minus Rahmlow himself) were sent to Grizedale Hall, a POW camp in the Lake District. Otto Kretschmer, the senior German officer in the camp, held a secret "court of honor" and found the first watch officer, Bernt Bernhardt, guilty of cowardice before the enemy. Bernhardt was given an opportunity to redeem himself by escaping from the camp and scuttling U-570 at her berth in Barrow-in-Furness, but he was shot and killed in the attempt. In 1942, after the failed Allied landing at Dieppe, Canadian soldiers were held in handcuffs, a violation of the Geneva Convention. German POWs at Bowmanville were ordered to don handcuffs in retaliation. Kretschmer, once again the senior German officer, refused and started a riot in the camp that has since become known as the Battle of Bowmanville. And it was Kretschmer who engineered the abortive escape attempt from Bowmanville in which a U-boat was to creep into the St. Lawrence River to pick up the escapees and ferry them to safety. To his men, he was magnificent; to his captors, Otto Kretschmer was a problem child who never got with the program.[27]

Oesten will not discuss his conversation with Otto Kretschmer, except to say that it was contentious. Kretschmer had no love for National Socialism and at the time of his capture at sea expressed himself bored and disillusioned with the war. But National Socialism—and its effects—had done nothing to dim his love for Germany or his pride in being a German. Presumably Oesten tried to convince Kretschmer that Germany's defeat was necessary to end National Socialism and that the country would benefit from it in the long term. Kretschmer would hear none of this, nor would

A.F. W.3006

SERIAL **B 132388**

PART I
Reverse

STAMP OF O/C P. OF W. COY. OR O/C MEDICAL UNIT.

GERMAN Nº 300 P.O.W. CAMP - 2 SEP 1946

GERMAN 18-10-194 17 CAMP

LODGE MOOR 28 OCT 1946 CAMP

Northern Command Letter
QRRO 3/3435 P/84
7 Jan 3-2-47

INTELLIGENCE OFFICE
28 FEB 1947
168 P.O.W. CAMP

WOUM, 1803/PWi of 18-12-40

A.F. W.3000   RF.255679

Prisoner of War   **B 132388**

Part I.   Group 24

To be completed by O/C Unit and retained by ... until the prisoner of war transferred. When the prisoner is transferred ... it will be handed to the escort for delivery to the new place of internment. The date of receipt of the prisoner of war should be recorded by office stamp on reverse.

STAMP OF
P/W CAMP
OR
MEDICAL UNIT.

Date of Arrival at Camp or Medical Unit.   3.6.45

Surname   OESTEN
Christian Names   Jürgen
Date of Birth   24.10.13
Place of Capture   Londonderry
Date of Capture   2.6.15
Particulars on Identity Disc   Jürgen Oesten
     Seeoffz 1933
Rank   Korv.Kpt.
Number or Name of Division   13. U-Flottille
Unit or Ship, Number of Regiment   U 861
Battn., Coy., Squad., Batty.   —

Nationality   German
Occupation   Regular Officer
Religion   ev.
Signature of Prisoner of War   Jürgen Oesten

Height   Weight   Complexion   Hair   Eyes
Feet Inches   lbs.
6 ft   74½   fresh   brown

Marks (if any)

Special observations

Personal Effects (if any) to be enumerated

Signature   Breitta
O/C COMD. 172 P.W. CAMP   LIEUT COL. R.A.

Date

RECORD OF TRANSFERS, CASUALTIES, ETC.

Date	Casualty	Authority
3.6.1945	from Londonderry Port to N o 172 PW Camp	
6.6.1945	from No 172 PW Camp to Kempton Park	
7 JUN 45.	Arrived K.P. Ex 172 CAMP.	
8 ... 1946	Transferred from No. 18 Camp to Camp No. *LDC* *LIM/M/9953 (PW)*	
7 SEP 1946	Transferred from No. 18 Camp to Camp No. *300* *VM/M/2264 (PW)* *26-8-46*	

DATE TRANS. ...1.5 OCT 1946
FROM No 300 CAMP
TO CAMP Nº ... 7 ...

OCT 1946   *Transf. to No 18 POW-Camp*

11 FEB 1947   Transferred from No. 18 Camp to Camp No. *168* *Northern Command* *Letter CRA/3/35/9 (P4)* *dated 3-2-47*   No. 18

18-2-47 transf. from 168 Camp to Hull WOUM/1803/PW for Repat.   *Serial 796.*   *18-12-46*

INTELLIGENCE OFFICE
28 FEB 1947
168 P.O.W. CAMP

(Opposite page, and above): A blizzard of typed entries, rubber stamps, and scribbled endorsements trace the path of Jürgen Oesten through two years of postwar captivity. (Jürgen Oesten)

two of Oesten's classmates, members of Crew 33 he also met at Lodge Moor. The reason for these negative reactions, he believes, is something he calls "barbed wire disease," an emotional condition brought on by prolonged confinement. "I studied the barbed-wire phenomenon to a certain extent, as I met many different types. . . . One thing seemed to me the same for all of them. The period of being [a] POW is like a black hole in their mental development. They stop in the position when they were taken prisoner, even if the possibilities for information and education are first class."[28]

Oesten had struggled to ensure that this did not happen to him. It had not always been easy. When he arrived, he was a nervous wreck, married, as he wrote, to uncertainty, a large chip on his shoulder. His position as a camp spokesman did not work out: he alienated more than a few of the men he had tried to help. He had his problems with Sulzbach, a man who seemed to have very little trouble dealing with anyone. His future was as cloudy as his new landscape.

But human beings are resilient by nature, and in the end, he did not allow any of these things to bother him. He began to improve. He knew he was getting better; he could see it in himself and by looking at other people, like Kretschmer, who had not changed. He had become more relaxed, more circumspect. He dislikes the term "cynical" and denies that it ever applied to him, but he was more open and willing to take at face value the opinions of other people, and he found that others were listening to him again and paying more attention to what he had to say. As he traveled around rural Northumberland matching men to jobs, he could see beauty in the country and in the daily lives of its people. "Lots of things happened," he continued in his letter to Eric Birley. "He met a milkman at the same corner at the same time early morning, walking through that rough and hilly countryside breathing in plenty of fresh air. Some of the country folk he met were not at all surprised but fitted him somehow into their picture of the globe, which was sensible and uncomplicated." [29]

A passage from Jürgen Oesten's last evaluation, signed by an interrogator at Featherstone Park named Philip Rossiter, is worth quoting. If, as Oesten believes, Herbert Sulzbach had anything to do with it, the evaluation can be regarded as reasonably accurate and very perceptive. "Oesten," wrote Rossiter, "used to be an enthusiastic sailor who did not worry his head overmuch about politics. He has come to his present positive but very realistic attitude by slow but sure steps. He is *most strongly* recommended for a job in youth or adult education where his outstanding ability to influence people has scope. He would also make an excellent [leader] of some rehabilitation group. Above all, Oesten is a very decent chap." Clearly, he had recovered. [30]

In early 1947 Jürgen Oesten was moved from Featherstone Park to Camp 168, a transit camp, to prepare for repatriation. From Camp 168 he would be sent to Hull, then placed on a ship for Bremerhaven, and finally, after eighteen months of questionably legal confinement as a "prisoner of peace," released. Most German prisoners of war came home between 1946 and 1948. Oesten believed they were released with the same mind-set they had when they were captured. If this is true—and the point is debatable—many of them were ill-equipped to handle freedom in a country that was very different from the one they had left so many years earlier. The Nuremberg trials were over. National Socialism had ostensibly been purged from society. A postwar government was in place and a new constitution was being written. Soviet control of Eastern Europe was complete and the first major confrontation of the Cold War, the Berlin Airlift, was under way. The country was still poor, but the first stirrings of a tremendous economic revival could be felt in the air. Everything had changed; a man who still believed as he had in 1940 or 1941 would be out of place in such an environment, like Oesten's woodcutter, "drifting between two entirely different lives, the one behind and the one ahead."

Happily, this was not the case with Oesten himself or with most of his fellow prisoners at Featherstone Park. Because of the camp's enlightened management, its open walls, and its wealth of diversions, the men who eventually emerged from it were better adjusted and more prepared than most to deal with the changes they encountered. When Oesten arrived at Featherstone Park, he was a tired, bitter man, confused, apprehensive, and emotionally drained. When he left he was spiritually refreshed, self-confident, and at peace with himself. Any physical confinement is unpleasant. Becoming a prisoner in a foreign country, without a crime, without a trial, with no indication of a release date or even a condition for release, can destroy a man. Jürgen Oesten did not allow this to happen and ended his captivity in triumph.

Conclusion

I hope that people will see, after all the emotions have died down, that Germany's only meager chance in a naval war (which was unavoidable in a conflict with England) was the U-boat, and that the U-boat men who went to sea did so in all good faith to fight for their Fatherland.

—Gottfried König

OESTEN arrived in Germany in the first week of March 1947. It was, he states, the beginning of his second life. For him and for his comrades in the U-Bootwaffe, the war was finally over, and as far as he was concerned, it was time to start again.

Not everyone took this attitude. For some of them the war never ended. For others who (to use a modern term) were unable to get a life, the war may have been over, but their part in it required them to continue fighting on other fronts. There was an image to protect, reputations to uphold, misconceptions to set right; sometimes the effort was ugly, and sometimes people were hurt. These skirmishes still take place—inside and out. The rift in the U-Bootwaffe described in this book is real and more pronounced than the usual differences that occur in communities of proud men. The open battle between Lothar-Günther Buchheim and Karl-Friedrich Merten is only the most egregious instance of it.

After a relatively long literary silence, Lothar-Günther Buchheim recently published an epic novel about the U-boats entitled *The Fortress*. But Karl-Friedrich Merten is not there to criticize it. He died in May 1993. Merten was a gentleman, forthcoming in his correspondence, generous with his advice, and patient with young historians. When he finally realized that his public squabbling with Erich Topp was becoming counterproductive and embarrassing to his comrades, he met with Topp. The two men agreed to refrain from further argument, and both lived up to the agreement. It is disappointing that Merten did not come to realize that his debate with Buchheim had become equally counterproductive, but it is consoling to think that he could have made such a decision.[1]

Aside from the image of the U-boat commander itself, the main reason for disagreement is Karl Dönitz. Most U-Bootwaffe veterans regard him as a saint, the rest as a sinner; the two sides will not be reconciled in this century. To his credit, Dönitz tried to stay above it all and encouraged his men to remain united for the good of the country and the service. He was convicted at Nuremberg on two counts of war crimes and served ten years in Spandau Prison. Afterward he lived quietly near Hamburg until his death in 1980 at the age of eighty-nine. He wrote three books, all self-exculpatory, critical of others, economical of the truth, and rather boring. When he died, his funeral was ignored by the state but attended by thousands of the officers and men he had once led. He was buried as a Christian next to his wife under a huge stone crucifix.

When Victor Oehrn was captured in the North African desert, Dönitz asked his fiancée, Renate von Winterfeld, how long she would wait for him. "After all," he told her, "it might be ten years." Renate was unmoved. "If it takes ten years," she said, "I will wait." The memory of this remark, Dönitz told the Oehrns after the war, helped him through his ten years in Spandau. The love it describes has made for a marriage now well past its fiftieth year, and both Victor and Renate Oehrn seem as happy now as they were on that last evening in the Casino Valadier.[2]

Of all the major players in the U-Bootwaffe, Victor Oehrn has doubtless had the most interesting career, but unlike many of his comrades, he has not written a book about himself and has directed that his draft memoirs not be made public until after his death. The genre is all the poorer for it but no less populous. At least a dozen U-boat biographies have appeared since the war. The most famous, of course, is Buchheim's *The Boat,* which describes his experiences as a photojournalist under the cover of U-boat fiction. Of the others, the most popular is either Herbert Werner's *Iron Coffins* or Terence Robertson's *Night Raiders of the Atlantic* (Otto Kretschmer's biography), but books about Erich Topp, Peter Cremer, Reinhard Hardegen, Heinz Schaeffer, Werner Henke, Reinhard Suhren, and Wolfgang Lüth are also available. The biography of Henke, *Lone Wolf* by Timothy Mulligan, demonstrates as well as anything the futility of holding the U-boat commander hostage to an image.

In 1955 a new German navy, the Bundesmarine, was formed. Most of its officer corps was commissioned before the war. Many U-boat commanders became Bundesmarine officers, including several of the great aces. Otto Kretschmer and Erich Topp rose to flag rank in the new navy and held NATO commands. Others, including Theodor Petersen, joined but did not rise to the top. Still others, for various reasons, chose not to join. Jürgen Oesten, for example, did not join the Bundesmarine because he wanted nothing to do with certain people, such as Hans-Rudolf Rösing, and Gottfried König declined because he could no longer reconcile himself to the naval profession. "My attitude towards war and the military has changed completely," he wrote. "I haven't become a pacifist, but I consider the military . . . a necessary evil. . . . Today I am appalled that young men could have fought, sunk ships, and destroyed lives with such ease and thoughtlessness, and I hope that one day war as a means of solving problems will no longer be an option, even if the condition of the world today might raise legitimate doubts about such a thing."[3]

Oesten became a successful businessman, König a headmaster. Of the other commanders mentioned in this book, no two have gone the same way. Heinz Lehmann-Willenbrock, the model for Buchheim's Old Man, entered the new Handelsmarine after the war. Heinz Schaeffer finished out his life in Argentina. Herbert Werner emigrated to the United States and now operates a commercial submarine business in Florida. Hans-Joachim Rahmlow, who surrendered U-570 in 1941, lay low for several years, surfaced briefly in the 1950s to defend himself in the pages of the German magazine *Kristall*, then vanished for good. Peter Hansen, the witness who slips in and out of these pages like a ghostly *Schimmelreiter*, is in Germany again after many years in Florida. Never a famous man, he is nonetheless often consulted by other writers and historians.

The Scheherazade, nightclub and unofficial watering hole for U-boat officers in western France, is now closed; its owner, the mercurial Vladimir, has vanished and is doubtless dead. The U-boat pens in the Biscay harbors, made of concrete many feet thick, stand today. The battleship *Royal Oak* rests at the bottom of Scapa Flow, and a ceremony is held every year to remember the men entombed in her hull. The Marineschule Mürwik reopened as an academy for Bundesmarine officer candidates in 1956; there is a memorial for Wolfgang Lüth on the grounds, a large boulder with his name on it, not far from where he was shot on the Black Path. The U-boat memorial itself, an awkward red stone structure in Möltenort, now displays on its curving walls the names of 938 boats and their crews: 199 lost in one war, 739 in another. Like the much more beautiful Navy Memorial in nearby Laboe, it is open to visitors. A memorial of a different kind, the U-Boat Archives in Cuxhaven, can also be visited if prior arrangements are made, but one has to be diplomatic once inside and ready to listen.

TWO statements were made in the introduction to this book. The first was that no two U-boat commanders were the same and it was a futile exercise to force them into a single class with a common image. This futility becomes clear in tracking the careers of several officers before and during the war; glimpses of their postwar lives only strengthen the argument. None of the men described in this book was anything like the others. None fitted any of the images in common currency. The experience of someone like Oehrn or Lüth or Oesten is not the picture we have of the stereotypical commander in the books we read or the movies we watch.

The second statement was that images, even if false, are still important. They can uplift and inspire. They color our history and bring it to life. They can become tradition and legend for future generations. But false images can also burden people and communities of people with reputations they do not deserve. For this reason people are driven to create and maintain their own images of themselves. Merten had an image of the U-boat commander he was willing to fight for. Buchheim is still polishing the image he wants to show the world. Topp and König and Werner all keep in themselves the pictures of how they were and how they wanted to be. For many of these men the preservation of image has become a part of their lives.

We are left finally with Horst Bredow, the sage of Cuxhaven. Bredow suffered a massive heart attack in 1992 and is now restricted in his movements. Instead of sixteen hours every day, he works six, and instead of twelve months a year, he is in the archives for only ten; but when he is at work he operates the same way he always has. The archives are his life's work; he has built them up and kept them going by force of will. Whatever one may think of Horst Bredow, his personal opinions, or his attitudes toward those who do not agree with him, one has to agree that he has done more to preserve the image of the U-boat commander, for better or for worse, than any man alive. He is in the archives now, frowning, letter in hand, looking among the crowded corridors and dusty bookshelves for a smiling officer in a white cap, a lost crew, and the gentle benediction of history. And he is happy.

Notes

Introduction

1. Michael Hadley, *Count Not the Dead: The Popular Image of the German Submarine* (Annapolis: Naval Institute Press, 1995); letter, 29 November 1995. Unless otherwise indicated, all letters are to the author.

2. Reinhard Reche, letter, 21 June 1992; Eberhard Godt, letter, 10 June 1992. Passages from *Wallenstein* in this chapter are taken from the Charles E. Passage translation (New York: Unger, 1958).

1. The Monsters of the Sea

1. The term "commander" (*Kommandant*) is preferred over "captain" (Kapitän), and I have tried to use it whenever practicable. Kapitän is more often used to refer to the captain or master of a merchant ship or as the accepted form of address for any of three German naval officer ranks up through Kapitän zur See.

2. "Kriegstagebuch" [War diary] of SM U-9, 22 September 1914, Marineschule Mürwik, inventory no. 4023.

3. Winston Churchill, *The World Crisis* (New York: Scribner's, 1951), 1:352.

4. Charles F. Horne, ed., *Source Records of the Great War,* Vol. 2, *AD 1914* (New York: National Alumni, 1923), 296.

5. *Harper's Pictorial Library of the World War,* Vol. 1, *The War on the Sea* (New York: Harper and Brothers, 1920), 207.

6. Horne, ed., *Source Records of the Great War,* Vol. 3, *AD 1915,* 60.

7. The *Lusitania* was in the blockade zone. Her captain knew when she sailed that she would be subject to attack, and as it turned out she was carrying war materials, including arms, when she was sighted off the coast of southern Ireland. Legally, Schwieger was on stronger ground than many people realized.

8. As most readers will know, the German name for the Battle of Jutland is Skagerrak. Because it was considered a victory in Germany, the Battle of the Skagerrak became an important part of German naval tradition, and Skagerrak Day was routinely celebrated as a holiday in the fleet.

9. Ajax, *The German Pirate: His Methods and Record* (New York: George H. Doran, 1918), 122.

10. Hadley, *Count Not the Dead,* 60–62; Lowell Thomas, *Raiders of the Deep* (New York: Garden City Publishing Company, 1928).

2. "We Were a New Start!"

1. Oehrn, letter, 18 March 1992.

2. Oesten, personal diary, 29 March 1933, in Oesten's possession. All new Reichsmarine recruits were directed to open and maintain personal diaries, which were reviewed from time to time during their training. The habit became so ingrained that many officers kept diaries for the rest of their lives.

3. Oesten, letter, 2 April 1992.

4. Karl Daublebsky von Eichhain, letter, 17 September 1992; Hans-Diedrich von Tiesenhausen, letter, undated; Helmut Witte, letter, 21 June 1992. Georg von Trapp is better known as the husband of Maria von Trapp and father of the von Trapp Family Singers. After the *Anschluss* he received orders to take command of a German warship. He and his entire family fled Austria at once for the United States, where he died in 1947.

5. Eric C. Rust, *Naval Officers under Hitler: The Story of Crew 34* (Westport, Conn.: Praeger, 1991), 36.

6. Michael Gannon, *Operation Drumbeat* (New York: Harper Perennial, 1991), 17–18.

7. Oehrn, letter, 23 August 1992.

8. Oehrn, letter, 7 November 1991.

9. Peter Hansen, letter, 30 January 1994. Forstmann was cagey. The conversation continued: "Then he looked at me somewhat mischievously and asked, 'Will that do for your assignment? As you will appreciate, this has to be between us verbally only. I would never put it in writing, though I wish Dönitz success because of Germany! Now let's have tea and discuss something else.'"

10. Oehrn, "Dönitz, Nähe Gesehen" [Dönitz up close], unpublished manuscript, 14.

11. Karl Dönitz, *Ten Years and Twenty Days* (New York: World, 1959), 151.

12. Hadley, *Count Not the Dead*, 71–75.

13. Oehrn, letter, 15 January 1992.

14. Oehrn, "Dönitz, Nähe Gesehen," 6.

15. Oehrn, letter, 10 August 1992.

16. Reche, letter, 21 June 1992; von Tiesenhausen, letter, undated.

17. Erich Topp, *The Odyssey of a U-Boat Commander: Recollections of Erich Topp* (Westport, Conn.: Praeger, 1992), 125.

18. Jürgen Oesten, letter, 17 January 1992.

19. Dönitz, "Bei der Trauerfeier für Kapitän zur See Wolfgang Lüth" [At the memorial service for Kapitän zur See Wolfgang Lüth], address delivered in Flensburg-Mürwik, 16 May 1945.

20. Wolfgang Lüth and Claus Korth, *Boot Greift Wieder An* [Boat attacks again] (Berlin: Erich Klinghammer Verlag, 1944), 22.

3. The Epiphany of an Ace

1. Lohmann, Vizeadmiral, "Die Ausbildung des Marineoffiziers" (The training of a naval officer), Marineschule Mürwik inventory no. 14718, 29.

2. Victor Oehrn, "Navigare Necesse Est," 1, unpublished memoirs.

3. Ibid., 2.

4. Quoted in Oehrn, "Dönitz, Nähe Gesehen," 15.

5. Dönitz, *Ten Years and Twenty Days*, 47.

6. There is some confusion over who was responsible for the idea and the planning of an attack in Scapa Flow. As Dönitz explains in his memoirs, he did it all, with only the initial encouragement of Victor Oehrn: "I remember how I was one day sitting in front of a map of Scapa and thinking about it, when suddenly my glance fell upon Lieutenant Commander Oehrn, the Staff Officer, Operations, on my staff and a man with an exceptionally clear and determined mind. In his characteristically decisive manner he turned to me and said: 'You know, sir, I'm pretty sure we could find a way to get in.' This opinion, expressed by the man whose judgment I trusted most out of all the officers on my staff, gave me just the final impetus I required to tackle the problem in earnest and in detail" (*Ten Years and Twenty Days*, 67–68. But Oehrn writes in "Navigare Necesse Est": "By studying the charts and *Seehandbücher* [nautical almanacs, tide and current tables, and so on] and the first set of aerial photos from the Luftwaffe, I was able to find a realistic solution" (6). And in a letter he wrote: "Certainly I was heavily involved, from the idea through the planning, but the deed was Prien's and the responsibility was Dönitz's" (letter, 14 August 1991). See also quote at the end of this chapter.

7. Dan Van der Vat, "Günther Prien," in *Men of War*, ed. Stephen Howarth (New York: St. Martin's Press, 1992), 394–404; Hadley, *Count Not the Dead*, 81–83, 89–90.

8. Peter Hansen, letter, 9 September 1993.

9. Ibid.

10. Oehrn, letter, 11 October 1991.

11. Oesten, letter, 30 June 1993.

12. This account of the passage to Scapa Flow comes from an account, unidentified but probably from the German magazine *Stern* in the mid-1950s, of Günther Prien's life.

13. Actually Prien had been sighted as he was entering Scapa Flow, caught in the headlights of an automobile whose drive subsequently tried to pass the alarm.

14. *Time*, 30 October 1939, 16.

15. BBC News, 14 October 1939. Used with permission.

16. *Das Ritterkreuz des Eisernen Kreuzes*, the Knight's Cross of the Iron Cross, was instituted on 1 September 1939, along with new 1939 versions of the Iron Cross, First and Second Class. None of the old imperial decorations were retained. On 3 June 1940 a higher award, the Knight's Cross with Oak Leaves, was instituted. This turned out to be the rough equivalent of the old Pour le Merite, the latter of which 687 were awarded during World War I and 853 of the former during World War II. Because Prien was awarded the Knight's Cross for the *Royal Oak*, it seemed only fair to give it to Otto Schuhart for the *Courageous*, and he was duly hauled in and decorated in May 1940. The idea of medals was a sore spot for Dönitz. He told Oehrn that the best system would be to give every award in existence to each man in the U-Bootwaffe and then to take them away, one at a time, whenever some laudatory deed warranted it. "That way," he said

wickedly, "whoever ends up with an empty chest first would obviously be the best man" (Dönitz, Nähe Gesehen," 22).

17. Hitler was referring to the internment of the Imperial Fleet in Scapa Flow in 1919. The man who gave the order to scuttle that fleet, Admiral Ludwig von Reuter, was to telegraph Prien: "I am happy that I have been allowed to live to experience the revenge" (*Time*, 30 October 1939, 16).

18. *Stern*, date unknown.

19. *New York Times*, 19 October 1939.

20. Accounts of the day were taken from *Time*, 30 October 1939, the *New York Times*, 18 October 1939, and *Stern*.

21. Quoted in Douglas Botting, *The U-Boats* (New York: Time-Life Books, 1979), 100.

22. Gus Britton, letter, 13 January 1992.

23. Horst Bredow, interview, 16 June 1991.

24. Oehrn, "Navigare Necesse Est," 10.

25. Ibid., 5.

4. On Patrol with the *Westward Ho!*

1. Oehrn, "Dönitz, Nähe Gesehen," 23.

2. Furthermore, there was much circumstantial evidence that the same torpedoes caused the loss of at least two U-boats in 1939, ruined "sure thing" attacks on the aircraft carrier HMS *Ark Royal* in September 1939 and the battleship HMS *Nelson* in November 1939, and caused Günther Prien to miss HMS *Royal Oak* on his first run in Scapa Flow. Even worse, Dönitz thought for some years afterward that Winston Churchill had been on board the *Nelson* when it was spared by the magnetic pistol, although this was not the case (Dönitz, *Ten Years and Twenty Days*, 99).

3. Oehrn, "Navigare Necesse Est," 13.

4. Werner Hartmann, Crew 21, was assigned to Oehrn's position as BdU A1. He "cursed like a tugboat captain," wrote Peter Hansen, at being made a staff officer, but he eventually regained command of a larger boat, did well, and survived the war in spite of spending its last days commanding a naval infantry regiment on the Lüneberg Heath (Hansen, letter, 20 February 1994).

5. Oehrn, "Navigare Necesse Est," 18.

6. Ibid., 19. This incident, according to Oehrn, was used as evidence at Nuremberg to prosecute Karl Dönitz.

7. Dönitz, *Ten Years and Twenty Days*, 102.

8. Oesten, letter, 3 March 1993.

9. Oehrn, "Navigare Necesse Est," 23–24.

10. The incident involving the *Severn Leigh* described here, part of which has been dramatized, is taken from Oehrn's manuscript "Navigare Necesse Est," 16–18. No corroborating account is available to the author.

11. Theoretical because although 100,000 GRT was widely known to be the requirement for the Knight's Cross, it was also widely ignored (more often later in the war than sooner).

12. The name Lorient is a corruption of the French word *l'Orient*, so called

because the port gained its initial significance during the heydey of the French East India trade. The term "Port of Aces" is used in Gannon, *Operation Drumbeat,* 30.

13. That is, he reported hitting three ships simultaneously.

14. Donald Macintyre, *The Naval War Against Hitler* (New York: Charles Scribner's Sons, 1971), 65.

15. S. W. Roskill, *The War at Sea, 1939–1945,* Vol. 1, *The Defensive* (London: Her Majesty's Stationery Office, 1954), 354–55.

16. Oehrn, "Navigare Necesse Est," 23.

5. The Capturing of Souls

1. See Gannon, *Operation Drumbeat,* Appendix B, for an excellent description of this process.

2. Oesten, letter, 3 March 1993.

3. The concept of Baubelehrung was not unique to the U-Bootwaffe; it still exists today, for example, in the United States Navy PCU crew, although these consist of only a few officers and senior enlisted personnel. The difference was that an entire crew participated in Baubelehrung.

4. Lüth and Korth, *Boot Greift Wieder An,* 255.

5. Hansen, letter, 30 January 1994.

6. Ceremony described by Oesten in letter, 20 September 1993.

7. Karl-Friedrich Merten, "Answers to Questions," 5. These are answers to a set of questions submitted by an unknown correspondent (possibly South African) to Merten, probably in late 1980. The cover letter for Merten's response is dated 23 January 1981. Copies are in possession of the author.

8. Topp, *Odyssey,* 74.

9. This happened many times. See the author's *U-Boat Ace* (Annapolis: Naval Institute Press, 1990).

10. Merten, "Answers to Questions," 4.

11. Oesten, enclosure to letter, 28 June 1991.

12. By the time he was given his last boat in 1944, Oesten had become most adept at finding and keeping the men he wanted: "When I was exercising my last boat in the Baltic in the beginning of 1944, there was a sort of parade in a Baltic port for Admiral von Friedeburg. He went around and saw, I think, eight U-boat crews, all brand new. At each boat he asked how many of the respective crew had experience on a fighting boat already. Two, or at a maximum three or four, hands went up. When asked my crew, thirty out of 64 hands went up. He said 'hands down' very quickly, as he had to realize that this result had been achieved by unconventional means" (letter, 20 January 1991).

13. Lüth and Korth, *Boot Greift Wieder An,* 253; this speech seemed to be a favorite of his and one he used on more than one occasion.

14. Merten, letter, 15 March 1991.

15. U-106's movements during the last three months of 1940 are taken from her Kriegstagebuch (war diary), a copy of which was supplied by Jürgen Oesten.

16. Description of Günther Sachs taken from Theodor Petersen, interview, 24 July 1984, and Hansen, letter, 14 January 1991.

17. Oesten, letter, 20 September 1993.

18. Timothy P. Mulligan, "German U-Boat Crews in World War Two: Sociology of an Elite," (*Journal of Military History*, 56 (April 1992): 261–81; Hansen, letter, 30 January 1994. Mulligan's study is based on a sample of 619 U-boat crewmen captured and processed during the war. As Mulligan points out, there are few such studies available, certainly none as exhaustive as Rust's of Crew 34, for example, and his own is only preliminary.

19. Oesten, letter, 20 January 1991.

20. Hansen, letter, 30 January 1994.

21. Hansen, letter, 30 January 1994; see also Richard Compton-Hall, *The Underwater War, 1939–1945* (Poole, Dorset: Blandford Press, 1982), 69–70.

22. Bredow, interview.

6. The Tide, the Games

1. Information on the movements of convoy HX 156 is from Patrick Abbazia, *Mr. Roosevelt's War* (Annapolis: Naval Institute Press, 1975), 293–308.

2. Hansen, letter, 30 January 1994.

3. *Stern*, date unknown.

4. Kretschmer, letter, 15 October 1985.

5. Poem courtesy of Eric Rust, who does not know the author but speculates that the poem was in general circulation by the summer of 1941.

6. Van der Vat, "Günther Prien," in *Men of War*, ed. Howarth, 404. *Kristall*, in 1956, ran a series about the Battle of the Atlantic entitled "Denn Wir Fuhren." In one segment, "U-47 Antwortet Nicht" (*Kristall*, 540/12), the author discussed, and rejected, several rumors about Prien and his crew, including one that he had died in a concentration camp. Prien's status in wartime Germany may be understood more clearly when one realizes that the only recent celebrity for whom similar sightings have been reported is Elvis Presley.

7. Barrie Pitt, *The Battle of the Atlantic* (New York: Time-Life Books, 1977), 66–67.

8. Lothar-Günther Buchheim, telephone interview, 20 May 1991.

9. Peter Hitchens, *International Express*, 2–8 June 1993.

10. Van der Vat, "Günther Prien," in *Men of War*, ed. Howarth, 396; Peter Padfield, "Grand Admiral Karl Dönitz," ibid., 184; Hansen, letter, 9 September 1993.

11. Bodo Herzog, "Otto Kretschmer," in *Men of War*, ed. Howarth, 383–93; Peter Padfield, *Dönitz, the Last Führer* (New York: Harper & Row, 1984), 226; Donald Macintyre, *U-Boat Killer* (Annapolis: Naval Institute Press, 1976), 52.

12. Hadley, *Count Not the Dead*, 85.

13. Wolfgang Lüth, "Menschenführung auf einem Unterseeboot" (Problems of leadership on a submarine), lecture presented 17 December 1943 in Weimar, Germany, translated by the Office of Naval Intelligence, Navy Department, Washington, D.C., document 11746, 1946.

14. Oesten, letter, 17 January 1992.

15. Topp, *Odyssey*, 118.

16. Topp, letter, 8 July 1991.

17. The war, wrote Merten as late as 1982, was considered by most Germans as simply "bad luck," a miscalculation based on an underestimation of Britain's "intransigence and hypocrisy," and therefore a struggle forced upon Germany.

18. Bodo Herzog, "Das Historisch-Politische Buch," Vol. 39 (1991): 80.

19. Bredow, interview.

20. Petersen, letter, 20 March 1988; Daublebsky von Eichhain, letter, 29 July 1992.

21. Oehrn knew the Russian mind as well as anyone in the Wehrmacht; he points out that in the early days of the invasion German troops were welcomed "with bread and salt" in the belief that they were there to bring down the government of Joseph Stalin and free the Soviet Union from communism; if this had been declared policy, he maintains, and if the Germans had accepted the gratitude of the people as freely as it had been given, Barbarossa would have been a success. As far as he could see, this was not happening; the occupation forces moving behind the tanks, operating with brutal effectiveness, prompted fewer cheers than plaintive cries: "You are saving us from Stalin, but who will save us from you?" ("Navigare Necesse Est," 35–36).

22. Oesten, letter, 15 November 1993.

23. Topp, *Odyssey*, 57.

24. Quoted in Macintyre, *The Naval War Against Hitler*, 97.

25. Time in the *Reuben James*, not in U-552.

26. Abbazia, *Mr. Roosevelt's War*, 300.

27. It was an understandable mistake because she was of the same class, *Clemson*, as many of the destroyers sold by the United States to Britain in 1940.

28. Topp, *Odyssey*, 3.

29. Thomas A. Bailey and Paul B. Ryan, *Hitler vs. Roosevelt: The Undeclared Naval War* (New York: Free Press, 1979), 207.

30. Observations on the Scheherazade were made by Peter Hansen in letters, 30 January and 20 February 1994. Hansen, as an officer working for the Abwehr, had been assigned more than once to investigate the nightclub and its patrons.

31. Ibid.

32. Topp, *Odyssey*, 81.

7. Fighting for an Image

1. "Lothar-Günther Buchheim fühlt sich betroffen!" (Lothar-Günther Buchheim feels betrayed!), transcript of telephone call from Buchheim to Karl-Friedrich Merten, 22 May 1985.

2. Lothar-Günther Buchheim, *The Boat* (New York: Knopf, 1975), 308.

3. Hadley, *Count Not the Dead*, 142. Hadley has devoted an entire chapter to Buchheim's effect on the postwar image of the U-boats. It is very well done and should be consulted for additional information.

4. Hansen, letter, 25 July 1994; Topp, *Odyssey*, 166. The controversy surrounding *The Boat* arises in part from the impression that this patrol in U-96 was

Buchheim's only significant combat experience in a U-boat, but he did make two other short patrols, both in 1944, and the combined length of the three was enough for him to be awarded the Frontspange, the U-boat badge.

5. Wolfgang Ott, *Sharks and Little Fish* (New York: Pantheon, 1958).

6. Buchheim, *The Boat*, 86, 100.

7. Ott, *Sharks and Little Fish*, 320.

8. Buchheim, *The Boat*, 169.

9. *New York Times Book Review*, 29 June 1975, 14.

10. Hansen, letter, 25 July 1994.

11. Buchheim, interview, 29 May 1991.

12. Oesten, letter, 18 March 1991; Reche, letter, 21 June 1992; Kretschmer, letter, 28 June 1991.

13. Oesten, letter, 18 March 1991.

14. Bredow, interview, 16 June 1991.

15. Hansen, letter, 5 March 1991. Presumably Hansen took the term "steel-helmets" from Stahlhelm, a prewar German organization made up of former servicemen and characterized by conservative opinions and extreme nationalism.

16. Merten, letter, 8 May 1984. Padfield is unrepentant. "The reaction in Germany [to *Dönitz*] was very mixed, as you say," he wrote in 1991, "for the good reason that the U-boat men have been mythologizing Dönitz for some 45 years now—that's a polite way of putting it!—and I imagine they actually believe it after all this time" (letter, 28 March 1991).

17. For a list of books considered suitable by Horst Bredow for use by historians, see Bredow, "Bücher Über die U-Bootwaffe" (undated, but no earlier than 1990; later editions are no doubt available for the asking). It seems unnecessary to observe that none of the books discussed in this paragraph are on the list.

18. Merten, letter, 1 April 1991.

19. Ibid.

20. Merten, letter, 15 March 1991.

21. Merten, "Betr: Film 'Das Boot' und Fernsehauftritt des Autors Buchheim" (Re: The film "Das Boot" and the venture into television of the author Buchheim), *Ritterkreuz* magazine, date unavailable, but probably mid-1985.

22. Hadley, *Count Not the Dead*, 161.

23. Merten, "Betr: Film 'Das Boot.'" The review of *Zu Tode Gesiegt* followed that of *The Boat* in the same issue of *Ritterkreuz*.

24. Merten, review of *Die U-Bootfahrer* (Bertelsmann, 1985), *Ritterkreuz*, I/86. So incensed was Merten by *Die U-Bootfahrer* that he and Kurt Baberg published a book of their own in which they tried to rebut everything Buchheim had written. See Hadley, *Count Not the Dead*.

25. Merten, review of *Die U-Bootfahrer*; Bredow, letter, 10 January 1991. "Obviously such a man wouldn't have been liked by the crew," concluded Bredow. Wrong, counters Buchheim, the crew did like him, "but they are easily led. They were made to say all those awful things about me and then, when I called each of them up afterwards, they all said 'we're sorry, we didn't mean to say those things'" (interview, 29 May 1991).

26. Hadley, *Count Not the Dead*, 169.

27. Merten, letter, 15 March 1991.

28. Topp, *Odyssey,* 167.

29. Bredow, letter, 10 January 1991.

30. Hansen, letter, 14 January 1991.

8. The Test of Gold

1. The primary source for the events described in this chapter is the manuscript "Navigare Necesse Est," Victor Oehrn's unpublished memoirs. All direct quotations used in this chapter are taken from "Navigare Necesse Est" unless otherwise noted.

2. Quite literally, for he was staying at a hotel by that name.

3. Peter Hansen states that Dönitz actually reported Oehrn's assignment to Berlin as "interim, acting" but, he added, "it is quite possible that Oehrn was never told this or [was made] aware of this administrative situation, as Dönitz treated such matters often as secondary." If this is true, then Oehrn was made to be more disappointed than necessary (Hansen, letter, 15 September 1994).

4. Gannon, *Operation Drumbeat,* 389. Strictly speaking, 397 ships were sunk in the Eastern, Gulf, Caribbean, and Panama Sea Frontiers in the six months beginning 11 December 1941 and ending 21 June 1942. These frontiers were contiguous, and the Eastern Sea Frontier extended two hundred miles east into the Atlantic Ocean. Additional ships were sunk in other parts of the world. See Gannon's book for details.

5. Perhaps the most selfless example was U.S. Navy Captain John P. Cromwell, who in November 1943 elected to go down with the damaged submarine USS *Sculpin* rather than be captured by the Japanese. Cromwell, who was briefed for Ultra and knew all about the upcoming invasion of the Gilbert Islands, did not trust himself to stand up to Japanese torture.

6. This was the same Albert Loycke who had served as the second commander of Flotilla Weddigen in 1936 (see Chapter 2).

7. From Oehrn's description of him, "a Catholic priest with red *kappi,* obviously rather high in rank," the man might have been a bishop.

8. Shortly afterward, as protocol dictated, Victor Oehrn and Renate von Winterfeld announced their engagement in Berlin. Renate's mother sent out one announcement for herself and her daughter, and a second was sent on Oehrn's behalf with the return address "Currently in British captivity: Middle East Egypt. Serial No. 23759ME."

9. Every Day a Sunday

1. Lüth and Korth, *Boot Greift Wieder An,* 96.

2. Petersen, letter, 7 October 1986.

3. Merten, letter, 11 February 1991; Walter Pfeiffer, letter, 18 May 1984; Buchheim, interview.

4. Oesten, letter, 6 January 1991.

5. Oehrn, letter, 18 May 1991.

6. Hansen, letter, 12 June 1991.

7. Oesten, letter, 20 May 1994.

8. Reche, letter, 21 June 1992.

9. Oesten, letter, 6 January 1991; Merten, "Answers to Questions," 5; Lüth, "Problems of Leadership"; Topp, "Philosophy of a Submarine," lecture outline, undated, 5–6. All further quotes in this chapter attributed to Wolfgang Lüth are taken from "Problems of Leadership" unless otherwise noted.

10. Oesten, letter, 20 May 1994.

11. Merten, letter, 15 March 1991.

12. Oesten, letter, 20 May 1994.

13. Karl Dönitz felt the need to insert a footnote (his only one) into written copies of "Problems" at this point, stating that Lüth's patrols were a special case and that his disciplinary methods were not necessarily applicable to all boats.

14. Topp, "Philosophy of a Submarine," 4.

15. Ibid., 5.

16. Merten, "Answers to Questions," 10.

17. Ibid., 11.

18. Ibid.

19. Oesten, letter, 20 May 1994.

20. Hansen, letter, 14 January 1991.

21. See Harald Busch, *U-Boats at War* (New York: Ballantine, 1982); Botting, *The U-Boats;* Compton-Hall, *The Underwater War* (Poole, Dorset: Blandford Press, 1982), 32; and Bodo Herzog and Günter Schomaekers, *Ritter der Tiefe/Graue Wölfe* [Knights of the Deep/Gray Wolves] (Munich: Verlag Welsermühl, 1976).

22. Reche, letter, 21 June 1992; Topp, letter, 27 January 1991; Merten, letter, 15 March 1991.

23. Merten, letter, 15 March 1991.

24. Edward L. Beach, letter, 28 November 1994. "It was my reaction," wrote Beach, "that [Lüth] actually fell into a good thing, that the area where he made his reputation was one of easy pickings. . . . He was a completely experienced profession with functioning weapons, suddenly descended on an inept and unsuspecting enemy. Had we been experienced to an equal degree, and with his weapons instead of ours in our submarine service at the start of the war, we'd have had easy pickings too."

25. Franz Persch, letter, 2 January 1984; Walter Schmidt, interview, 23 December 1983.

10. A Bunch of Arabs

1. Herbert Werner, *Iron Coffins* (New York: Holt, Rinehart and Winston, 1969), 199. All quotes attributed to Werner in this chapter are from *Iron Coffins* unless otherwise noted.

2. Werner, telephone interview, 20 March 1992.

3. König, letter, 18 May 1986.

4. "It was a hard blow," Werner wrote, to be taken so soon from his first boat, but the order saved his life. On his very next patrol, Paulssen managed to break

through into the Mediterranean Sea, and in December he sank the British cruiser HMS *Galatea,* but shortly afterward he and his entire crew were killed when U-557 was accidentally rammed and sunk by an Italian torpedo boat.

5. Oesten, letter, 20 January 1991.

6. Hansen, letter, 19 February 1991; Hadley, *Count Not the Dead,* 133; Bredow, letter, 26 August 1991.

7. Werner, letter, 6 June 1991.

8. Werner was not the only man in his crew to write a book. See Heinz Schaeffer, *U-Boat 977* (New York: Norton, 1952). Schaeffer, like Werner and König, belonged to Crew XII/39, and his career followed the same pattern as theirs. He received command of U-977 in December 1944. Schaeffer's book is not as good as Werner's, however; his disregard for historical accuracy is more blatant, and the narrative is not as personal. One interesting difference is that whereas *Iron Coffins* carries a relatively friendly foreword by Edward L. Beach, *U-Boat 977* was given a distinctly hostile one by Nicholas Monsarrat, a former Royal Navy officer and the author of *The Cruel Sea.* "If *U-Boat 977* were not two things," wrote the surly Monsarrat, "a readable book and an engrossing piece of war history—I would not touch it with a depth charge." U-boat crewmen, he stated, were Nazis of the worst stripe, and any opinion to the contrary was "rubbish."

9. Topp, *Odyssey,* 58. Topp does not say when he learned that this reversal had occurred, although it must have been increasingly obvious as the war went on.

10. Rust clarified this point in a letter dated 13 January 1995.

11. Daublebsky, letter, 29 July 1992.

12. Reche, letter, 21 June 1992.

13. Rust, letter, 13 January 1995.

14. König, letter, 17 June 1991.

15. Oesten, letter, 3 March 1993.

16. Werner, *Iron Coffins,* 109. *Iron Coffins* has been widely criticized and often condemned for its factual errors. It is a valid criticism. He claims, for example, that U-230 reported sinking two ships from convoy SC 121; the *Egyptian* at 0240 on 9 March, the second an unidentified steamer at 2325 the same day. In reality, only the *Egyptian* was sunk, at 0210 on 7 March. The second ship, probably the Norwegian steamer *Jamaica,* was hit instead by another U-boat's torpedo.

17. Quoted in Macintyre, *Naval War Against Hitler,* 319–20.

18. Peter Cremer, *U-Boat Commander* (Annapolis: Naval Institute Press, 1984), 131. Peter Erich "Ali" Cremer was almost killed in October 1942 when U-333 was rammed by HMS *Crocus.* He recovered and returned to U-333 in June 1943.

19. See Eberhard Rössler, *The U-Boat: The Evolution and Technical History of German Submarines* (Annapolis: Naval Institute Press, 1981), for more information on this subject.

20. Petersen, letter, 11 November 1994. Lüth's friend was actually Harald Jeppener-Haltenhoff, a member of Crew 33 who served briefly as commander of U-24 in 1939, then for the remainder of the war as *Offz.-Personalreferent* (officer detailer) for the U-Bootwaffe.

21. König, letter, 18 May 1986.

22. Wrote Peter Hansen, "U-415, a Danzig-built U-boat, had already made and survived too many patrols to have really any chance to remain afloat much longer. Danzig built U-boats were not as well-constructed as those built by either Blohm and Voss in Hamburg or Germania-Howaldt yards in Kiel and hardly any of them survived long at the front. I would have moved heaven and hell, if I had ever been assigned to a Danzig built boat, to get off as quickly as possible and transfer elsewhere" (letter, 23 January 1995).

11. Dragon's Teeth

1. Oehrn, letter, 29 May 1992.
2. Oehrn, letter to Peter Padfield, 31 May 1982.
3. Oesten, letter, 6 January 1991.
4. Quoted in Padfield, *Dönitz,* 339.
5. Werner, interview.
6. Hansen, letter, 15 August 1991.
7. Oehrn, "Dönitz, Nähe Gesehen," 37–38.
8. Ibid., 38–39.
9. Cremer, *U-Boat Commander,* 134.
10. Padfield, *Dönitz,* 311.
11. Oehrn, letter, 29 May 1992.
12. See Heinrich Walle, "Individual Loyalty and Resistance in the German Military: The Case of Sub-Lieutenant Oskar Kusch," in *Germans Against Nazism: Nonconformity, Opposition and Resistance in the Third Reich, Essays in Honour of Peter Hoffmann,* ed. Francis R. Nicosia and Lawrence D. Stokes (New York: Berg, 1990), 323–49. Quotes pertaining to Kusch are taken from Walle.
13. Ironically, Kusch's principal accuser, Ulrich Abel, had died two weeks earlier when the boat he had just taken command of, U-193, was bombed and sunk by British aircraft. (Peter Hansen observed that it was unfortunate that fifty-eight other men had to die as well.)
14. Quoted in Walle, "Individual Loyalty," 345–46.
15. Merten, letter, 20 January 1992; Topp, quoted by Walle, "Individual Loyalty," 345–46; Topp, letter, 21 March 1991. "The hesitation in rehabilitating Kusch," wrote Walle, "is understandable in the sense that all who were involved in his condemnation . . . looked for a personal excuse. Therefore they try even today to show that Kusch would have been guilty not from a political point of view but for military misconduct" (letter, 27 March 1991).
16. Padfield, *Dönitz,* 360. The quote at the beginning of the paragraph (and the beginning of the chapter) is taken from Stephen Vincent Benet, *Litany for Dictatorships,* 1935.
17. Quoted in Cremer, *U-Boat Commander,* 179.
18. Ibid., 180.
19. Werner, *Iron Coffins,* 236.
20. Busch, *U-Boats at War,* chap. 16.
21. *Bredow,* letter, 26 August 1991.
22. Hansen, letter, 5 March 1991; Werner, *Iron Coffins,* 285.

23. Peter Cremer quotes Rodger Winn, director of the Submarine Tracking Room in London, who was listening to German Enigma traffic during the invasion: "The reaction of the C-in-C U-boats to the Invasion is prompt and energetic, but confused. The disposition of the boats now deviates in numerous points from the plan originally laid down by the U-boats. In several cases issued orders have been countermanded. But all boats have been instructed to attack ruthlessly" (*U-Boat Commander*, 181). Herbert Werner in U-415 had still not received his orders at 1000 on D-Day. "New orders were issued and cancelled within minutes. Confusion grew as more time passed. The boats were still at the pier at noon. Rumors and false alarms chased each other like steers in a stampede" (*Iron Coffins*, 241).

24. Padfield, *Dönitz*, 297.

25. Topp, *Odyssey*, 164.

26. Ibid.

27. Oesten, letter, 4 April 1991.

28. Topp, *Odyssey*, 165. See Padfield, *Dönitz*, for a fairly conclusive discussion about Dönitz's attendance at the Posen Conference of October 1943.

29. Dönitz, quoted in Padfield, *Dönitz*.

30. Oehrn, "Dönitz, Nähe Gesehen," 50–52. Oehrn cites Erich Raeder as an example of how badly a senior Wehrmacht commander might fare in attempting to hold onto his honor by keeping his distance from Hitler. It is a good point if one is willing to concede that honor is less important than military effectiveness.

31. Ibid., 38.

32. Dönitz, quoted in Padfield, *Dönitz*, 370.

33. Oesten, letter, 20 May 1994.

34. Oesten, letter, 19 September 1991.

35. Werner, *Iron Coffins*, 263, 306–30. The comment about party membership is from Hansen, letter, 14 January 1991. If true, it represents a radical departure from old Kriegsmarine policy, which was designed by Raeder to keep officers separate from party politics in fact as well as by inclination.

36. Letter to the editor, *Marineforum*, Heft 6 (1994): 213. The name of the officer involved in this incident, a member of Crew 35, is at the bottom of the letter and thus a matter of public record, but no purpose is served by revealing his name here. Needless to say, his opinion of Lüth is entirely negative.

37. Karl Peter, *Acht Glas: Ende der Wache* (Eight Bells: End of the Watch) (Stuttgart: Preussische Militär-Verlag, 1988), 158.

38. Schaeffer, *U-Boat 977*, 134.

39. Werner, *Iron Coffins*, 310.

12. The Woodcutter

1. Oesten, personal diary, entry of 29 March 1933.

2. Oesten, interview, 16 June 1991 and follow-up letter.

3. Hansen, letter, 10 December 1994.

4. König, letter, 17 June 1991.

5. Translation and quotation from Dan Van der Vat, *The Atlantic Campaign*

(New York: Harper & Row, 1988), 381. Much of the confusion resulted from the unauthorized transmission of a signal containing the codeword *Regenbogen*, "rainbow," the prearranged order to destroy all U-boats. It was countermanded almost immediately, but approximately 250 boats were scuttled by their crews in the first week of May, prompted by honor, exigency, and the veiled encouragement of their superiors. It was not a valid signal, said Dönitz's adjutant, Walter Lüdde-Neurath, when two U-boat commanders asked him to clarify it. "But if I were a U-boat commander, I certainly would know what to do and how to act" (Hansen, letter, 14 May 1995).

6. Werner, *Iron Coffins*, 337.

7. Schaeffer, *U-Boat 977*, 145.

8. Technically, the Allied governments were still allowed to hold enemy personnel as prisoners of war even though the war was over. Germany had surrendered and an armistice was in effect, but the Geneva Convention provided for repatriation of prisoners only after a peace agreement was signed, and such an agreement would not exist for several years.

9. This exchange between Oehrn and Dönitz is described in "Dönitz, Nähe Gesehen."

10. Oesten, letter, 24 June 1991.

11. Oesten, letter, 19 September 1991.

12. Matthew Barry Sullivan, *Thresholds of Peace* (London: Hamish Hamilton, 1979), 192. The figure of seventy is known with some certainty because of an interesting incident that occurred several months later. By the end of 1945 it had become common knowledge at Featherstone Park that certain senior Wehrmacht officers, including Karl Dönitz, were on trial for war crimes. This was regarded in the U-Bootwaffe as highly unjust, and in January 1946 a letter was written and signed by most, if not all, of the U-boat commanders in the camp, including Oesten. It was addressed to Dönitz's defense team, and it is essentially a blanket denial that Dönitz ever issued orders to any of them that involved the killing of survivors.

13. Oesten, letter to Eric Birley, 17 August 1946.

14. The journey to Argentina is described in the latter part of Heinz Schaeffer's book *U-Boat 977*. According to Peter Hansen, it is the only part of the book to be trusted.

15. Burkard Baron von Müllenheim-Rechberg, *Battleship Bismarck: A Survivor's Story*, trans. Jack Sweetman (Annapolis: Naval Institute Press, 1990), 398. Von Müllenheim-Rechberg was the senior surviving line officer of the *Bismarck*.

16. Sullivan, *Thresholds of Peace*, 192.

17. Petersen, letter, 29 April 1986; C. S. Lewis, *The Last Battle* (New York: Collier, 1970).

18. Otto Erxleben, quoted in Sullivan, *Thresholds of Peace*, 66.

19. Oesten, letter, 21 August 1995.

20. Sullivan, *Thresholds of Peace*, 195.

21. Oesten, letter, 19 September 1991. Oesten says he was appointed deputy camp spokesman because of his skill in English—the spokesmen dealt with the camp commander regularly—and not because of his seniority (as a Korvettenkapitän, he was actually rather low on the pole).

22. Oesten, letter, 16 May 1991.

23. Sullivan, *Thresholds of Peace,* 197.

24. Oesten, letter, 4 April 1991.

25. Oesten, letter, 19 September 1991.

26. Ibid.

27. The story of Otto Kretschmer and his activities at Grizedale Hall and Bowmanville has been told several times, and at least one movie, *The McKenzie Break,* is based loosely on his career. See Terence Robertson, *Night Raiders of the Atlantic* (New York: E. P. Dutton, 1956), for a good overview.

28. Oesten, letters, 4 April 1991, 19 September 1991, and 22 March 1995.

29. Oesten, letter to Eric Birley.

30. Philip Rossiter, PW Division COGA, endorsement of 11 January 1947 (courtesy Jürgen Oesten).

Conclusion

1. Merten, letter, 20 January 1992.

2. Oehrn, "Dönitz, Nähe Gesehen," 36.

3. Oesten, interview, 16 June 1991; König, letters, 17 June 1991 and 12 April 1995.

Bibliography

Published Sources

Abbazia, Patrick. *Mr. Roosevelt's War*. Annapolis: Naval Institute Press, 1975.

Ajax. *The German Pirate: His Methods and Record*. New York: George H. Doran, 1918. Wartime propaganda—read with caution.

Bailey, Thomas A., and Paul B. Ryan. *Hitler vs. Roosevelt: The Undeclared Naval War*. New York: Free Press, 1979.

Botting, Douglas. *The U-Boats*. New York: Time-Life Books, 1979.

Buchheim, Lothar-Günther. *The Boat*. New York: Knopf, 1975.

Busch, Harald. *U-Boats at War*. New York: Ballantine, 1982.

Chesneau, Roger, ed. *Conway's All the World's Fighting Ships, 1922–1946*. New York: Mayflower Books, 1980.

Churchill, Winston. *The World Crisis*. 4 vols. New York: Scribner's, 1951.

Compton-Hall, Richard. *The Underwater War, 1939–1945*. Poole, Dorset: Blandford Press, 1982.

Cremer, Peter. *U-Boat Commander*. Annapolis: Naval Institute Press, 1984.

Dönitz, Karl. *Ten Years and Twenty Days*. New York: World, 1959.

Frank, Wolfgang. *The Sea Wolves*. New York: Ballantine Books, 1955.

Gannon, Michael. *Operation Drumbeat*. New York: Harper Perennial, 1991.

Giese, Otto. *Shooting the War: Memoirs of a World War II U-Boat Officer*. Annapolis: Naval Institute Press, 1994.

Gilbert, Martin. *The Second World War*. New York: Henry Holt, 1989.

Hadley, Michael. *Count Not the Dead: The Popular Image of the German Submarine*. Annapolis: Naval Institute Press, 1995.

Herzog, Bodo, and Günter Schomaekers. *Ritter der Tiefe/Graue Wölfe* [Knights of the Deep/Gray Wolves]. Munich: Verlag-Welsermühl, 1976.

Horne, Charles F., ed. *Source Records of the Great War*. New York: National Alumni, 1923.

Howarth, Stephen, ed. *Men of War*. New York: St. Martin's Press, 1992.

Lüth, Wolfgang, and Claus Korth. *Boot Greift Wieder An* [Boat Attacks Again]. Berlin: Erich Klinghammer Verlag, 1944. Again, read with care—propaganda, but not as bad as some.

Macintyre, Donald. *The Naval War Against Hitler*. New York: Charles Scribner's Sons, 1971.

———. *U-Boat Killer*. 1956. Reprint. Annapolis: Naval Institute Press, 1976.

Merten, Karl-Friedrich. "Betr: Film 'Das Boot' und Fernsehauftritt des Autors Buchheim" [Re: The film 'Das Boot' and the venture into television of the author Buchheim]. *Ritterkreuz* magazine, date unavailable; but probably mid-1985.

———. Review of *Die U-Bootfahrer*. *Ritterkreuz*, I/86.

von Müllenheim-Rechberg, Burkard. *Battleship Bismarck: A Survivor's Story*. Translated by Jack Sweetman. Annapolis: Naval Institute Press, 1990.

Mulligen, Timothy P. "German U-Boat Crews in World War Two: Sociology of an Elite." *Journal of Military History* 56 (April 1992): 261–81.

———. *Lone Wolf: The Life and Death of U-Boat Ace Werner Henke*. Westport, Conn.: Praeger, 1993.

Nicosia, Francis R., and Lawrence D. Stokes, eds. *Germans Against Nazism: Nonconformity, Opposition and Resistance in the Third Reich, Essays in Honour of Peter Hoffmann*. New York: Berg, 1990.

Ott, Wolfgang. *Sharks and Little Fish*. New York: Pantheon, 1958.

Padfield, Peter. *Dönitz, the Last Führer*. New York: Harper & Row, 1984.

Peter, Karl. *Acht Glas: Ende der Wache* [Eight Bells: End of the Watch]. Stuttgart: Preussische Militar-Verlag, 1988.

Pitt, Barrie. *The Battle of the Atlantic*. New York: Time-Life Books, 1979.

Robertson, Terence. *Night Raiders of the Atlantic*. New York: E. P. Dutton, 1956.

Rohwer, Jürgen. *Axis Submarine Successes, 1939–1945*. Annapolis: Naval Institute Press, 1983.

Rössler, Eberhard. *The U-Boat: The Evolution and Technical History of German Submarines*. Annapolis: Naval Institute Press, 1981.

Rust, Eric C. *Naval Officers under Hitler: The Story of Crew 34*. Westport, Conn.: Praeger, 1991.

Schaeffer, Heinz. *U-Boat 977*. New York: Norton, 1952.

Sullivan, Matthew Barry. *Thresholds of Peace*. London: Hamish Hamilton, 1979.

Thomas, Lowell. *Raiders of the Deep*. New York: Garden City Publishing Company, 1928.

Topp, Erich. *The Odyssey of a U-Boat Commander: Recollections of Erich Topp*. Westport, Conn.: Praeger, 1992.

Van der Vat, Dan. *The Atlantic Campaign*. New York: Harper & Row, 1988.

Von der Porten, Edward P. *The German Navy in World War II*. New York: Galahad Books, 1969.

Werner, Herbert. *Iron Coffins*. New York: Holt, Rinehart and Winston, 1969.

Unpublished Sources

Dönitz, Karl. "Bei der Trauerfeier für Kapitän zur See Wolfgang Lüth" [At the memorial service for Kapitän zur See Wolfgang Lüth]. Address delivered in Flensburg-Mürwik, 16 May 1945. Marineschule Mürwik.

Lohmann, Vizeadmiral. "Die Ausbildung des Marineoffiziers" [The training of a naval officer]. Marineschule Mürwik, WGAZ inventory number 14718.

Lüth, Wolfgang. "Menschenführung auf einem Unterseeboot" [Problems of leadership on a submarine]. Lecture presented 17 December 1943 in Weimar, Germany. Translated by the Office of Naval Intelligence, Navy Department, Washington, D.C., document 11746, 1946.

Merten, Karl-Friedrich. "Answers to Questions." Cover letter dated 1981.

Oehrn, Victor. "Dönitz, Nähe Gesehen" [Dönitz up close]. Undated. Copy in possession of the author. Oehrn has kindly allowed this manuscript and "Navigare Necesse Est" listed below to be used on the conditions that all direct quotations are credited to him, he be informed in advance of all quotations used, and no further use be made of either manuscript.

―――. "Navigare Necesse Est." Memoirs of Victor Oehrn. Undated.

Topp, Erich. "Philosophy of a Submarine." Lecture outline. Undated. Copy in possession of the author.

Interviews and Correspondence

Edward Beach, Horst Bredow (Stiftung Traditionsarchiv Unterseeboote), Gus Britton (Royal Navy Submarine Museum), Lothar-Günther Buchheim, Karl Daublebsky von Eichhain, Eberhard Godt, Michael Hadley, Peter Hansen, Gottfried König, Otto Kretschmer, Karl-Friedrich Merten, Victor Oehrn, Jürgen Oesten, Peter Padfield, Franz Persch, Theodor Petersen, Walter Pfeiffer, Reinhard Reche, Jügen Rohwer, Eric Rust, Eberhard Schmidt (WGAZ, Marineschule Mürwik), Walter Schmidt, Jack Sweetman, Hans-Diedrich von Tiesenhausen, Erich Topp, Helmut Witte.

Index

About the Author

Jordan Vause grew up in southern California and graduated from the U.S. Naval Academy in 1978. A software engineer by profession— a writer by avocation— he began working on his first book, *U-Boat Ace: The Story of Wolfgang Lüth* (Naval Institute Press, 1990) in 1982. Nine years later, he began researching *Wolf*. At this rate of production, he does not anticipate a career in historical writing and is content to spend what little free time he has with his wife, his five children, and his garden in San Jose, California.

THE NAVAL INSTITUTE PRESS is the book-publishing arm of the U.S. Naval Institute, a private, nonprofit, membership society for sea service professionals and others who share an interest in naval maritime affairs. Established in 1873 at the U.S. Naval Academy in Annapolis, Maryland, where its offices remain today, the Naval Institute has members worldwide.

Members of the Naval Institute support the education programs of the society and receive the influential monthly magazine *Proceedings* and discounts on fine nautical prints and on ship and aircraft photos. They also have access to the transcripts of the Institute's Oral History program and get discounted admission to any of the Institute-sponsored seminars offered around the country.

The Naval Institute also publishes *Naval History* magazine. This colorful bimonthly is filled with entertaining and thought-provoking articles, first-person reminiscences, and dramatic art and photography. Members receive a discount on *Naval History* subscriptions.

The Naval Institute's book-publishing program, begun in 1898 with basic guides to naval practices, has broadened its scope in recent years to include books of more general interest. Now the Naval Institute Press publishes about 100 titles each year, ranging from how-to books on boating and navigation to battle histories, biographies, ship and aircraft guides, and novels. Institute members receive discounts of 20 to 50 percent on the Press's nearly 600 books in print.

Full-time students are eligible for special half-price membership rates. Life memberships are also available.

For a free catalog describing Naval Institute Press books currently available, and for further information about subscribing to *Naval History* magazine or about joining the U.S. Naval Institute, please write to:

Membership Department
U.S. NAVAL INSTITUTE
118 Maryland Avenue
Annapolis, MD 21402-5035
Telephone: (800) 233-8764
Fax: (410) 269-7940
Web address: www.usni.org